The Cavan Leahys: Origins

David Leahy M.Sc.

Dedicated to my father George Robert Leahy (1932-1986), my mother Emily Elizabeth Leahy (nee Semple) (1935-1999), my Uncle John Charles 'Jack' Leahy (1926-2015) from 'The Cross' Aghakilmore, and to my daughter Evanna who might one day be interested in her origins

Also, by same Author:

The Cavan Leahys: 1800-1950, 2018, ISBN-13 978-0995663046
Leahy Land Deed Notes 1708-1950, 2016, ISBN-13:978-0995663015
Sheelin: (Historical Novel): ISBN-13: 978-0-9956630-5-3

David Leahy M.Sc.

Contents

         David Leahy M.Sc.

List of Figures

List of Tables

Acknowledgements

Over the last 5 or 6 years myself and my cousin Caroline have been visiting Cavan to talk to descendants from these early Lahys who still live in the area. We are in debited to them for their generosity and local knowledge and enthusiasm about the research. It's all part of their story and they're entitled to know the origins of their family line. I'm also in debt to Francis Sheridan for allowing me access to his private deeds collection.

"The truth is out there...." (X-Files)

David Leahy M.Sc.

1 Introduction

This is the book I wanted to buy 5 or 6 years ago, when I wanted to know how it all started, where the Leahys came from, who were they? where did they live? How they came to be in County Cavan and were they connected to each other at all? As I couldn't find it (the closest I came to was Shirley Lahey's *'The Laheys'* [1] I decided to find out myself and write it myself! This work is partly about pulling together my research in a structured format to help me understand it! I could wait until more evidence becomes available for early Lahys, however nothing significant has come to light the past few years so I'll risk publishing now rather than run the risk of never-ending research which never sees the light of day.

Shirley Lahey in her book *The Laheys: Pioneer settlers and sawmillers* (self-published) – [1] began her story with the 'Irish Dawn' where she attempted to record the history of the Leahy/Lahey/Lahy family in Cavan. She did a very comprehensive job and to date it is to my knowledge the best documented account of the early Lahy family in Cavan. However, I believe she did a lot of her research in the 1970s and 1980s, when there wasn't a lot of access to records that are now available (on-line and elsewhere). One major data source she didn't seem to have been able to access is the Registry of Deeds records at Henrietta Street in Dublin. This is quite an important data source as far as the Lahey family is concerned because they owned land, and they bought and sold it and gave it away in dowries for at least a hundred and fifty years. Although it wasn't obligatory to record the land transactions in deed format, I'm guessing they did it should any 'dispute' arise as to who owned the land (although the exact boundaries are never given in the deeds!). In addition, although Shirley's account is quite comprehensive it focuses (as the title suggests) mainly on the Australian Lahey immigrants who launched a successful saw milling enterprise in Queensland.

This book is an attempt to focus more on the Irish genesis of the Lahys of County Cavan (and theorize about what came before) and tries to locate the various different Lahys at different times as far back as I can get documentary evidence as well as recording some of the more interesting characters in the story. Where there isn't documentary evidence, I will try and use logic to theorize what may have occurred but obviously this could be overruled with future discoveries of documentary evidence. I'll also describe a little more of the area the Lahys inhabited as they didn't move around very much (which made them easier to trace!). I will try to fill part of that gap although like all genealogy research it is a 'work in progress' – so there will be a second edition! In addition, there may be another data source that becomes 'available' in the future, and so I'll leave it to another to write an update based upon that!

Many people probably have knowledge of one or two people at the top of their 'Lahy' tree in County Cavan. This was the case when I first started researching the Lahys in County Cavan – there were a few individuals who popped up in Will calendars from the 1700s – but that was all. There was nothing to identify who they were or who they were connected to. There are still a number of individuals who cannot be 'connected' however this research uniquely attempts to bring together all of the Lahy / Leahy families of

County Cavan into one family tree - as I believe that they are all connected. I have use a combination of Church Records, Wills, Census Reports, Land deed records, privately held deeds and earlier research by other genealogists in this area checking that the resultant tree accommodates those sources and that the data cross-correlates.

Previous research performed in the 1990s identified 'some' Lahys in the Cavan area mainly from Church and census records. They therefore naturally tried to 'connect' these individuals without supporting evidence which was understandable as it was all they had to work with. I have been able to access all publically available land deeds as well as some in private collections which has provided a lot more information and facilitated 'cross checking' to verify individual's relationships and locations. There are still lots of holes and unsubstantiated relationships. No one will ever know the 'whole' story but we can work towards that goal with a view to providing the most accurate picture possible. There are still many gaps however my objective was to create as accurate a representation as possible using the data sources available to me at this time.

It is not a *'Unified Leahy tree'* for the whole of Ireland as I don't have evidence that supports the premise of a unified 'Leahy' tree. Uniquely, I believe that the Cavan Leahys were an isolated 'group' with few (if any) links to the other main Leahy clans in Ireland - namely those that exist in Tipperary, Kilkenny, and Cork. They did however overspill into neighbouring counties to Cavan - such as Meath, Westmeath, Leitrim, Longford and the city of Dublin.

It has taken years to get to this point – to eventually make connections to what initially appeared to be an unrelated group of the Lahy family in County Cavan and I thank everyone that has talked to me and contributed material.

I intend to tell the story in 2 volumes - this being the first, from earliest origins theories and evidence through to about the year 1800. From 1800 onwards, there is a lot more data (and photographs of Lahys and their dwellings) and I will organize that by townland area and show how the major branches spread out from the 7 or 8 main branches highlighted in this volume. The exact relationships and connections are known from roughly 1800 onwards although there are still a number of isolated 'Lahys' that I can't connect to any of the known branches. Some children were born out of wedlock and raised by friends of the family etc. and some 'holes' will always exist as there are few written records other than the census and church records. Interestingly the court records of the late 1800s give insight as to which families were in dispute with each other. There are also some court data which can't be explained and perhaps we'll never know what took place. If you're reading this and hoping to find you're Lahy / Lahey / Leahy line then you may be disappointed especially if you don't know the townland area they hailed from. As I said not all the Lahys in the area at the time will be represented here - especially if they didn't contribute to any official documentation such as land deeds, or wills etc. Your family ancestors may be present in the next Volume covering 1800s onwards.

David Leahy M.Sc.

1.1 Name variations

It may seem confusing at first, the variations on the name: Lahy, Laghy, Lahey, Leahy etc. It should be noted that in some documents the same person's surname is spelt in different way, suggesting it was more a function of the author of the document than accuracy of the surname spelling. I have noticed a pattern in that the earliest records of Cavan Leahys spelt the name as '**Lahy**' or '**Laghy**', '**Laughy**', '**Loughey**' or even '**Lahie**'. It wasn't until the mid to late 1800s that the 'Leahy' spelling became more prevalent. I have a suspicion that the extra 'e' was added as the Cavan Lahys were mostly Protestant and that by adding an extra 'e' the surname matched an existing established Irish (mostly Roman Catholic) surname ' Leahy' [mostly hailing from Counties Cork and Tipperary] and so more acceptable and easier for the mostly Protestant Cavan Leahys to assimilate into the majority Roman Catholic population in the Republic of Ireland.

1.2 TimeLines

As I gathered a lot of the evidence for the existence of various people in various places at various times it very quickly became apparent that in order to make sense of this data and perform any kind of analysis it is necessary to represent it graphically, not just in terms of a family tree format (which is the best for showing the people relationships) but also in a timeline format. The timeline format although not showing every single person, depicts key people in key places at certain times from a number of different sources. In a sense these have become my '*master frameworks*' upon which to place people. Sometimes different data sources position an individual in the same place at the same time which is always good. In some other cases logic can be used e.g., about known family relationships to position certain individuals in a certain place at the same time. I believe this is a key tool for helping to 'visualise' the puzzle and try and fit the pieces into place – and identify where the holes are – the loose ends etc. Today such a representation would be very confusing due to our geographical mobility, however a few hundred years ago people tended to stay close by to where they were raised and only moved if they had a very good reason – for example the famine! I have shown the timelines for completeness in Appendix A.

1.3 Land Deeds

Much of the data presented here is extracted from Land Deeds - I spent many hours in the Registry of Deeds in Dublin my arms were sore from lifting the big heavy books containing all the old land deeds and I felt the eyes of my ancestors looking down on me from the shelves silently screaming to be heard. They are difficult to read and contain a lot of legal language which is difficult to understand and somewhat ambiguous. Thus, rather than transcribe in details the deeds, I made notes on the key elements within them related to names, places and relationships, as well as witnesses. These notes [up to the year 1800] are shown in Appendix B – section 24. In addition, I have included the actual transcriptions from a few key deeds to give the reader a flavour and insight to the transaction. I have also published the notes I made on all of the existing deeds to the year

1950 [120]. There are obviously lots of gaps and there were more Lahys around than we have records for - but hopefully in the future new records will come to light and resolve some of the outstanding questions. The deeds are Indexed by the 'Seller' rather than the purchaser and thus I have seen all of the 'Seller' deeds but may not have accessed all of the 'purchaser' deeds.

David Leahy M.Sc.

2 Origins Earliest Origins Theories

2.1 *Summary Table of Likely Origins*

From my research to date there are a number of different origin theories that have come to light. A summary of these are listed in Table 1.

Table 1 Summary of Earliest Origins Theories

1	Huguenot Origin - Delahydes - / Dublin		
Medieval family names De lahayde in Dublin			
Evidence For	**Evidence Against**	**Conclusion**	
<ul><li>Lahy' in middle portion of name</li><li>Huguenots (requested books from Ronel in France)</li><li>Important family - Nat Archives papers (had money to buy land)</li><li>Documentary evidence for them in Dublin in early 1500 Dublin Archive Records</li><li>Buying land in Dublin in 1700s</li><li>The Delahayes of Cork are descendants of one Walter de la Haye (C. Parker - Local Cavan Historian)</li><li>Pedigrees of Delahays in Dublin going back to the 1200s and 1300s (NLI) - [2] & Figure 1.</li></ul>	<ul><li>In the 1700s the name was either Delahayde or Delahoode (by this stage the Lahys are already documented in Cavan)</li><li>No documentary evidence for Delahydes in County Cavan (but no records in cavan < 1700!)</li></ul>	Probably on an equal footing with the Huguenot Delahaye theory - documentary evidence of them in Dublin (but not Cavan), but family story also has a weighting!	
2	Descended from the Cork Leahys		
Evidence For	**Evidence Against**	**Conclusion**	
<ul><li>Name - Leaghy / Leaghie</li><li>Some were Episcopalian / Protestant</li><li>Some were in the Masonic</li></ul>	<ul><li>Most were Roman Catholic</li><li>No evidence linking them to Cavan</li></ul>	Possible but unlikely	
3	Descended from the Tipperary Leahys		
The highest concentration of Leahys in Ireland			
Evidence For	**Evidence Against**	**Conclusion**	
<ul><li>Name - Leahys!</li></ul>	<ul><li>Religion - Tipperary & Cork Leahys are predominantly Roman Catholic (unlike Cavan Leahys who are predominantly Protestant)</li><li>No documented Birth / Marriage / Death links</li><li>Unlikely that they</li></ul>	Possible but unlikely	

	would change their name to Lahy when they moved to Cavan?	

4	**Kilkenny Descendants**	

Small group of Lahys in the Kilkenny region may be linked.

Evidence For	**Evidence Against**	**Conclusion**
• Thomas Lahy - 1570s land grant by the duke of Ormonde [75-77]	• Little documentary evidence linking the Kilkenny Lahys to Cavan • The Kilkenny 'Leahys' today are mostly Roman Catholic, whereas the Cavan 'Leahys' mostly Protestant.	A possible contender but the difference in religion contradicts Cavan connection.

5	**Wexford Descendants**	

Evidence For	**Evidence Against**	**Conclusion**
• John O'Lahy 1581	• Little documentary evidence linking the Wexford Lahys to Cavan • The Wexford 'Leahys' today are mostly Roman Catholic, whereas the Cavan 'Leahys' mostly Protestant	A possible contender but the difference in religion contradicts Cavan connection.

6	**Huguenot Origin - Lahayville**	

Francois Delahaye and his 11 Children emigrated to County Cavan (possibly via England) - from Lahayville in Lorraine France after persecution by the Roman Catholic King.

Evidence For	**Evidence Against**	**Conclusion**

• 'Lahy' in middle portion of name
• The Leahys are Protestant
• Shirley Lahey family story (passed down) [1]
• Independent sources identify the Cavan Lahys as being of Huguenot Descent:
  A/ Shirley Lahey
  B/ Bill Graham (well respected local genealogy researcher)
  C/ New York Newspaper Article [Mary Lahy Walker - section 2.8]
  D/ Michael Leader Letter [Section 2.9]
  E/ Drumeeny Leahys 'hearsay'
• Naming conventions: 'Francis' common name throughout the Lahy men
	• No documentary evidence prior to 1667!	A good contender and no evidence so far refutes this story

Note - what is meant by 'hearsay' is that this 'origin' story has been passed down the family line.

2.2 Dublin De LaHayes - Origin Theory 1

In 1169 the Normans made Dublin the centre of their activities following their successful invasion of Ireland. Delahydes were one of the Anglo-Norman families who settled in the country.

In the course of my research, I was contacted by a local Cavan historian Ciaran Parker who had this to say of the 'Cork' De La Hays:

"The Delahayes of Cork are descendants, as far as I know of one Walter de la Haye. He was an Englishman, though obviously of Norman descent, who lived in the mid thirteenth century. He joined the administrative staff of king Henry III (I suspect he as in them back to the treasury. In short, he was the king's representative in the minor orders) and was sent to Ireland where his skills enabled him to be appointed to the office of sheriff of Waterford in 1269. He held this job, along with the sheriff's office of Co. Cork for thirteen years, a record at the time and a testament to his efficiency. The sheriff in those days was far more than his modern equivalent. He was the head of whatever passed for local government. He was responsible for collecting taxes and fines and transmitting locality. De la Haye was unusual; he could be trusted to do the job, but there was not exactly a long list of budding candidates wanting to take it on. There were many people in the localities who wanted it, as they saw it had immense opportunities for graft. Not only could tax money be siphoned off into the holders' pockets, but the sheriff had a considerable role in the mechanisms of law and order. presided over the county court and if the sheriff was on your side you could more or less do anything and get away with it. When Walter left the southeast he entered the administration of the lordship of Ireland in Dublin where his skills were especially needed during the preparations for Edward I's wars in Scotland - something which bankrupted the Irish lordship. We last hear of Walter c. 1306 when he has retired but when he is still being pursued for money that it was claimed he owed. However, Walter thumbed his nose at these investigations. He had no known legitimate offspring, but he had at least one son whom he recognised called Simon. He had been granted lands by his father in counties Cork and Waterford. I can't tell you whereabouts exactly, though I think it was somewhere in the eastern part of the county. It is from this Simon Delahaye that most of the Cork Delahayes are descended. They continued to play a minor role in local politics, and holders of the name stick their heads over the parapets of anonymity to appear as jury members. They were never big landholders, and certainly would never has been able to challenge the power of Sadly we don't know as much about them (or any other minor
family) as we'd like because the sources start to get a bit patchy."

A few hundred years later a **Walter Delahayd**e is mentioned, in the Civil Survey of Wexford. Calloghe O'More in 1574, was granted *"the Lordship and Manor of Ballynaa, Colnoghe, Thomastown, Cadameston, Ballynemone, Norney, Cloneaghe and Toneragye*

*Co Kildare with all rests services customs and temporal hereditaments to the said manor belonging - the Estate of **Walter Delahyde** attained. To hold to him and his heirs by the tenth part of a knight's fee rent £27:8:0 - 3rd August 1574."*

The Delahaye pedigree [2] shown in Figure 1 is difficult to decipher but clearly very old. The writing in the column to the right mentions lands in Cambridge and 'Caxton' (near Cambridge) - possibly a stopping point for the Delahays before they moved to Ireland?

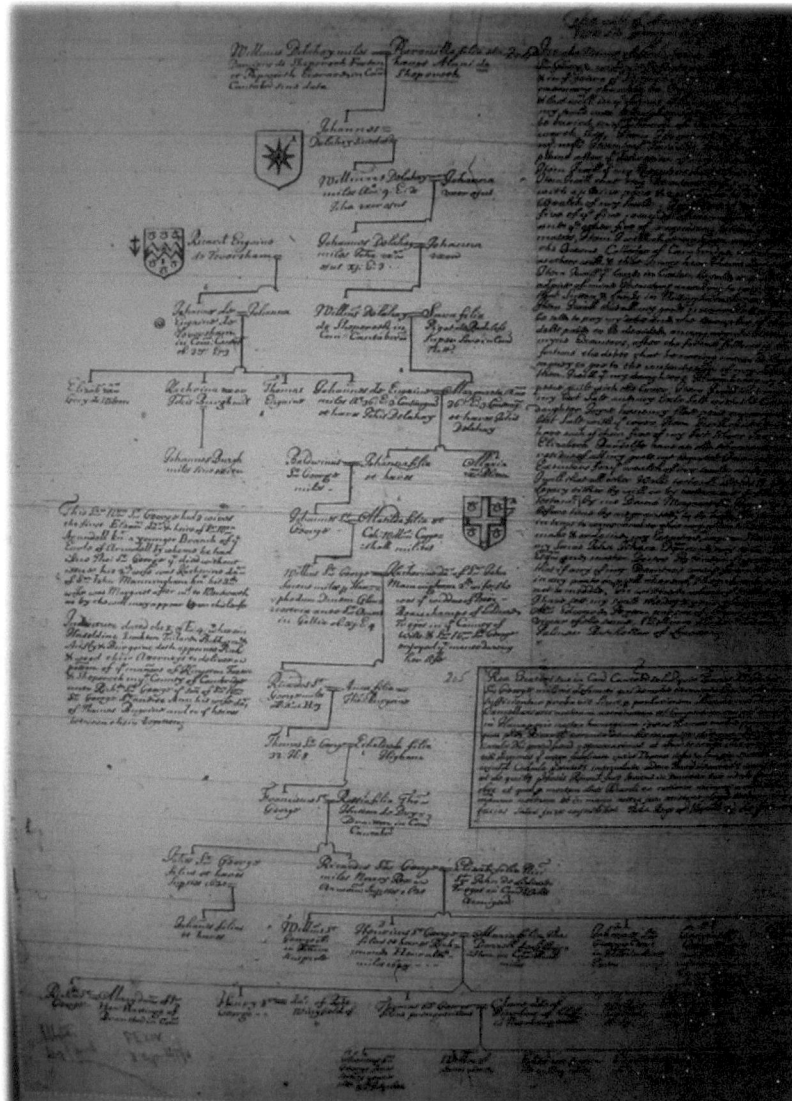

Figure 1 Delahayes Pedigree - [Courtesy NLI]

It is not known if the 'Cavan Lahys' are related to the Cork Leahys although my uncle [John Charles Leahy] seemed to think so.

2.3 Descended from Cork Leahys - Origin Theory 2

[116] describes the Leahys of County Cork being of ancient Munster origin - name being derived from the Gaelic *Loag(d)ha*, meaning heroic. They were descendants of the Kings of Ulster, line of Clan Colla; House of Hermon, and early in Irish History were chiefs of Caladh in the Barony of Kilconnel, County Galway. In the 8th Century the name was common in the Clans of Thomond in Munster.

About 600AD St Finnbarr founded the Celtic Monastery of Cork. In 863AD the Vikings raided the Monastery and *'Donald O'Leahy'* the Abbot of Cork and Lismore was slain.

From notes on the Cork Leahys [116] the Leaghies or Leaghys in the 15th Century were engaged in fishing, trading and shipping out of Kinsale. In the reign of King Henry VII, while at sea they spotted a Spanish Fleet about to invade. They out-sailed the Spaniards and raised the alarm and warning fires were lit along the coast dissuading the Spaniards from invading. For this service, the Leahys were granted a Fishing Right by the King to a certain length of Coast line probably between Youghal, Cork and Kinsale from which they earned an income from all cargos of fish landed. The original holders of the fishing grant were probably names Thomas, John or William O'Leaghie and born circa 1480.They held this right until Charles I granted it to one of his favourites. Despite the Leahys appealing, they never regained this right. [116] goes on to describe Heny VIII being in Kinsale in 1480-1500 and *"waiving a sword around (like Mahomet)"* inspiring most of the inhabitants to become Episcopalians.

There is a lot more information on the Cork and Youghal in [116] including Leahys who were members of Masonic Lodges in Youghal and some who were rebels against Cromwell (e.g. John O'Leaghie 1657) and the forbearer of the famous Admiral Leahy who accompanied President Roosevelt at Yalta in 1945.

I believe that the Cork/Youghal Leahys were a mixture of Episcopalian and Roman Catholic communities. However, at no stage in [177] is there any mention of a 'County Cavan' connection. Also at no stage where they referred to as 'Lahy' - always 'Leaghie' or 'Leaghy'. Also, it seems that the Cork Leahys have a much longer ancient descendancy (within Ireland) than the Cavan Leahys. For these reasons I don't believe that the Cork / Youghal and Cavan Leahys are connected. But I'm willing to re-appraise this conclusion should future evidence present itself!

2.4 Descended from Tipperary Leahys - Origin Theory 3

I don't have any specific evidence for this theory other than it is possible. The county of Tipperary has the largest concentration of Leahys in the country, and it's possible that a group (or even just one family) of them moved north to County Cavan for some unknown reason. There were a few 'Lahys' who came from Tipperary and perhaps it was they who moved north. Predominantly the spelling of the name is 'Leahy' in county Tipperary, and they are almost 100% Roman Catholic in religion. This to me makes it an unlikely origin, in that the Cavan Leahys are predominantly Protestant (although about 1/5 were Roman Catholic) and the Cavan Leahys were known as Lahy or Lahy - and didn't go by the name 'Leahy' until at least the mid-1800s.

2.5 Kilkenny Descendants - Origin Theory 4

2.5.1 Thomas Lahy Prior of Kells-

The earliest reference to a Lahy I have found in the 16th century is to a Thomas Lahy of [115] Ballytobin and Mallardstown (parish of Dunnamaggan) - also written as Lathy who was a prior of Kells in County Kilkenny from 1492 until his death in 1507 [3]. The old parish church of Kells was used as a Protestant place of worship till about 1850, when it was deserted; it is now a ruin.

THE PARISH OF DUNNAMAGGAN.   63

William O'Hedian became Bishop of Elphin, Dec. 5th, 1429, and was translated thence, Nov. 7th, 1449, to Emly, which latter See he governed till his death in 1477.   He appears to have been unsuccessful in the controversy over the Priorship of Kells.

Edmund Stapulton, otherwise Archer, clerk, of Cashel Diocese, was appointed by Papal Brief of July 1st, 1471, to be Prior of the Monastery of the Blessed Mary of Kenlys, in Ossory ; 100 marks stipend.[1]

John Carne was Prior for 17 years.

Thomas Lahy (also written Lathy) was Prior for 16 or 18 years.   He was Prior of Kells, March 18th, 1501-2.[2] ; also in 1506.

Patrick Baron, otherwise Fismoris of the Geraldines (de Geraldinis), Prior, died about 1531.   He was evidently of the Barons, otherwise Fitzgeralds, otherwise Fitz Morrises, of Burnchurch.

Philip O'Holohan, one of the Canons of the Monastery of the Blessed Mary of Kenlis, of the Order of St. Augustine, in Ossory, was, by Papal Brief of April 30th, 1531, appointed Prior of the said Monastery (vacant by the death of Patrick Baron otherwise Fismoris de Geraldinis) ; whose fruits with those of its annexes are £60 sterling.[3] He was still Prior on the 8th March, 1540, when he surrendered the Priory to the Commissioners of Henry VIII.[4]   His enforced surrender must have been attended with circumstances displeasing to the agents of the Crown, as they made no provision for his future maintenance.   They granted pensions to only three members of the dissolved community, one of whom, Nicholas Tobin, they strangely style Prior of the House, thus :

" 1540 (April 20). Grant for Edmund Laghnan, conventual person of the late priory of the B.V.M. of Kenles, County Kilkenny ; of a pension of 40s. ; and for Nicholas Lahy, conventual person of the same, a pension of 26s. 8d. ; issuing out of possessions in Kenles." [5]

Figure 2 Lahy's of Kells / Kilkenny (courtesy [115])

There is also [3] a reference in 1540 to "*Edmund Laghnan conventional person of the late priory of the B.V.M of Kenles a pension of 40s and Nicolas Lahy conventional person of the same a pension of 28s 8d. issueing out of possessions of Kenles."* This may refer to consequences of Henry VIIIs dissolution of the monasteries.

In the National Library of Ireland there are 3 deeds referencing a Thomas Lahy in Kilkenny in the 1570s – it seems likely that this Thomas was a descendant of the Thomas Prior of Kells. The Deeds are titled as follows:

1. Grant by Sir Thomas Lahie, vicar of Kells, to James Archdeacon of the whole vicarage of Kells (in Ossory), Feb. 13, 1570. [75]

2. Grant by the Earl of Ormonde to Sir Thomas Lahy of the town of the Grange of Kenlis, Co. Kilkenny, for 21 years, July 20, 1572. [76]

3. Grant by Richard Shee, as attorney of the Earl of Ormonde, to Peter Shee and Sir Thomas Lahie, of the altarage of Kilrye and Donnamogane, Co. Kilkenny with all tithes, lands, etc. belonging thereto, for 21 years, Feb. 2, 1578. [77]

I obtained a copy of the second Grant [76] from the National Library of Ireland (shown in Figure 3). It is quite difficult to translate as it is written in secretary script (flamboyant style of European handwriting developed in the early sixteenth century). Although I've circled in red Thomas Lahy's mention in the text and it is also signed by him at the bottom.

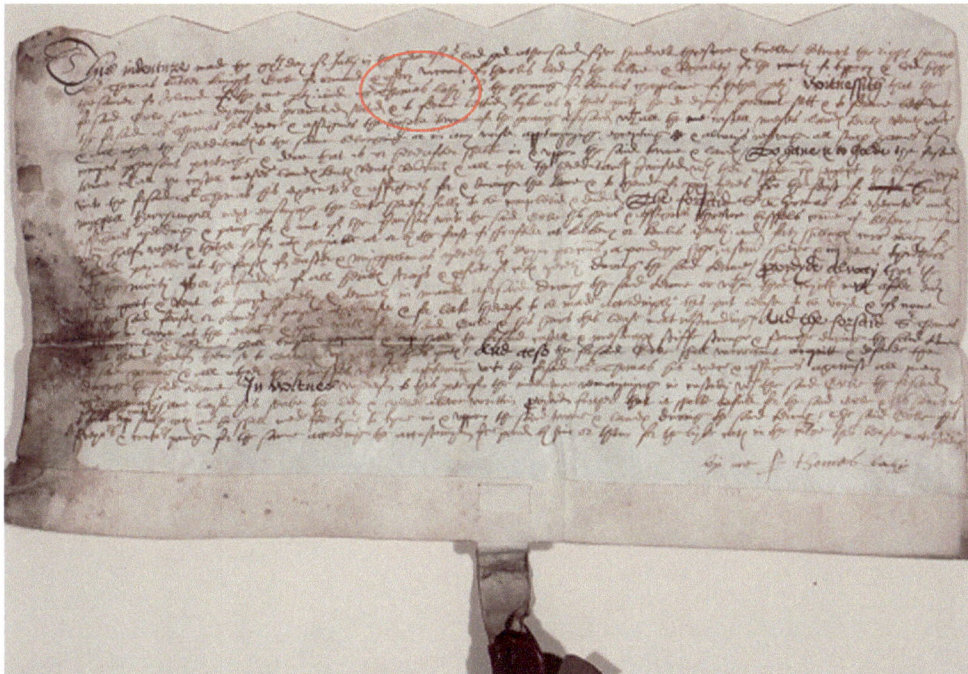

Figure 3 Thomas Lahy - Kilkenny Deed 1752(Courtesy National Library of Ireland)

Thomas Lahy (also written Lathy) was Prior for 16 or 18 years. He was Prior of Kells, 1501-2; also in 1506.

* 1540 (April 20). Grant for Edmund Laghnan, conventual person of the late Priory of the B.V.M. of Kenles, County Kilkenny; of a pension of 40s; And for Nicholas Lahy, conventual person of the same, a pension of 26s. 8d.; issuing out of possessions in Kenles." 5

Later evidence [101] lists a few Wills of Lahys in the Kilkenny area:

> *178: Admin of the goods of Philip Lahy late of Kilkenny, Victualler, granted 16th January 1758 to Anne Lahy his widow. Inventory to be returned 16th July next, and an acct. when required.*

> *433: Admin, granted 7th March 1777 of the goods and c. of Patrick Lahy late of Muckully in the County of Kilkenny, farmer to John Lahy, brother, and next of kin of said deed.*

Archive Newspaper [102] records in 1755 show:
> *Robert Lahy, late of Rofiberean in the county of Kilkenny, Victualler.*

Victualler is an old Irish term for butcher. Perhaps Philip and Robert were related as they had the same profession.

2.6 Wexford Descendants - Origin Theory 5

The Wexford Martyrs were Matthew Lambert, Robert Myler, Edward Cheevers, Patrick Cavanagh (Irish: Pádraigh Caomhánach), **John O'Lahy**, and one other unknown individual. In 1581, they were found guilty of treason for aiding in the escape of James Eustace, 3rd Viscount Baltinglass; for refusing to take the Oath of Supremacy which declared Elizabeth I of England to be the head of the Church; and for conveying Catholic priests, laymen, and a Jesuit out of Ireland. On 5 July 1581, they were hanged, drawn and quartered in Wexford, Ireland. They were subsequently Beatified by Pope John Paul II. [117].

2.7 Huguenot Origins - Origin Theory 6

2.7.1 Who Were the Huguenots?

Huguenots were French Protestants inspired by the writings of John Calvin (Jean Calvin in French) in the 1530s. The majority of Huguenots endorsed the Reformed tradition of Protestantism. As Huguenots gained influence and more openly displayed their faith, Catholic hostility grew, in spite of increasingly liberal political concessions and edicts of toleration from the French crown. A series of religious conflicts followed, known as the Wars of Religion, fought intermittently from 1562 to 1598. One such battle was the St.

Bartholomew's Day Massacre of 24 August – 3 October 1572, when Catholics killed thousands of Huguenots in Paris – (see Figure 5).

The wars finally ended with the granting of the Edict of Nantes [1598], which granted the Huguenots substantial religious, political and military autonomy.

Renewed religious warfare in the 1620s caused the political and military privileges of the Huguenots to be abolished following their defeat. They retained the religious provisions of the Edict of Nantes until the rule of Louis XIV, who progressively increased persecution of them until he issued the Edict of Fontainebleau (1685), which abolished all legal recognition of Protestantism in France, and forced the Huguenots to convert. While nearly three-quarters eventually were killed or submitted, roughly 500,000 Huguenots had fled France by the early 18th century.

Source: [Wikipedia]

The symbol for the Huguenot plight is the Maltese cross with attached 'Dove' representing the 'flight' to escape persecution (see Figure 4).

Figure 4 The Huguenot Symbol

2.7.2 De La Haye Name Origins ?

According to www.surnamedb.com:

"De La Haye
This interesting and unusual name is of Norman origin and was introduced into England after the Conquest of 1066. As a French name it is locational from any of the various places named with the Olde French word "haye", meaning "hedge", of Germanic origin and ultimately equivalent to the Olde English pre 7th Century "(ge)haeg", meaning (hedged) enclosure. The places in Normandy generating the surname include "Les Hays" and "La haye", while Robert de Haia (1123), founder of Bexgrove Priory in Sussex, came from "Haye-du-Puits", La Manche. The Olde French word was usually used to denote an enclosed forest. The modern surname is found as "De La Haye", "de la Hay", "Delahaye" and "Delhay". In the late 16th Century, the name was reintroduced by French Huguenot refugees as in Jermyde la Haye, christened in London 1603. The first recorded spelling of the family name is shown to be that of Ranulf de Lahaia, which was dated 1199, in the "Records of the Abbey of Colchester", Essex, during the reign of King Henry 1, known as "The Lion of Justice", 1100 - 1135. Surnames became necessary when governments introduced personal taxation. In England this was known as Poll Tax."

2.7.3 François La Haye

In Shirley Lahey's book [1] she mentions a story told to her by her grandfather 'David Lahey' regarding their forbearers, supposedly a story handed down the generations. It basically states that Francois La Haye, a French Huguenot lived in Normandy in the Lorraine region probably in a town called Lahayville or Lahaycourt. David Lahey went on to state that Francois's forbearers came from La haye du Puits in 1103. In France there are a number of towns with the name Lahay including Lahaymeix, Lahayville, Laheycourt and a Lahaye in Holland.

To continue with Francois La Haye, according to Shirley Lahey the story handed verbally down the family line was that;

> *"Jean, eldest son in Francois's family of twelve, was killed in one of the battles that led up to the Massacre of St Bartholomew's Day in August 1572. Jean's death occurred in 1564 when he was about nineteen years old. Francois was said to have been a prominent Huguenot "blessed with a fair share of the world's goods and doubly blessed with a fine family""*

The latter statement is taken from an 'account' written by George F. Nicklin titled The Laheys of Queensland dated 1929 – however I haven't been able to obtain a copy of this 'account'.

Shirley goes on:

"after the death of Jean, "pride of his father's heart", Francois "broken hearted, sold his property as quickly as he could, left his country, changed his name to Francis Lahey and crossed with his family to the north of Ireland"

Other stories Shirley recounts include a family member being burnt at the stake.

Figure 5 Painting by François Dubois of the Saint Bartholomew's Day Massacre 1572

2.7.4 Huguenot Origin Logic

The 'logic' argument for the Huguenot origins could go as follows:

In the mid-17th century, the whole of Northern Europe was embroiled in the Catholic / Protestant religious wars. People didn't usually convert from one side to the other without good reason (some who were starving converted for bread and soup or winter clothes). Very often the 'converted' then converted back to their original religion a short time after (having consumed or acquired the religious bribe). Thus, although there were conversions and it is possible that some Leahys converted to Protestantism they must surely be too few to account for the mass of Protestant Lahys in County Cavan. In addition, why would they change their name from Leahy to Lahy? It makes much more logical sense that the Cavan Lahys are imported Protestants, and the name change progressed from De Lahaye (Huguenot original) to Lahay or Lahy – anglicised when the family moved to Britain / Ireland. The final name change (to Leahy) occurred around the 1870s. There could be several reasons for the final change.

1. The population were mainly farmers and not very literate and spelling consistency was pretty bad.

2. When Official documents (such as baptisms/ wedding / land deeds etc) were written, the name was often spelled as it sounded to the scribe – very often the same individual's surname is spelt in different ways in the same document!

3. The local Protestant Lahys will obviously have been aware that the Irish Leahys were catholic and may have wanted to 'fit in' with the local catholic population (who vastly outnumbered them in Cavan).

4. Griffiths' valuation of the late 1850-70s. Griffiths tended to lump all the variants of a name together (Lahy, Lahey, Leehy, Lahiff, Lahay, Leahey, Lahye, Laghy, Laughy, Laghie, Laghee, Laghey, Lahe, Lahey, Leahy, Lehy, Lihie Etc) and output a 'standard' format – in this case Leahy

In any case several variations of the name still exist (principally Lahey and Leahy) however most remaining in the Lough Sheelin area today are Leahys. I know that in my own family, the Leahys of 'The Cross' were still referred to as the 'Lahys' even up to the 1930s.

2.7.5 Known Huguenot Settlements in Ireland

There were significant Huguenot settlements in Dublin, Cork, Port Arlington, Lisburn, Waterford, Youghal and Killishandra. I visited the old Huguenot cemetery located in the centre of Dublin, off St. Stephen's Green, but found no Lahys or Delahays listed as having been buried there. I also visited the old cemetery at Killishandra (dating from 1688). It has restricted access however in Cavan town genealogy centre they let me look through a listing of the gravestones there and I found no Lahys or Delahays listed as having been being buried there.

It is not easy to trace the Huguenot movements, especially as no passenger lists exist for short term sea crossings such as the English Channel or the Irish Sea at the time. According to Gwynn [96]:

"The task of assessing the number of Huguenots seeking refuge in later Stuart England is exceptionally difficult. They left France by stealth, so no emigration lists exist. French names could be anglicized almost immediately on arrival across the Channel or otherwise changed beyond recognition, and marriage and burial records concerning Huguenots are often entered in the registers of English churches rather than those of the French congregations themselves. As refugees the mobility of the Huguenots was great. Guesses as to the numbers reaching England, exaggerated in the eighteenth century and since reduced, have varied from 20,000 to 150,000. A study of surviving baptismal records, in conjunction with other evidence including informed contemporary estimates, suggests that some 40,000–50,000 Huguenots settled in England between the late 1670s and the reign of Queen Anne. Refugee communities were located south of a line drawn from the Severn to the Wash. Almost all were near the sea, normally in towns rather than

in the countryside. By far the largest concentration was in London; living for the most part in the eastern and western suburbs, Huguenots comprised about 5% of the total population of the capital at the end of the seventeenth century."

2.7.6 Why Ireland?

The Stick
The Edict of Nantes, issued on April 13, 1598, by Henry IV of France, granted the Calvinist Protestants of France (also known as Huguenots) substantial rights in a nation still considered essentially Catholic. This was revoked in October 1685 by Louis XIV prompting a mass exodus by the Protestant Huguenots.

However clearly the Lahys were already in Cavan well before the later. So, although this revocation prompted an exodus of Protestants the Cavan Lahys (or Delahays) obviously left France well before the revocation and possibly even left before the Edit of Nantes. If the Francois Delahaye story is to believed they left France around the time of the St. Bartholomew's Day massacre in 1572 – following the murder of Francois's Eldest son Jean. Thus, they probably fled for their lives.

The Carrot
According to Froude [4] *"In 1662, the Duke of Ormond sent agents to France to attract Huguenots, French Presbyterians, to come to Ireland, promising them the preservation of their Calvinist ecclesiastical polity on condition that the congregations would officially conform to the Church of Ireland. At the same time, the Irish Parliament enacted that for a period of seven years Protestant Strangers would be enabled to become naturalized citizens and freemen of towns and guilds if they agreed to take the oaths of Allegiance and Supremacy. This proposal of collective naturalization made Ireland a much more attractive place of refuge than England, where a similar opportunity was not available until 1709. By contrast to late 17th and early 18th century Scottish Presbyterians, who were seen as a threat to the established order, French Huguenots were perceived to be an ideal group to strengthen the Protestant interest, provided they could be incorporated in some fashion into the national Church."*

2.7.7 Why Cavan?

The Land: Lake
Lahayville in Normandy (where Shirley Lahey suggested the Cavan Lahys originated from) is located next to a large lake – *Lac De Madine* (Figure 6 & Figure 7) It could be that Francois De Lahaye and his family having entered the country via a port (probably Cork or Dublin), that they wanted to buy land near a large lake in the country away from the city where they could continue their farming profession. Lake Sheelin would be a prime candidate for such a move. Why they chose that lake and that land is still unknown

however again assumptions can be made (see next chapter) in that the high ground around the lake would be easily defended.

Figure 6 Lac De Madine

Figure 7 Lac De Madine - Near Lahayville

There are many towns in France with a 'La Haye' in the name, (see Table 2):

Table 2 'La Haye' Towns in France

La Haye	Les Hayes, Loir-et-Cher
La Haye	La Haye-Bellefond, Manche
La Haye-Piquenot	La Haye-Comtesse, Manche
La Haye-Aubrée	La Haye-Pesnel, Manche
La Haye-Malherbe	La Haye-d'Ectot, Manche
La Haye-de-Calleville	La Haye-du-Puits, Manche
La Haye-de-Routot	Haye-Pesnel, Manche

La Haye-le-Comte	Hayes, Moselle
Le Haye-du-Theil	La Haye-des-Allemands, Moselle
La Haye-Saint-Sylvestre	L'Hay-les_Roses
La Haye-Descartes	Val de la Haye, Rouen

It should also be noted that the French name for The Hague in Netherlands in '*La Haye*'. As such, some people from The Hague have taken the 'La Haye' surname, for example the 16th Century painter Corneille de La Haye.

However, in the absence of alternative evidence, the four towns listed in Shirley Lahey's book [1] where the Lahays potentially originated were as follows:

1. Lahaville
2. Lahaycourt
3. Lahaymeix
4. La Haye-Du-Puits (Cherbourg Peninsula)

The first three are all in the Lorraine / Meuse region of Eastern France – near Lac De Madine,

Figure 8 Meuse Region in Lorraine   **Figure 9 La Haye-du-Puits in Manche / Normandy**

The fourth La Haye-Du-Puits – on the Cherbourg peninsula is included as one of Shirley Laheys relatives – David Lahey reportedly is on record as saying that the family hailed from the Normandy region of France – specifically La Hay De Puits in 1103.

Figure 10 Relative locations of Lahaycourt (on left). Lahaymeix (centre) and Lahayville (Right)

(Courtesy of Google Maps)

Lahayville

Lahayville is a very small town (or commune) in the Meuse region, situated very close to Lac De Madine as can be see in Figure 10 above. As one can see from Figure 11 and Figure 13, it's essentially a two-street town with a church. Its current population is about 30 people, and when I visited the town, only 2 donkeys were available for comment, however neither spoke English! In the 1500s when Francois De Lahaye and his family of twelve supposedly lived here it may have been a much larger village. Today this is quite a poor region of France, and so may have become depopulated. Due to the small size of the town there is very little recorded history of the town apart from its mention in World War 1 when there were gas attacks here. Like most of the towns in this region there is a 1st World War memorial.

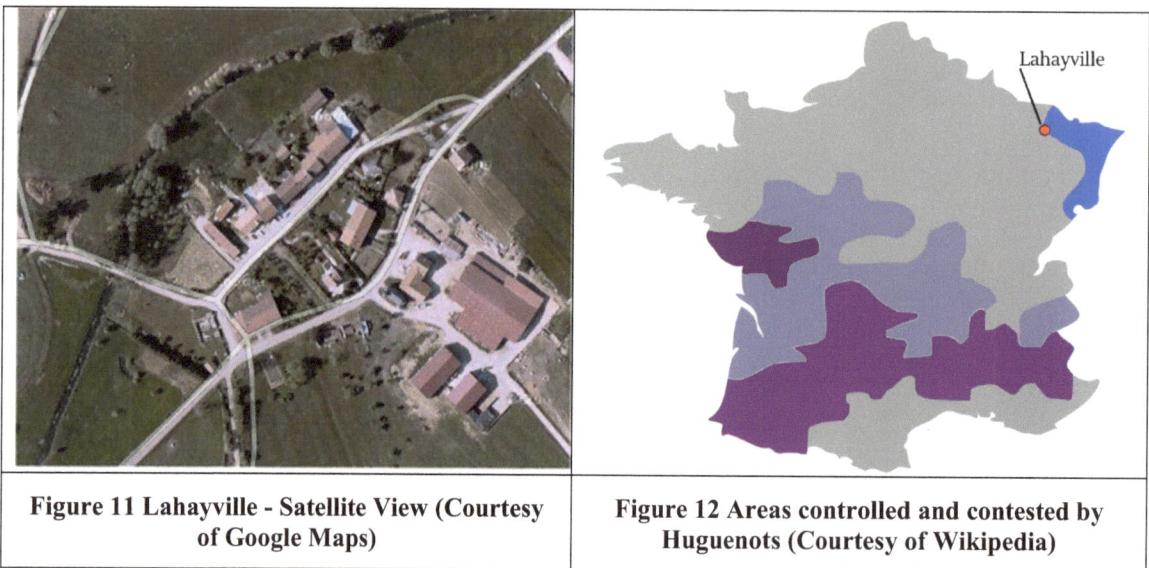

| Figure 11 Lahayville - Satellite View (Courtesy of Google Maps) | Figure 12 Areas controlled and contested by Huguenots (Courtesy of Wikipedia) |

Figure 13 Lahayville in 2011

Lahaymeix

Lahaymeix is another small town located half an hour drive from Lac De Madine in the middle of a forest region. It has a population of about 100 today, however on my visit there were only a few people around. There's a church with a graveyard which I investigated, however there were no Lahays buried there – it is probably a Roman Catholic Church.

Figure 14 Lahaymeix Satellite view (Courtesy of Google Maps)

Figure 15 Lahaymeix in 2011

Lahaycourt

Another half hour drive west of Lahaymeix is Lahaycourt, a town centred on a cross roads. It's the largest of the Meuse Lahay towns with a population of about 400.

Figure 16 Lahaycourt Satellite view (Courtesy of Google Maps)

Figure 17 Lahaycourt in 2011

I can find no references to Huguenots in these Meuse towns.

David Leahy M.Sc.

La Hay De Puits

On the Cherbourg peninsula lies La Haye-Du-Puits, which David Lahey (In Shirley Lahey's book [1]) recalled as being the origin of the family. It is much larger than the other three towns with a population today of about 1700. It has a castle dating back to the 11th century and was probably inhabited at some point by William the Conqueror prior to his invasion of England in 1066.

Figure 18 La Haye-Du-Puits Satellite View (Courtesy of Google Maps)

Figure 19 La Haye-Du-Puits in 2011

2.8 Mary Lahy Walker

On the 13th of June 1895 the New York Times [113] published an obituary for Mary Lahy Walker born 1818 and died 8/6/1895. It states that *"She was a descendant of the De La Hayes, a Huguenot family who fled from France and settled in various parts of Great Britain"*. A similar obituary was published in The Churchman journal [114] and the Brooklyn Daily Eagle (Figure 20). Obviously, the immediate family would have provided the information for the obituaries and the 'Huguenot origin' story passed down the generations.

In 1821, Mary would have been about 4 years old. Fortunately, most of this census (for County Cavan) has survived. On a search of the 1821 Census of the whole of Ireland, only one Mary Lahy is listed as being 4 years old in house No 12 in **Clonlohan** townland in the parish of **Drumlumman** County Cavan, she is listed as shown with the rest of her family in Table 3.

Table 3 Mary of Clonlohan in 1821 Census

Name	Age
John	36
Anne	36
William	13
Margaret	10
James	8
David	6
Mary	**4**

The only other close in age listed Mary Lahy in Ireland in this census is Mary Lahy of Mullagh (County Cavan) - who was 5 years old in 1821 - see Mullagh Lahys (Section 16). I think it more likely she was the Clonlohan Mary as it is closer to the 1818 birth date given in the Newspaper article. We can't say for sure that this was definitely Mary 'Lahy' Walker (as not all counties records in the1821 census survived) but it would seem likely.

We know from the 1860 census that Mary's eldest child (William) was born in New York in 1839 thus she must have emigrated from Ireland before that date.

Passenger Ship to New York
 A search of the **New York passenger list 1835** [112] shows a Mary Lahy aged 18 (estimated birth year 1817) on a ship named John Linton bound for New York. This is the only Mary Lahy of the correct age in the records bound for New York before 1839 thus it must be her. On the same ship is a *'Margaret Lahy'* who just happens to be the same age as Mary's sister Margaret, so I think it is quite likely that it is her.

On the same ship there is a '*James Lahy*' (labourer) aged 29 listed. Mary had an older brother James, who was 4 years older than her (not 12). It is possible her brother James lied about his age, however on a search of the 1821 census there is only one James Lahy listed of the correct age - James Lahy of No 28 **Mullaghboy**. Mullaghboy is very close to

Clonloaghan, so it is likely that this James (perhaps a friend or more likely cousin) went along with Mary and her sister as an older male chaperone for the potentially dangerous journey.

Her marriage to James Walker (also Irish origin - potentially from No 39 Kelgala, Drumlumman) according to the Newspaper article took place in 1837 however I can't find a record of this marriage in either Ireland or New York. However, given that she was listed on the Ship manifest as Mary Lahy (not Walker) I presume she married James in New York or elsewhere in the USA.

The US census reports for 1860 and 1870 show both Mary and James were born in Ireland. Table 4 shows Mary's family in the 1st District 6th Ward Brooklyn, Kings, New York. The age of Mary is a few years out, but that is not unusual in these types of records.

Table 4 Mary 'Lahy' Walker in the New York 1860 Census

Name	Age
James Walker	40
Mary Walker	**40**
William D Walker	21
James H Walker	19
John T Walker	16
Jane Walker	14
Samuel	11
Emma H Walker	6
Alfred Walker	4
Agnus Walker	0

I'm quite confident that I have found the correct 'Mary Lahy' as her age and that of her sister Margaret match up to the 1821 census in Clonloaghan (and also James the cousin?) who travelled with them. Thus, here is clear evidence - reported in a late 1800s Newspaper that a 'Lahy' probably from Cavan, Ireland is descended from the De La Hayes Huguenot family. See section 12 on the Clonloaghan branch of Lahys.

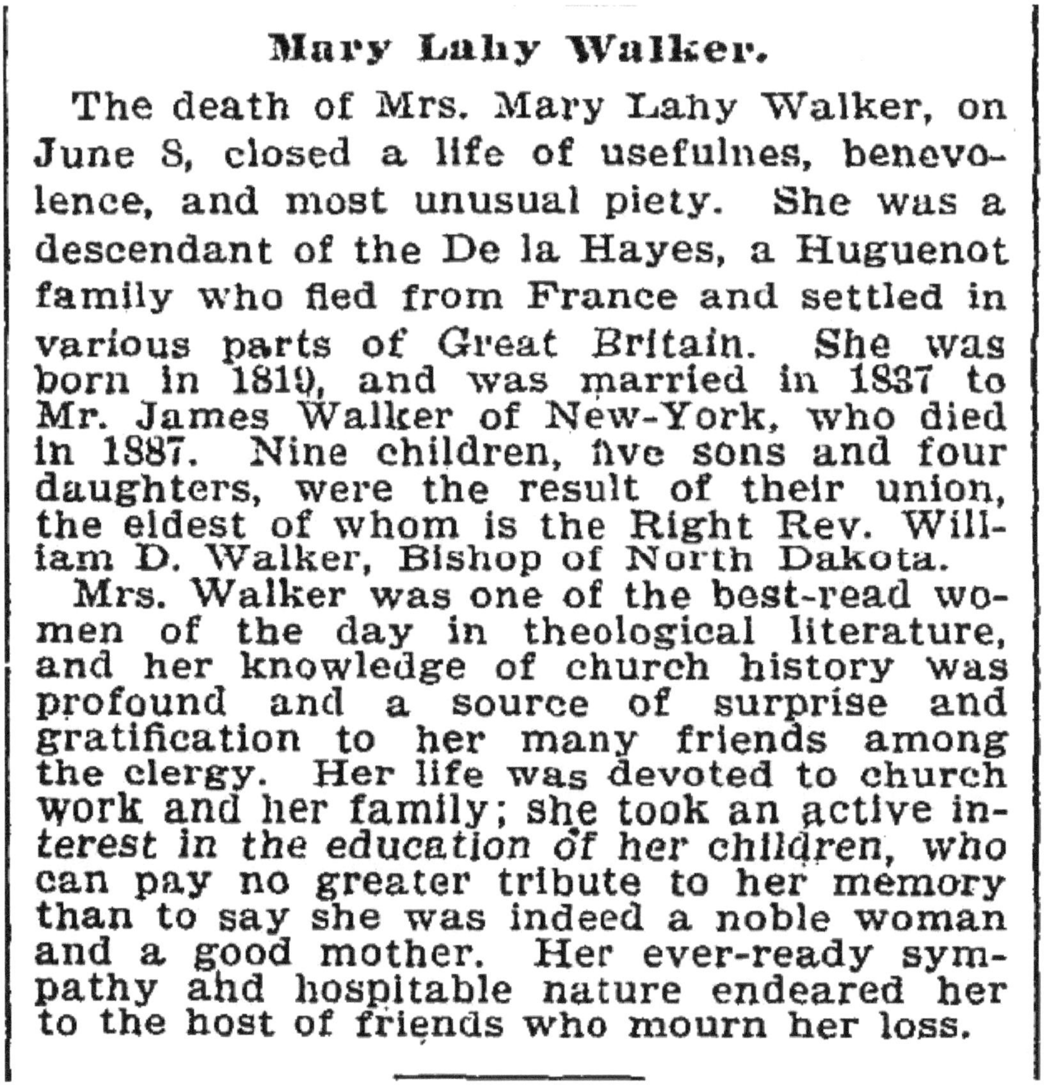

Mary Lahy Walker.

The death of Mrs. Mary Lahy Walker, on June 8, closed a life of usefulnes, benevolence, and most unusual piety. She was a descendant of the De la Hayes, a Huguenot family who fled from France and settled in various parts of Great Britain. She was born in 1819, and was married in 1837 to Mr. James Walker of New-York, who died in 1887. Nine children, five sons and four daughters, were the result of their union, the eldest of whom is the Right Rev. William D. Walker, Bishop of North Dakota.

Mrs. Walker was one of the best-read women of the day in theological literature, and her knowledge of church history was profound and a source of surprise and gratification to her many friends among the clergy. Her life was devoted to church work and her family; she took an active interest in the education of her children, who can pay no greater tribute to her memory than to say she was indeed a noble woman and a good mother. Her ever-ready sympathy and hospitable nature endeared her to the host of friends who mourn her loss.

Figure 20 Obituary of Mary Lahy Walker - Brooklyn Daily Eagle 12/6/1895

2.8.1 Mary's Brother Nicholas

I have not been able to obtain Mary's marriage certificate to confirm her origins as County Cavan, however new evidence has come to light (from the USA) which identifies Nicholas Lahy as being a brother of Mary Ann Walker and also written evidence that he was from Clonloaghan – thus verifying that the Mary Ann (Lahy) Walker was indeed one of the Cavan Leahys as suggested.

There is a birth record in Ballymachugh Church of Ireland of Nicholas Lahy, son of John and Ann in 1827 (Figure 21) and his brother John in 1822 (Figure 22).

David Leahy M.Sc.

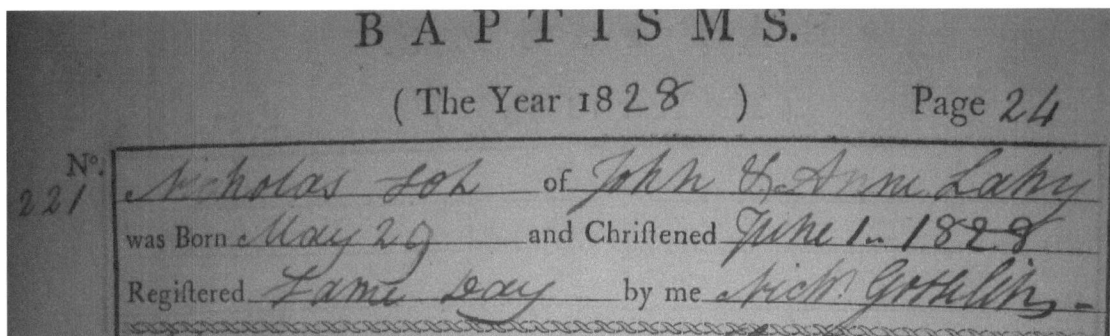

Figure 21 Nicholas baptism in Ballymachugh Church of Ireland 1828

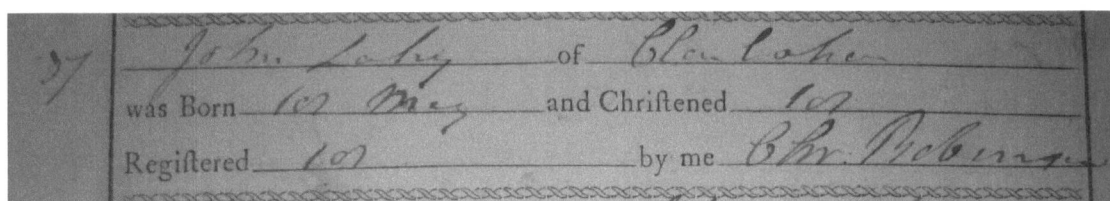

Figure 22 John baptism in Ballymachugh Church of Ireland 1822

John and Ann took a ship (The Eliza Anne) from Liverpool on 11/6//1844 to New York together with their sons Nicholas and John. Nicholas (17) [listed as 15 - perhaps it was a cheaper fare!] and John [listed as 22].

Figure 23 Passenger record of the Eliza Anne to New York 1844

Presumeably, they stayed with their daughter who were already in New York. Military discharge papers (Figure 24) stated that he was from Clonloaghan, Cavan. The only John and Ann in Clonloaghan at that time were the parents of Mary Lahy Walker (who travelled toNew York with her sister Margaret in 1835. He and his brother John were not listedin the 1821 census as obviously they were not born yet [John born 1822 (Ballymachugh Church Records]. This mustbe the same family as they were the only Lahy family listed as living in Clonloaghan in 1821 and the only John and Anne Lahy in Clonloaghan.

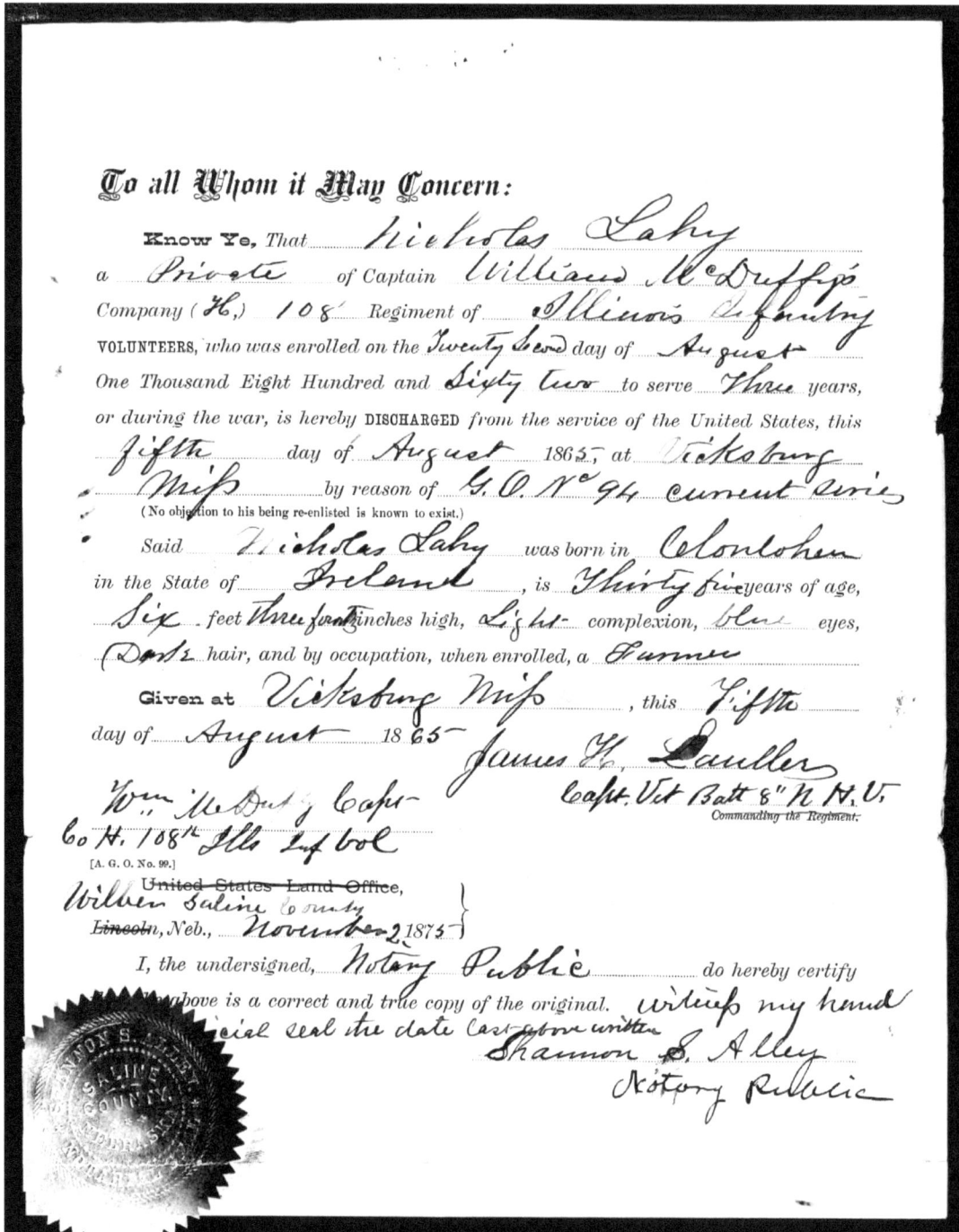

Figure 24 Nicholas Lahey - US Army discharge paper 1865 [https://glorecords.blm.gov]

Thus, there can be no doubt that Mary (Lahy) Walker – claimed Huguenot descendant of the De La Haye family originated from the Cavan Lahys. Further information on the fate of the Clonloaghan family is presented in the next Volume.

2.9 Michael Leader Letter - Edward Lahee

In the Irish Genealogical Research Society (IGRS) archives [116] there is a letter from Michael Leader, dated 1990 to Trinity College Dublin on behalf of a client of his 'Miss Lahee' researching an ancestor of hers - *Edward Lahee* (of Fenagh) (born approx. 1849) who was enrolled at Trinity College Dublin. The letter stated that:

> "*The family has always assumed it had Huguenot origins*"

There are a few locations in Ireland named 'Fenagh'. One is near Antrim in Northern Ireland and the other in in County Leitrim - just west of County Cavan - see Figure 25. I can find no trace of Edward Lahee in the enrolment registers of Trinity College Dublin. However, in the England and Wales Census of 1881 there is an Edward Lahee born in Ireland in 1849 living in 33 Windsor Road, Islington London (Railway Clerk). By 1891 he and his family have moved to Gordon Lodge, Enfield, London. In 1901 they are still in Enfield and Edward is now a Commercial Accountant. In the Ireland 1901 census there are no Lahee families in either the Antrim or Leitrim Fenaghs.
It is not known if this Edward Lahee came from Fenagh - however the birthplace says Ireland.

Figure 25 Relative location of Fenagh to Lough Sheelin (Courtesy Google Maps)

3 The 1600s – De Lahayes

Like the 1500s, the 1600s left very little written evidence of Lahys in Ireland - there whereabouts or travels. There are a few references to De Lahayes in this period, but mainly residing in England. I have nevertheless collected some evidence

3.1 1600s: Miscellaneous Evidence

According to [95]:
"Lists of foreign Protestants and aliens resident in England, 1618-1688 ". In Kent it lists;

> *"French refugees during the reign of James 2nd made free denizens by order dated 16.12.1687. De la HAYE, John - John, Thomas, Charles, Moses, Adrian,& Peter his children"*

Huguenots in Ireland, pre-1643

De La Haye is mentioned in a list of French refugees (and their descendants) who settled in Great Britain and Ireland before 1643. These surnames were obtained from "Irish Pedigrees", vol.2, by John O'Hart which was published in 1892 in Dublin [5]. Hay (De la Haye, H., Dover, 1622) is listed in the appendix to Fosdick's' The French blood in America' [6].

3.2 The Pirate: Jacquotte Delahaye

Jacquotte Delahaye was a pirate, or buccaneer, active in the Caribbean sea, daughter of a French father and a Haitian mother. To escape her pursuers, she faked her own death and took on a male alias, living as a man for many years. Upon her return, she became known as "back from the dead red" because of her striking red hair. She led a gang of hundreds of pirates, and with their help took over a small Caribbean island in the year of 1656, which was called a "freebooter republic". Several years later, she died in a shootout while defending it. - [Source: Wikipedia] There's no record of her being in Ireland, and it is not known if she was descended from 'Francois De Lahaye' from Lahayville, but it is always nice to think there may have been a pirate in the family lineage.

3.3 1630 Move to Ireland?

Bill Graham, a local Cavan historian who did a lot of genealogy research in the local area stated in [1] that: "The Lahys were free settlers, not planters – a professional educated family moving from England around 1630. They paid for Aughakilmore with *cold hard cash*. The Lahy females were sought after brides because they were of good stock and had dowries"!

3.4 William Delahaye - Back Pay Claim

In 1660 there is a record of a William De Lahaye making a claim for back pay in the arms in Dublin (Figure 26).

Order by the Lords Justices of Ireland upon the petitions of Robert Morris; of James Graham; of *William de la Haye*; and of Christopher Bell and others, respectively, all relating to arrears of military pay [95].

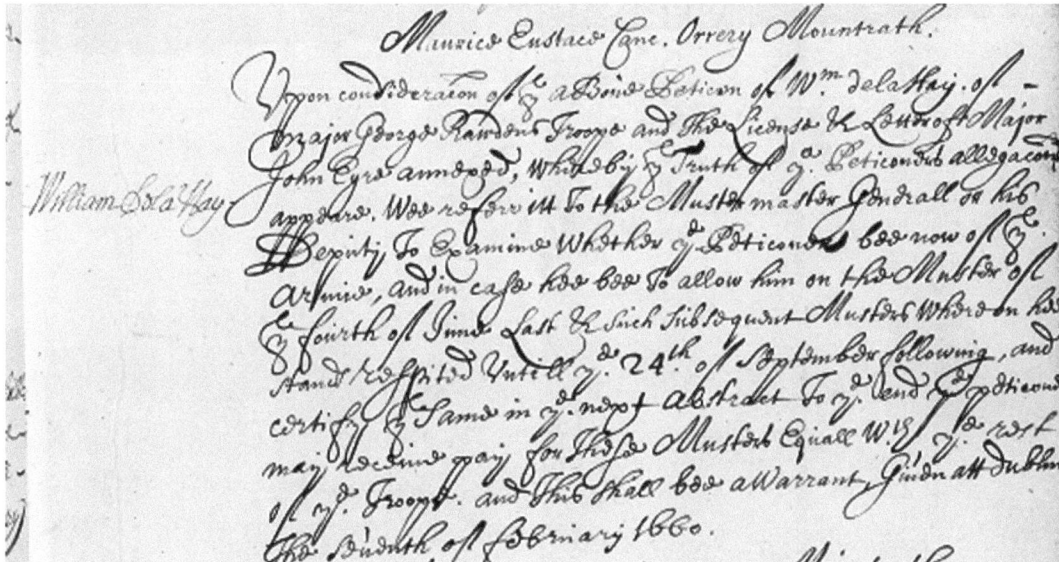

Figure 26 William De Lahaye Back Pay Claim 1660 [95]

3.5 Captain De La Hay

The Parliamentary Army (Cromwell) under the Earl of Essex 14 September 1642 lists:

> Lieutenant: Captain **John de la Hay**

Edith Lahey (a relative of Shirley Lahey) in her book: 'The Laheys of Bellissima Forest' [7] made reference to a family story of a Colonel La haye who fought with Cromwell *"The next La-Haye of whom I have heard [after Francis] is a Colonel La-Haye, a descendant of Francis La-Laye, who fought with Cromwell in 1649 when the latter went to Ireland to quell the Rebellion."* According to Shirley, Edith Lahey was told a lot of family stories by some of her 'American' ancestors; however, I have searched the military archives at Kew in London and can find no trace of this Colonel La-Haye, which is surprising as it is quite a high rank not to be documented. There is however a John De La hay listed as a Lieutenant in Cromwell's Parliamentary Army under the Earl of Essex 14 September 1642 (although confusingly it names him as 'Captain' John de la hay, so it is unclear if his rank was Lieutenant or Captain).

In Peacock's [8] The Army Lists of the Roundheads and Cavaliers, Lieutenant Colonel John De La Hay is listed as being part of the parliamentarians, under Command of **Colonel William Earle of Bedford**, his captain being Arthur Evelin. It is conceivable that he was promoted to Colonel later in his career – so perhaps we've found the 'Colonel La hay' mentioned by Edith Lahey [7] – see Figure 27 below.

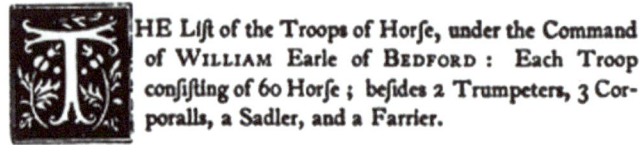

HE Lift of the Troops of Horfe, under the Command of WILLIAM Earle of BEDFORD : Each Troop confifting of 60 Horfe ; befides 2 Trumpeters, 3 Corporalls, a Sadler, and a Farrier.

COLONELLS AND THEIR OFFICERS.

Colonell, William Earle of Bedford.	Chirurg. James Swright.
Major.	Colonell, Bazil Lord Fielding.⁸⁴
Chirurgion, Hugh Ward.	Major, Robert Beckill.
Colonell, Sir Wil. Belfore.	Colonell, Lord Willoughby of Parham.⁸⁵
Major, Jo. Urrey.	Colonell, Sir William Waller.⁸⁶

[*PARLIAMENT.*]   49

31.
C. Arthur Evelin.
L. C. John de la Hay.

32.
C. Geo. Thompfon.
L. John Cofhe.
C. Iohn Upton.
Q. Will. Coufe.

33.
. C. Edwin Sandys.
L. John Cockaine.

34.
C. Anth. Milemay.
L. Hen. Hatcher.
C. Sam. Cofworth.
Q. Th. Varnon.

35.
C. Ed. Kyghley.
L. W. Cooker.
C. Tho. Loftus.
Q. Alex. Winchefter.

36.
C. Nath. Fines.⁶⁸

Figure 27 The Army Lists of the Roundheads and Cavaliers [8]

Thus, although there is some discrepancy in the different colonels / Generals of his regiment, there is clear evidence that a Lieutenant Colonel John De La hay fought for the Parliamentarians – alongside captain Arthur Evelin. However, I can find no further record of Lieutenant Colonel John De La Hay.

His regiment however saw action in 1642 at the Battle of Edgehill (Figure 28) which was an indecisive encounter at the beginning of the English Civil War. (Earl of Bedford's Regiment of Horse highlighted with red circle).

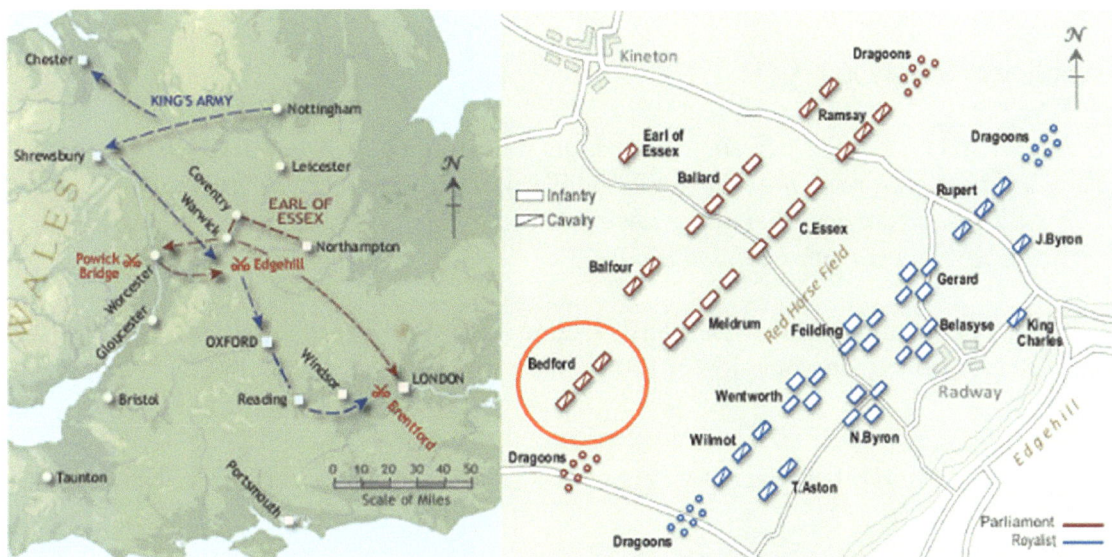

Figure 28 1642 Battle of Edgehill (Courtesy of http://www.british-civil-wars.co.uk)

In Figure 29 below one can see a listing of residents at the Royal Hospital at Kilmainham in Dublin in the year 1686, a home for retired soldiers. Here is listed a Francis De Lahay in the Duke of Ormonde's regiment of Horse [97].

Figure 29 Francis Delahay - Royal Hospital Kilmainham - Dublin 1686

According to Shirley Lahey [1]:

"*In 1693, about fifty French Huguenots who were retired military officers and soldiers, following the war of 1689-1691, were invited to settle in Youghal by the mayor and corporation of the town" Amoung the "principal families" were the Dehays – a variation of De La hays?"*

There is no mention of Lahy or De Lahy / DeLahaye in Daltons Irish Army Lists, 1661-1685 [9]. Nor is there any mention of Lahys in the 1630 Muster Rolls for County Cavan [10].

A reference in PRONI [11] details letters from a La Haye working with 'The King' in 1692 (see Figure 30):

Figure 30 1692 La Haye arrived with the King (courtesy PRONI [11])

David Leahy M.Sc.

"Arrived there with the king ten days ago. Acknowledge Lord C's letter of the 1st, and asks him to help Van Homrigh in looking after A's affairs in Ireland; the sooner he (A) can get his warrant and be put in possession of his property the better. The king has written to Lord C. and Porter thereupon. Says he will do his best for Lord C's interests; but it is said the King will not give anything away until next session of parliament. Will also do his best for the chief Baron. Will start tomorrow for the provinces of Ujtrect and Gueldres, where the King also intends to go in a few days. The French are very quiet; it is thought they will not do anything, as they have withdrawn their troops and are beginning to break up their magazines."

The King in this Case must have been William of Orange.

A *Charles des Moulins de la Haye* is listed as a Huguenot French officer stationed in Dublin around 1700 [118].

4 1600s – Loghy / Laughey 1st in Cavan

4.1 Commonwealth Survey Records of 1652

The survey as transcribed by William Mooney in 1835 covers the entire of County Cavan and is listed in order of barony. It appears to be a unique document, and no similar survey has been discovered for any other county. The format, purpose and content of this work differentiates it from other surveys from around the same era including the Civil Survey of Ireland 1654-56 and the 1659 Census of Ireland in which both sources, Cavan returns are not found. The 1652 Commenwealth Survey [121] lists **Pat Loghy** & Bryne in the townland of **Aughhakilmore Lower** in Ballymachugh as land owners. This is the earliest recorded Lahy in Cavan and must be the same Pat Lahy mentioned in the later land deeds. Thus, the Lahys were there before at least 1652 and probably much earlier.

4.2 Pender 1659 'Census'

This "census" was probably taken during Petty's survey between December 1654 and the year 1659. It details the names of the large estate owners and the numbers of Protestants and Catholics in each parish. The original clan names are also noted with the numbers of individuals of that surname. It is missing all of counties Cavan, Galway, Mayo, Tyrone and Wicklow, most of Meath (nine baronies) and four baronies in Cork. Nevertheless, there are little other data from this time period and the locations of the surname 'Lahy' and 'Leaghy' are shown in Table 5.

Table 5 1659 Penders Census Returns for 'Lahy' and 'Leaghy'

Name	County	Barony	Number of People
Lahy	Tipperary	Slevardagh	12
		Middlethird	12
		Baronyes of Eliogurty and Ikerim	53
Leaghy	Cork	Cork City	8
		Barrony of Kinalea	8
		Barony of Kierycurrihy	7
		Barony of Barymore	30
	Kerry	Barony of Maquinihy	9

David Leahy M.Sc.

4.3 Patrick & John Laughy at Tree Top

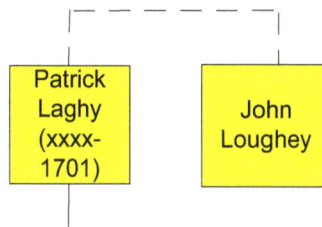

Figure 31 Patrick & John Laghy / Loughey

4.3.1 Dissenters to King James II

Since first publication, new information has come to light on Patrick and John at the top of the known tree. **Patrick** is first mentioned in a deed dated **1667** [12]. It is not known whether **John** was a brother, son or father. Patrick went on to have descendants (we know this due to the Rebecca Burrows marriage articles [20]) in which land is mentioned that is inherited from him. It is not known if John lived to produce any descendants, but I think that it's quite likely given the number of Leahys that emerged in Ballymachugh!

In 1688, the English (Roman Catholic) King James II (James VII of Scotland), driven off by the ascent of William and Mary in the Glorious Revolution, came to Ireland with the sole purpose of reclaiming his throne. After his arrival, the Parliament of Ireland assembled a list of names in **1689** of those reported to have been disloyal to him, eventually tallying between two and three thousand, (1305 of which lived in Ireland) in a bill of attainder [122]. Those on the list were to report to Dublin for sentencing. With the assistance of French troops, James landed in Ireland in March 1689.The Irish Parliament did not follow the example of the English Parliament; it declared that James remained King and passed a massive **bill of attainder** against those who had 'rebelled' against him.

> *"Persons here after named, being Persons who have notoriously joined in the said Rebellion and Invasion, and some of which are upon Indictments condemned, some executed for High Treason, and the rest ran away, or abscond, or are now in the actual Service of the Prince of Orange against your Majesty, and others kill'd in open Rebellion - Irish Protestants considered by the government of James II to be disloyal to the king".*

Patrick Laughy and **John Laughy** from Aughakilmore, Cavan were on the list! They were listed as Yeomen. Yeomen were likely to be freehold farmers - someone who was of slightly higher standing than copyhold or tenant farmers. He wasn't rich enough not to work on the farm himself and so wouldn't style himself as a gentleman farmer. Patrick and John were thus part of the **1305** 'rebellious' individuals named who lived in Ireland. In terms of the 'Top of the family Tree' it is the earliest reference to a 'John', thus John was probably either a brother or father of Patrick. It gives us more evidence of their Protestant (and potentially Huguenot) origins and also lets us know that there were only 2 of them (Lahys / Laughys) with land in Cavan at the time. Sources at the Ulster Historical Foundation [123] told me that *"the point of the list was so that those named would know they had been attainted"*.

In the column marked Code the references stand for: I Persons who have notoriously joined in the late rebellion [Against Catholic James 2nd]; II Persons who have absented themselves from this kingdom since 5 Nov last; III Persons who absented themselves before 5 Nov last; IV Persons absent because of sickness, infirmity, etc. The list included people from across the island of Ireland.

Patrick and **John** were listed under category I - *Persons who have notoriously joined in the late rebellion;*

The Bill of Attainder was according to [124] "*a declaration of war against the Protestants. The English Royalists warned James that the passing of the Bill would prejudice his interests in England, but it was in vain, and the dragoons followed by armed Irish, drove the Protestants out and seized their estates*".

"*Then there were other estates which Protestants had obtained by purchase [as opposed to land 'given' to the Planters by the British Government]. These were not held sacred. The Protestants must be driven out. A Bill was passed confiscating the property of all who had aided or abetted the Prince of Orange*" Patrick and John were, it is presumed part of this category, as we have information passed down the family line [Shirley Lahy [1] that they bought the land with 'cold hard cash'. Between 2-3000 people were affected by these acts of attainder.

They must have been quite traumatic times - as it was unclear who was going to win (of the two Kings (Protestant King William of Orange or Roman Catholic King James [2nd son of Charles I) - Patrick and John stood to lose everything they owned - including their lives – which must have been particularly frustrating given that they had 'bought' the land rather than allocated it as Protestant 'planters'. After William of Orange defeated James II at the battle of the Boyne the **bill of attainder** was made null and void in both the English and Irish parliaments probably much to the relief of Patrick and John.

Also interesting is the spelling of the name – **Laughy / Loughey** (Patrick in 1667 land deed spelt as Laghy)

4.3.2 Involvement in Williamite War

There is a record of Patrick and John 'Loughey' [125] as having participated as 'Defenders' at the **siege of Derry** in 1689. They were listed as 'Yeomen' and stated as being from Monaghan (rather than Cavan). They may have temporarily taken residence in Monaghan during the Williamite war, or possibly gave a 'wrong address' in case of reprisals in their home county of Cavan (in which they'd already been resident for at least 22 years).

They may also have been involved in the battles around Enniskillen. According to Wikipedia:

> *Williamite civilians drawn from the local Protestant population organised a formidable irregular military force. Operating with Enniskillen as a base, they carried out raids against the Jacobite forces in Connacht and Ulster.*

The rationale for 'participating' in the Williamite war is noted in [124].

> *"some of the minor country gentry came with whatever force they could command of men able to bear arms, an in many cases with their wives and families, who could not be exposed to danger of life if left behind in their country houses"*

In other words, the choice was simple – fight or be killed by the Jacobite armies roaming the countryside.

One such Jacobite was Sir Gerard Irving of Lowtherstown who (according to [124]) *"when disappointed in not being appointed to the command of the Inniskillen troops as Colonel, he went to Dublin and offered his services to the other side"*. He subsequently was offered Lieutenant-colonel rank and proceeded to Cavan on his way to his own estate. In Cavan he *"had such a number of swords, pistols, carbines and other equipment for the troop which he was to raise, that the Protestant inhabitants of Cavan became uneasy, and communicated the news to Belturbet. The Belturbet men acted promptly. Mr Daniel French and Mr Henry Williams set out with about 60 horse soldiers for Cavan, seized the arms, and accoutrements and took Sir Gerard Irving prisoner"*.

4.3.3 Cavan Town Rejects Irish Authority

"At a Quarter Sessions held at Cavan on the 8th of January, several Irish justices of the Peace being on the bench [created by the Jacobite leader 'Earl of Tyconnell] Captain Robert Saunderson, of Castle Saunderson with a body of 14 horse entered the town, and, mounting the Bench, demanded by what Commission they sat there? They answered, by that of King James. He told them the authority was not good, while the laws were unrepealed, and told them to return home"

"Tyconnell, being informed of this proceeding at Cavan, threatened to send some Troops of Horse into that rebellious country that would not submit to justices acting against the law, which so much terrified the people that almost every man put himself in Arms. And this was the cause of sending down Galmoy into that country, and of the fears and plight of the people"

Lord Galmoy was a much-feared commander on the Jacobite side, he had notoriously broken his word to 'give quarter' to surrendering captives only to murder them once they surrendered. With this sort of force on its way, it's no wonder that John and Patrick Loughey took up arms to defend themselves. Lord Galmoy entered the County of Cavan on 20th March 1689, stopping in Belturbet before proceeding towards Castle Crom to unsuccessfully lay siege and was defeated by the defending Enniskillen army.

4.3.4 Action at Cavan

According to [124]– History of Enniskillen]:

"As the Irish foot (soldiers) had not deserted the Castle at Cavan, Colonel Wolsely sent on 23rd March 1689-90 a party under command of Lieutenant-Colonel Earle and Major Billing, to take it. Making their way by Butler's -bridge, they pursued the usual Inniskillen method of travelling by night and attacking in the early morning. A party of horse and about 50 foot (soldiers) of Colonel Earle's detachment, beat the enemy (about 60) from their breastwork, and crossing the river pursued them, killing 20 and taking 16 prisoners, including the Irish Captain and one ensign with a loss of only one man. The horse (regiment) then joined the party proceeding to Cavan, which drove the Irish out of the houses that remained, killing between 60 and 80 of them, and set fire to the houses. The Inniskilleners lost only one officer, one ensign and eight men in this engagement.

In both the outposts at Belturbet and Ballyshannon the Inniskilleners were "straightened" for want of food. About the 23rd March Colonel Wolsey led out a force from Belturbet, which secured a thousand head of cattle, and for this reason were pursued by the Jacobites, who clung closely to those whom they called in consequence "cattle-stealers." The Inniskilliners killed 20 or 30 of their opponents and secured their prey."

The Enniskillen men were fierce fighters by all accounts and were feared by the Jacobite armies that lay before them. It's also interesting that securing cattle was a key resource for both armies.

4.3.5 Siege of Derry

In [124] it is recounted that after the 13 apprentice boys had slammed the City Gate closed in the face of King William's troops, that *"messages were sent, under cover of the following night, to the Protestant gentlemen of the neighbouring counties"*. No doubt Cavan was amongst these. He went on *"..it was evident that the country seats which the Protestant landowners had recently fortified in the three southern provinces could no longer be defended. Many families submitted, delivered up their arms, and thought themselves happy in escaping with life. But many resolute and high-spirited gentlemen and yeomen were determined to perish rather than yield. They packed up such valuable property as could easily be carried away, burned whatever they could not remove, and well-armed and mounted, set out for those spots in Ulster which were the strongholds of their race and of their faith. The flower of the Protestant population of Munster and*

Connaught found shelter at Enniskillen. Whatever the was bravest and most truehearted in Leinster took the road to Londonderry".

He goes on that *"Some of them attempted to make a stand at Dromore, but were broken and scattered. The flight became wild and tumultuous. The fugitives broke down the bridges and burned the ferryboats. Whole towns, the seats of the Protestant population, were left in ruins without one inhabitant. The people of Omagh their own dwellings so utterly that no roof was left to shelter the enemy from the rain and the wind. The people of Cavan migrated in one body to Enniskillen".*

According to [124] by March 20th 1689,

> *"Protestants from County Cavan had come to Eniskillen, including 3-4 troops of horse and 3-4 foot companies, together with terrified women and children. These too had received instruction from Colonel Lundy to leave Cavan and travel north, their actions given impetus by the presence of the Jacobite Lord Galmoy and a large part of the Irish army in Cavan."*

> *"By the 23rd the Co Cavan men had left the town to journey to Londonderry as ordered"*

No doubt **Patrick** and **John Loughey** were among them.

In [124] a more detailed account is given:

> *"Colonel Lundy had meanwhile ordered the garrison of Cavan to fall back on Derry, and when the Protestants of Cavan learned of the advance of James they became alarmed and resolved to march to Inniskillen they had four troops of horse and about four companies of foot [approx. 100 men in a company], pretty well armed and these, with women and children, set out in dreadful weather on their journey, and reached Inniskillen in great disorder on the 20th March in a most pitiable plight covered with mud and dirt, with tears and lamentations. Governor Hamilton had them immediately supplied with free quarters, and the Inniskilliners were uplifted with the hopes that these troops and companies would help them in their defence.*

> *The Inniskillen men hoped that these Cavan troops of horse and companies of foot would stand by them to defend the town; but the Cavan gentry and officers insisted on obeying the positive orders of Colonel Lundy; and the Cavan officers used their best endeavours to persuade Governor Hamilton to do the same thing, to forsake Inniskillen and flee to Derry. They tried to influence some of the Inniskillen men to adopt the same opinion - a policy which, if it had been followed, would as McCormack observed, "have ruined the whole Protestant interest in*

Ireland, and given the Irish army the opportunity of passing into Scotland or Ireland at their pleasure.

When the men of Inniskillen further reasoned further with the fugitives from Cavan, they discovered that Cavan men were moved not so much to obey Lundy as to avoid Lord Galmoy who was advancing at the head of a large army, and by means of his horse soldiers and dragoons had arrived at Belturbet, taking Dean Dixie's on his way. So, the men of Cavan only stayed three days at Inniskillen, sufficiently long to get refreshed after the fatigue of this part of their journey and proceeded to set out for Derry. Governor Hamilton, feeling disgusted at their cowardice, and wishing to save his supplies, insisted on their taking their wives and children with them, as if left behind they would be turned out of the town. This order had some effect, for most of the foot soldiers had wives and children, and, being unable to take their families with them, remained in the town; and these three or four companies swelled the Inniskillen forces, while the others were allowed to proceed to Londonderry."

I presume Patrick and John (as Yeomen) were part of the three or four companies. Thus, it appears that the Enniskillen men held the Cavan men's family's hostage to force them to fight with them (as opposed to going to the defence of Londonderry). Probably not the best motivation to install in your 'supposed' allies. It's not known whether Patrick and John Loughey travelled with the first party to Derry or stayed and fought at Enniskillen with their families – and then went to Derry? However, from this statement, we can assume that John and Patrick had no family with them if they proceeded on to fight in the siege at Derry.

It is estimated that 30,000 Protestants resided in the City of Londonderry when the siege began. As Lord McCaulay quoted in [124] goes on to say *"The number of men capable of bearing arms within the walls was seven thousand; and the whole world could not have furnished seven thousand men better qualified to meet a terrible emergency with clear judgement, dauntless valour, and stubborn patience."* – although I suspect it was as much about survival than fighting for the Protestant cause per se. At the end, the garrison was reduced to about three thousand. The be-siegers also lost a lot of men. The siege lasted 105 days with the besieged having to eat rats and chew on cow hides towards the end. A rat cost 6d, a mouse 1s and a cat 4s 6d. The blood of a horse was 2d per quart. The besieged let the cats and dogs feed on the corpses of their fallen comrades to fatten them up before killing and eating the dogs.

Interestingly one of the ships employed to break the blockade - The Dartmouth – was commanded by Captain John 'Leake' who went on to become an Admiral of the fleet. It's not known if he was connected to the Lahys (he was born in London).

After their victory at Enniskillen, according to Lord McCaulay quoted in [124]...*the Eniskilleners soon invaded the County of Cavan, drove before them fifteen hundred of James's troops, took and destroyed the castle of Ballincarrig reputed the strongest in that part of the kingdom and carried off the pikes and muskets of the garrison."*

David Leahy M.Sc.

It's not clear whether or not John survived the ordeal as there is no record of a 'John Loughey' after the siege. Patrick, however obviously did survive as there is a record of his Will in 1701 (see Figure 33 page 56).

Figure 32 Depiction of the Siege of Londonderry 1689 (taken from [124]

4.3.6 Name Spelling

The exact relationship between Patrick and John is not currently known but they must have been either father and son or brothers at the very least. The spelling '*Loughey*' is interesting and also appears spelt this way on Patrick's Will of 1701 [126]. However, in his land deed dated 1667 it was spelt as '*Laghey*'. It seemed to be interchangeable back then – as literacy wasn't commonplace it's not surprising there are variations. The key question is how the original name was spelled – and was it of French (Huguenot) origin.

4.3.7 Patrick's death

Ireland Diocesan and Prerogative Will & Administration 1595-1858 [126] lists a ***'Patrick Loughey'*** of Upper Aughakilmore as having made a Testamentary Will in the year 1701. Thus, he most probably died that year or the following one. It's unlikely that it still survives. Note the name Spelling - Loughey! – See Figure 33 Listing of Patrick's Will in 1701 (Courtesy NAI)and that he lived in *Upper Aughakilmore* (rather than Tawlaught) as the 1667 Land deed suggested.

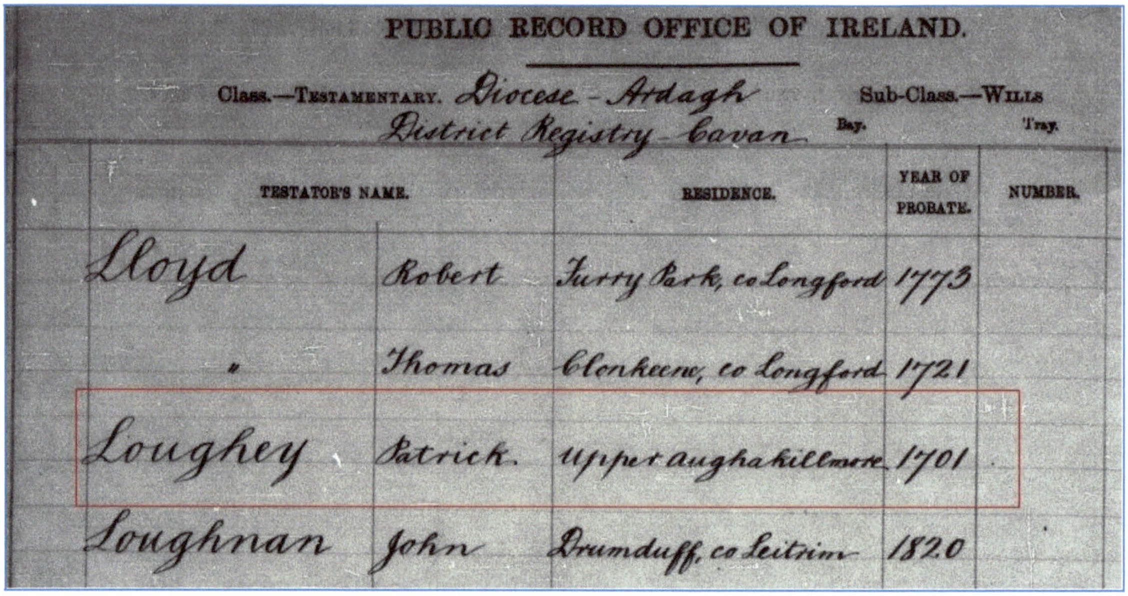

PUBLIC RECORD OFFICE OF IRELAND.

Class.—Testamentary. Diocese - Ardagh — Sub-Class.—Wills

District Registry Cavan — Bay. — Tray.

Testator's Name.		Residence.	Year of Probate.	Number.
Lloyd	Robert	Furry Park, co Longford	1773	
"	Thomas	Clonkeen, co Longford	1721	
Loughey	Patrick	Upper aughakillmore	1701	
Loughnan	John	Drumduff, co Leitrim	1820	

Figure 33 Listing of Patrick's Will in 1701 (Courtesy NAI)

4.4 Earliest Land Deeds

When the De Lahays / Lahys moved to Cavan occurred is unknown however if the dates in Shirley Lahey's account are to be believed then they moved sometime **after 1564** and **before 1652** when Pat Loghy is listed in the 1652 Commenwealth Survey [121] as a land owner in Aughakilmore Lower. Their whereabouts in the intervening 100 years is unknown - Shirley suggested they may have spent the time in England before moving to Ireland.There are two deeds [12 & 13] from a private source dating from the 1600s relating the Lahys in the area:

4.4.1 Pat Laghy and Thomas Coote 1667

[12] **Pat Laghy** of Tawlaught bought land from Thomas Coote in 1667: There are two versions of this deed, I have transcribed the shorter version here:

This indenture dated the first day of July the year of our lord God ----------- twentieth xxx year of the reign of out sovereign Lord Charles the second by the grace of God of England Scotland and Ireland, King Defender of the faith, Between Thomas Coote of Cootehill in the county of Cavan of the one part and **Patrick Laghy of Tawlaght** in the county of Cavan gentleman of the other part. Witness that the said Thomas Coote aforesaid in consideration of the sum of ten shillings ? of lawful money of England to him in hand payed porfetting hereof by the said Patrick Laghy herin whereof the said Thomas Coote doth hereby acknowledge hath bargained and sold and by he Gents doth bargain and sell ontfo the said Patrick Laghy all the land tenants and -------- hereafter mentioned (that is to say) out of Taughlawt fifteen acres and woods profitable plantation measured out, Out of Akhakilmore seventy two acres profitable lands of like Irish plantation measured out of Moydristan, sixty six acres and woods profitable land plantation measures all for lands and -------- are lying and being in the Barony ofClonmahon and County of Cavan and ------ in the one hundred and fifty acres and woods profitable land and plantation measured to two hundred forty six acres one root English measure. Together with all and singular the houses, Edifices, buildings, woods -------, bogs, mountains, heath, tenements ---------- commodation ------- and --------- in any way belonging or appointing to have and to hold the -------- mentioned or intended to be bargained and lands and every ------ snd psrt sll thereof with all and every ---------- commodation dadvantage and ------ belonging as to the said Pat Laghy his Exorata -------- and aligns for and during the ---- andsxard of two xxx yearor remmorroring from the day before ------ and from -----forth fully to ------- yelding and paving therfore unto the said Thomas Coote, his heirs and assigns during the said ---- and yearly rent of one xxxxxx found on the first day of November in arth of the said years if the same co lawfully demanded. An witnesse wherof tho said parties to presente into ---------- sell their lands and sealed the day and year first above.

Thus, Patrick purchased:
>   15 Acres Tawlaught
>   72 Acres Aughakilmore
>   66 Acres Moydristan
>   150 Acres (Irish)

This equated to 246 Acres English measure. Interestingly in the same year Patrick's address is given as the townland of Tawlaught [adjacent to Upper Aghakilmore] (not Aghakilmore as in the Walter Ward Deed). It is possible that there were two Patrick Laghys buying land in the same area but that would seem unlikely.

4.4.2 Pat Laghy & Walter Ward 1677

[13] **Pat Laghy** of Aughakilmore bought land from Walter Ward in 1677:

Figure 34 Pat Laghy / Walter Ward Deed (Courtesy F. Sheridan)

This Indenture made the eleventh day of January in the year of our Lord God one thousand six hundred seventy seven and in the nine and twentieth year of the reign of our Sovereign Lord Charles the Second by the grace of God of England Scotland France and Ireland King defender of the faith Between Walter Ward of Drogheda in the county and towne of Drogheda aforesaid Gent of the one part and Patrick Laghy of Aghakilmore in the barony of Clonmahon within the county of Cavan aforesaid Gent of the other part. Witnesseth that the said Walter Ward for and in consideration of the full sum of fifty pounds sterling, the receipt whereof the said Walter Ward doth here ---- acknowledged Hath bargained and sold and by there profits doth bargain and sell onto the said Patrick Laghy all the lands, tenants and ------ herein after mentioned that is to say out of Aghakilmore seventy acres profitable land plantation measure it lying and being in the Barony of Clonmahon within the county of Cavan together with and sinularly ----- houses and buildings woods, under woods, ways walks bogs, mountains --- tennaments ----- profits, commodities advantages and apprentices more unto in any way belong apportaining for ever without revocation and -- the said Walter Ward for him for life his heirs execs and aligns does covenant promise and grant to and with the said Patrick Laghy, his heirs execs and aligns that upon demand had on his land give and grant to and unto the ----- or assigns all deeds and convenences of and for the promise by the ---- in law of the said Patrick his --- be bought fit and lawfull and that at the ---- and strongest ofsaid Patrick , his heirs and assigns in witness thereof both parties have

Thus, in summary:

> Deed 11/1/1677 - 29th Year of Charles II Reign (His Reign is taken to have commenced the day his father Charles I was executed in 1649).
> **Parties:**
> 1. Walter Ward of Drogheda
> 2. Patrick Laghy of Aughakilmore
>
> Patrick gave Walter Ward £50 for 70 Acres in Aughakilmore.

Note that Patrick already had purchased 72 acres in Lower Aghakilmore 10 years before - thus he now possessed at least 142 acres in Lower Aghakilmore.

Signatories to the Deed included:

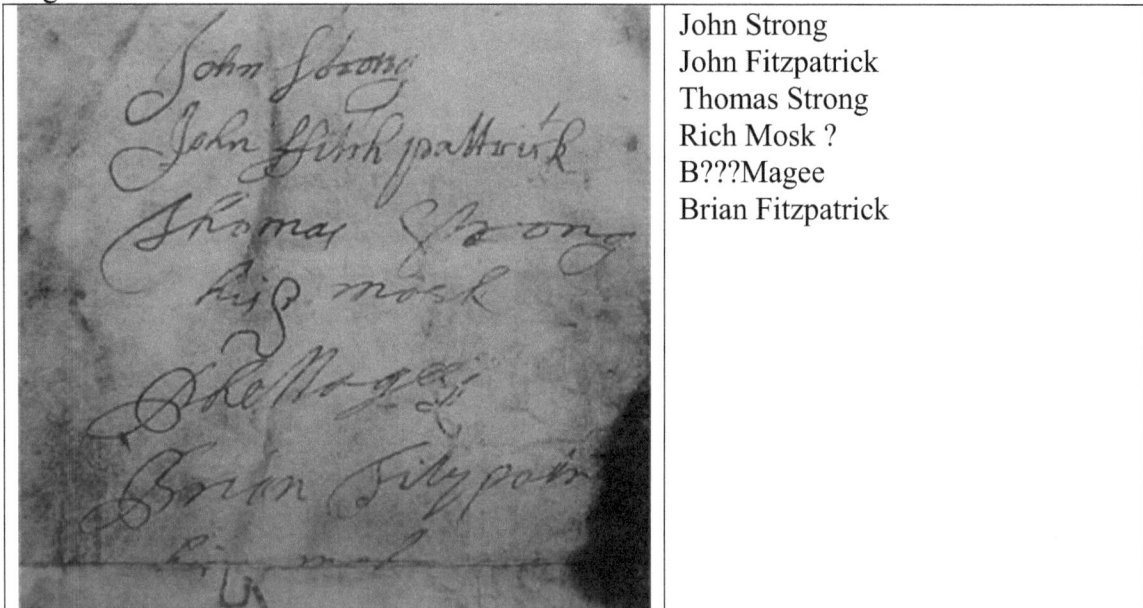

	John Strong
	John Fitzpatrick
	Thomas Strong
	Rich Mosk ?
	B???Magee
	Brian Fitzpatrick

Figure 35 Signatories to the Walter Ward Deed

Patrick was obviously a man of considerable means to be able to purchase such large quantities of land (and he may have made be other purchases we are not aware of). The Registry of Deeds records start at 1708, thus land purchased prior to this date only exist in private collections such as this one.

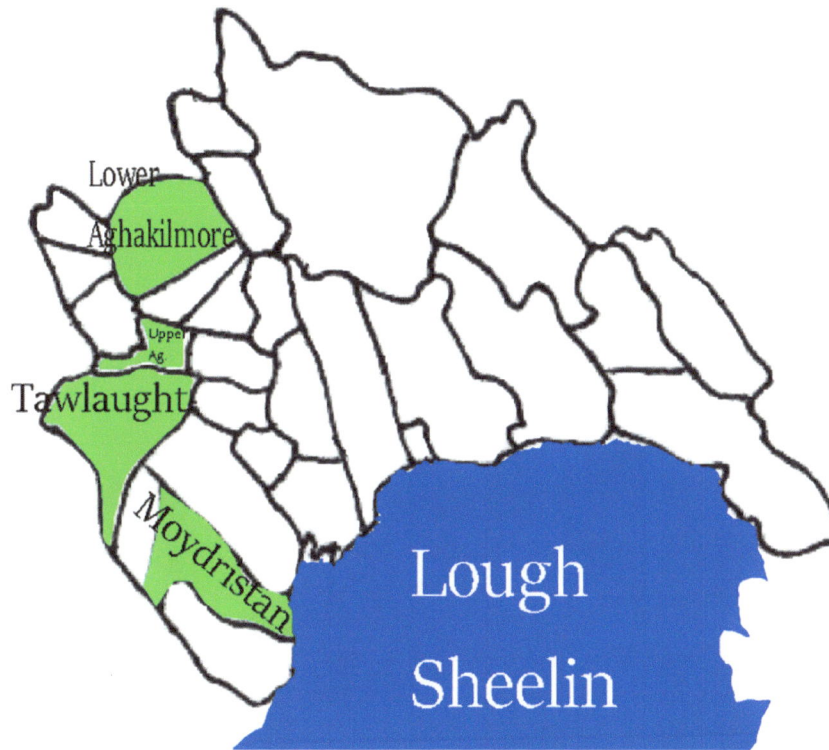

Figure 36 Townlands where Pat Laghy first purchased land in 1667

4.4.3 John

The earliest record of a 'John' Lahy/Laughy/Loughey apart from the Williamite war is that of John of Lower Aughakilmore's land deed [103] (his daughter Mary's marriage articles) in 1719. It's unknown if this is the same John, it could be the case that John was Patricks' father and died before 1700, unfortunately no records exist to confirm or deny this.

There is also a record of a John Loughy marrying Elinor Woods in 1722 in [127] It may not be the same John (as its over 30 years later), but interestingly it's the same unusual spelling of the name 'Loughy'. It was a protestant marriage and the Woods family certainly married into other early sections of the Lahy family. Thus, I think this John is either the same John or a close relative.

4.4.4 William Laughy – 1690

In Irish Marriage Records c 1660-1930 [128] there is a record of a William Laughy marrying Alice Murroe (of Derriaghy) at the Blaris (Lisburn) Church of Ireland on 20/2/1690. This William may or may not be related to John and Patrick Loughey from Cavan, however it could be that he was from Cavan and got married in the local church of his bride (Derriaghy is a suburb of Lisburn). In addition, 1690 was a turbulent year with much population movement due to the Williamite war.

4.5 Canadian Confirmation of Lahayville Origin Story

A North American descendant of Jean Lahie (1666 – 1738) very kindly got in touch with me and recounted how her father told her that they originally came from a town called Lahayville in France. Jean Lahie converted to Catholicism went he arrived in the new world and had a colourful life.

"What I heard for as long as I can remember is that we came from a place called Lahayville."

She stated that when her father told the children this that they laughed as they thought he had made it up. He apparently left behind a vast fortune in Ireland - reported to be in the Millions, though this seems highly unlikely. It is however, completely independent verification of Shirley Lahey's Lahayville origins of the Lahys. It is not known the connection between this Jean and the Cavan Lahys, but I'll assume for now that there must have been one, given the common origins story and the fact that Lahayville is a very small town!

A descendant of the 'Drumeeny' line [*Dorinda Askin*] also got in touch with me to state that her father had always told them that they were of Huguenot descent.

Another of the Lahey descendant from Killyfassey emigrated the to the USA and started a lace business (very traditional Huguenot business).

The wife of a descendant of Catherine Leahy (1842-1916), a daughter of Doctor James Leahy who married William Henry Sides in Australia also confirmed to me that:

"My mother-in-law used to speak of the boat ride across the Channel with as much jewellery as they could carry. She always insisted on a French connection in her family"

Marie Hartley (daughter of Georgina Leahy) also related to me that:

"...cousin Jerry (Tomas and Martha's son /Sallyhill) always had to lecture me that the Leahys were gifted and came from French lineage, I was young and took no notice of him but later on in life I began to think about it and without a doubt the Leahys are different to other Irish people in my opinion."

4.6 John Lahey Witness

A land deed dated 1738 (Pritchard to Haughton) has come to light in which lands of Williamstown (in County Waterford) are recovered and witnessed by **John Lahey (**see Figure 37**)** & John Meagher of the City of Dublin, Gent. It is not known if this John Lahey is connected with the County Cavan Lahys (63539 in [103]

Figure 37 John Lahey signature from 1738 Deed of 'Williamstown' in Waterford

4.7 Thomas of Upper Aughakilmore [Witness & Daughter?]

A land lease deed (dated 1730) (63769 in [103]) has come to light in which **Sarah Sizers** (alias Lahy) rents land in Kilgolagh (just south of Lake Sheelin) from Dillon Collard with (her presumed husband Oliver Sizers for a term of 31 years. Thomas Lahy (her presumed father) witnessed the deed (see Figure 38 and Figure 39) along with members of the Woods family. From this we can conclude that this is either Thomas (Senior) (in yellow in Figure 38) or Thomas (Junior) (in green in Figure 38)[as defined in [1] at the top of the tree. Thomas (senior) was probably still alive in 1730 as his death is not confirmed until 1734 in a later deed [103]. There is a mention in Thomas (Junior)'s 1766 Will [103] of a 'Sarah McClean' but this is presumed to be his niece. There is money left to 'Jane' in his will but not a 'Sarah Sizers'. It's possible that Sarah Sizer's husband Oliver died and she remarried a McClean. It's also possible that this Sarah is Thomas (Senior)'s daughter, I think this more likely to be the case. It's not known what became of Sarah after this date.

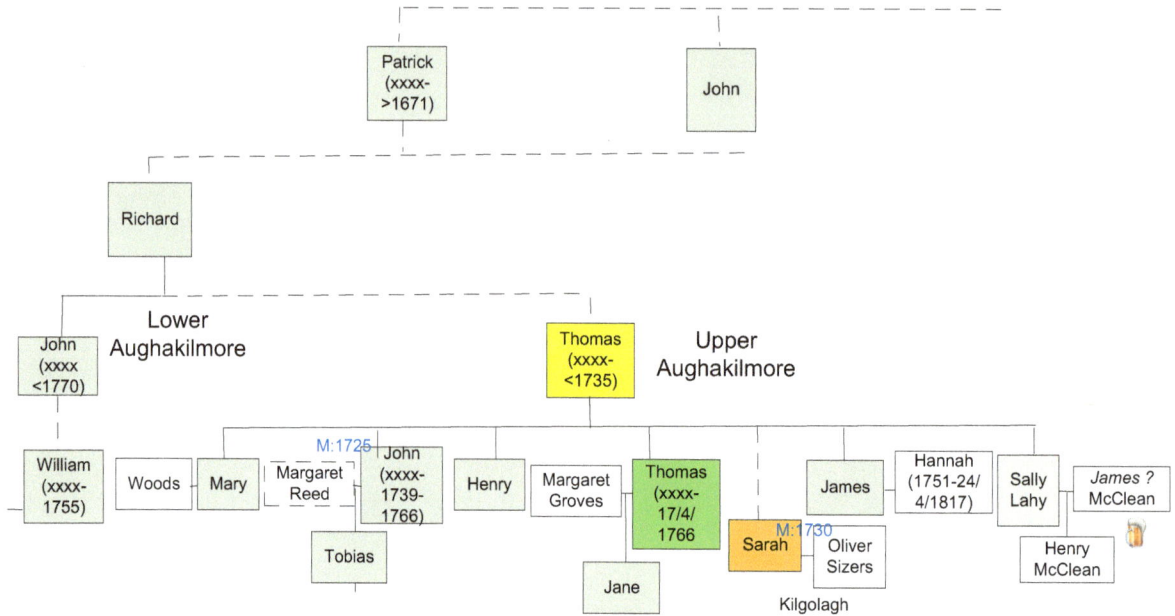

Figure 38 Possible parentage of Sarah Sizers (nee Lahy) of Kilgolagh

Figure 39 Thomas Lahy's signature from 1730 'Sizers' deed

4.8 Presumed sons of James of Upper Aughakilmore

My reasoning is that William of Lavagh traded in a lot of land - probably more than anyone else - and James of Upper Aughakilmore owned a lot of land in Lavagh - thus he probably inherited it from James. Also, James of Mullaghboy - was around at the same time - and traded with William and James of Upper Aughakilmore (and its very close to Lavagh) - and also the name 'James' links him. I think that these are reasonable assumptions and I will look for more evidence to back them up! James of Mullaghboy was also involved with a rental deed in 1782 with John of Lower Aughakilmore (and his sons Pat and William). James's son William is also mentioned in the same deed (1782 Aughafad Deed in [55]). Another possible 3rd brother (F. Sheridan possesses a document

David Leahy M.Sc.

that states there were 4 brothers) is Arnold, mentioned living in Lavagh in the 1821 census).

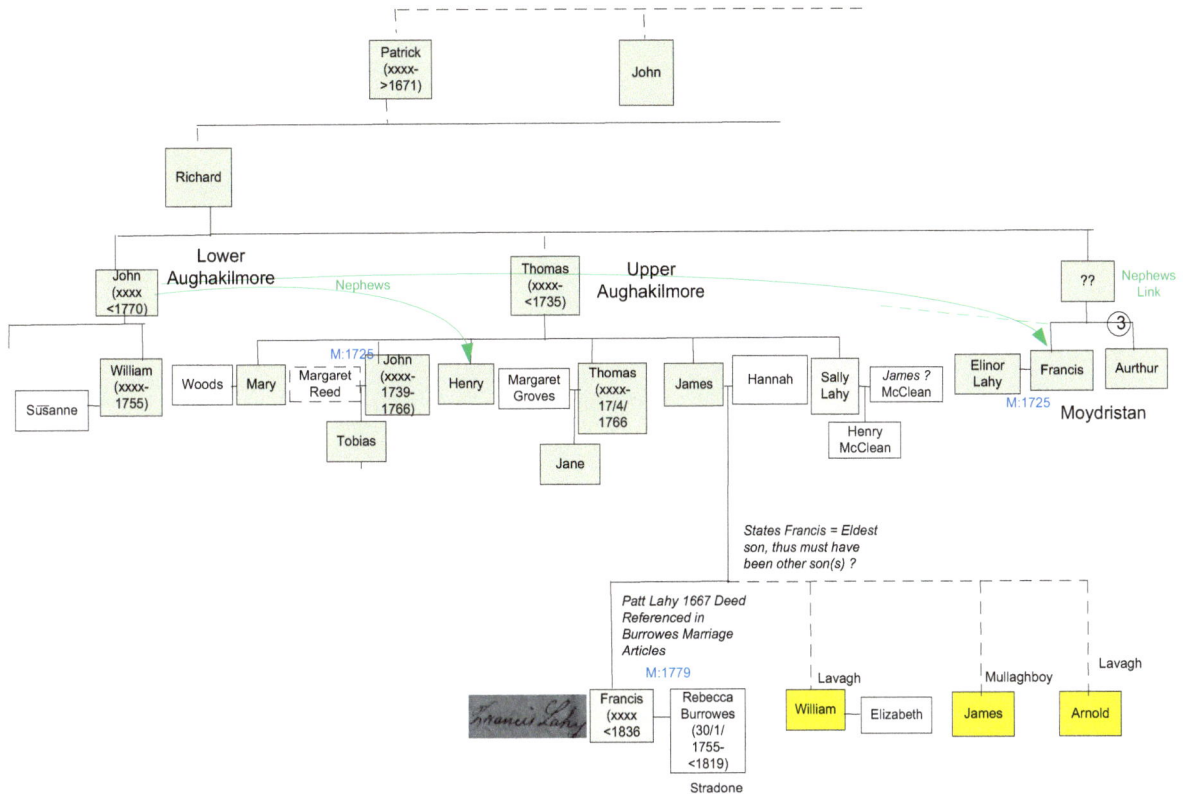

Figure 40 Potential connections of William of Lavagh and James of Mullaghboy

4.9 Other Land Deeds Evidence

4.9.1   1761 William of Tycullen

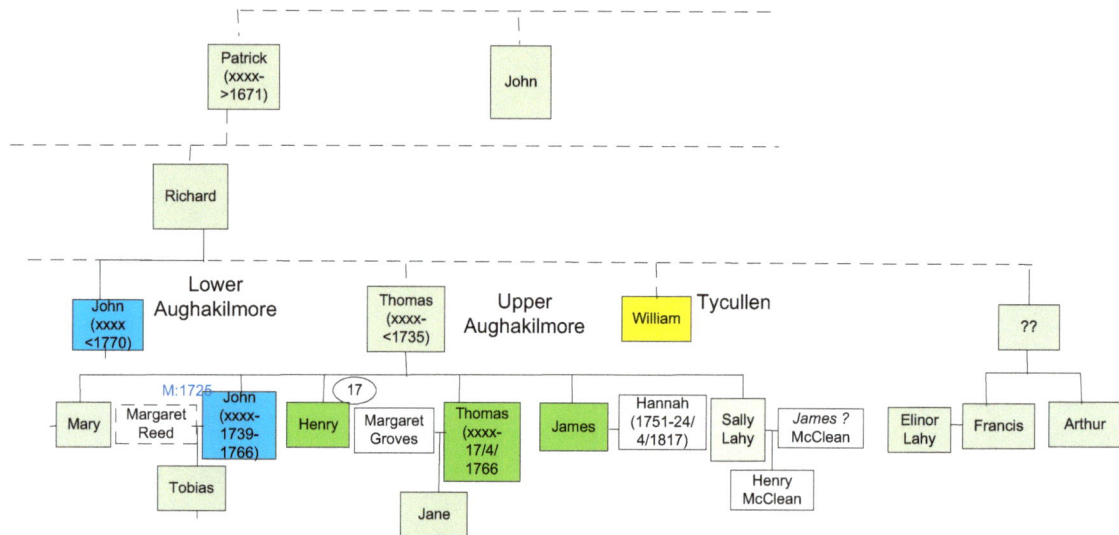

Figure 41 William of Tycullen Deed Participants

Further analysis of a Land deed dated 1761 [103] concerning William of Tycullen who sold his lands in Lower Aughakilmore to John Lahy (of Aughakilmore). The sum of £500 sterling was mentioned thus a lot of land must have been involved (in today's money that's worth over £70000). Unfortunately, it didn't specify which John (Upper or lower Aughakilmore) – both shown in blue in Figure 41. However, another land deed made a year earlier [103] listed William of Tycullen selling land (in Lavagh) to John of 'Lower' Aughakilmore – thus I presume this deed [146370 in [103]] also refers to John from 'Lower' Aughakilmore. A comparison of signatures seems to back this up – see Figure 42.

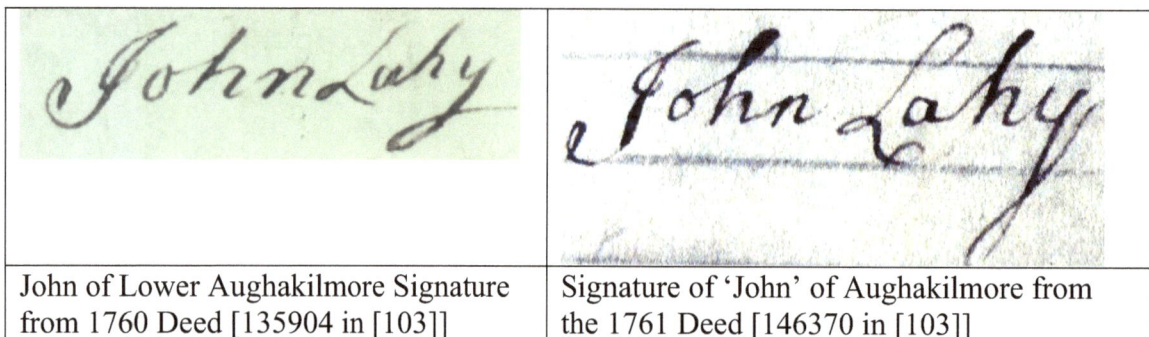

| John of Lower Aughakilmore Signature from 1760 Deed [135904 in [103]] | Signature of 'John' of Aughakilmore from the 1761 Deed [146370 in [103]] |

Figure 42 Signature comparison of Johns in the two Deeds

David Leahy M.Sc.

The deed did specify Witnesses of Thomas, Henry and James Lahy – who I presume to be the brothers shown in green in Figure 41 – potentially the nephews of William of Tycullen - which backs up an earlier assumption made in Volume 1 [1] that William of Tycullen was a brother of the Upper Aughakilmore Lahys. The only caveat would be that the deed stated Henry, Thomas and James were from *Lower* Aughakilmore – however given the relatively small size of Upper Aughakilmore, it's reasonable to assume that they expanded into the larger townland of Lower Aughakilmore. A comparison of the signatures of this Thomas Lahy Witness and that of Thomas (Junior) indicates that it's probably the same person – see Figure 43). In essence the deed basically ties the Tycullen Laheys in with the Upper and Lower Aughakilmore Laheys, to probably being brothers or nephews.

Thomas (Junior) Signature from his Will in 1766 [103]	Thomas signature from the 1761 deed [103]

Figure 43 Comparison of Thomas signatures

The recent discovery of an earlier 'John' Laughy / Loughey (see section 4.3 on page 49) makes it possible that the Tycullen Lahys were descended directly from this earliest John – rather than Patrick – that being said it is likely that the earliest Patrick and John were probably brothers.

4.9.2 1730 Departure?

Local historian Bill Graham told Shirley Lahey [1] that the Shantully/Tircullen Lahys moved to Aughakilmore about 1730. However clearly the Lahys were in Aughakilmore at least 60 years before this (see [1]), with Patrick Laghy being recorded buying land there in 1667. I think it's likely that a 'branch' moved to Tircullen (perhaps with a marriage dowry of land there), and then moved back to the 'safety' of Aughakilmore with the rest of their kin.

4.9.3 John of Shantully?

Before leaving the Tircullen/Shantully Lahys, it is worth including this record of a burial in the Kilmore Parish [14] in April 1799 (Figure 44). It's difficult to make out the surname but it appears to be John 'Lahy' (or potentially John Ladly) of Shantully. If we conclude 'Lahy' then this is the last recorded 'Lahy' in the Tircullen/Shantully area.

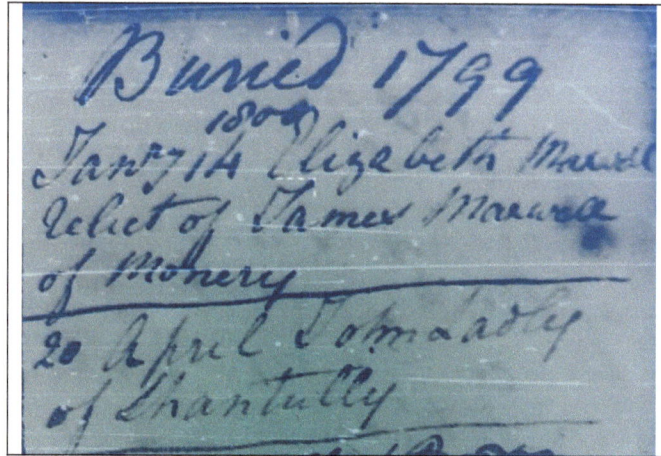

Figure 44 John 'Lahy'? Of Shantully buried 1799

4.9.4   James of Aughakilmore / Lavagh

James Lahy is first mentioned by his brother Thomas in his Will of 1766 [103]. He inherited substantial lands from his brother Thomas – in Upper Aughakilmore, Lavagh, Aughafad, Mote and Aughakilmore Middle (Capragh) in 1766. In 1775 it would seem that he consolidated his territory in Lavagh by buying more land in Lavagh and Aughacreevy from William and Elizabeth [203250 in [103]]. That is assuming it is the same James. Although his signature exists on this 1775 deed, it doesn't exist anywhere else (to my knowledge) thus we can't do a direct signature comparison (see Figure 45). The 1775 deed is Witnessed by Henry Lahy I presume to be his nephew (see signature comparison Figure 46).

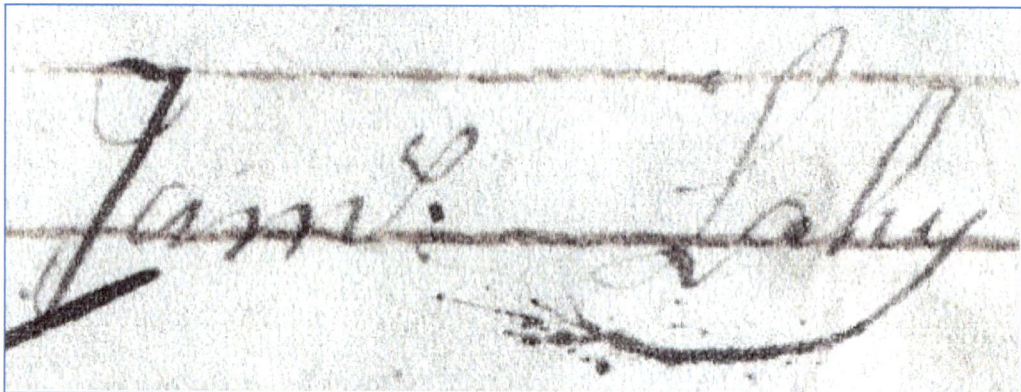

Figure 45 James Lahy of Aughakilmore Signature

David Leahy M.Sc.

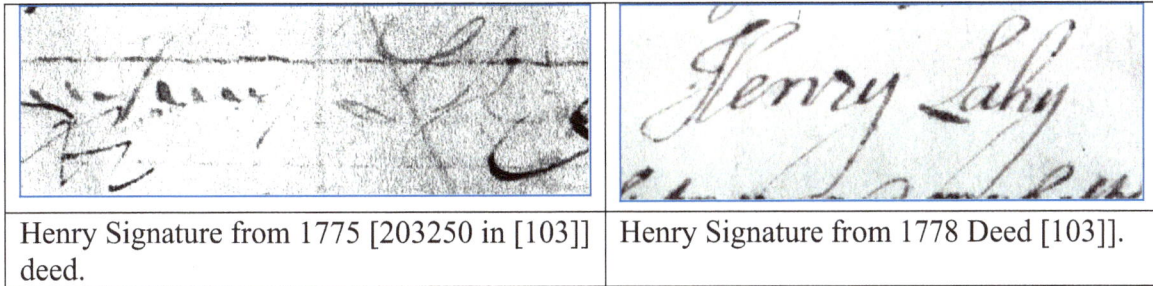

| Henry Signature from 1775 [203250 in [103]] deed. | Henry Signature from 1778 Deed [103]]. |

Figure 46 Henry Signatures Comparison

4.10 Henry to his Son Henry

In 1778 (one year before his death) Henry the Elder gave over half of his lands in Aughakilmore to his [second son] Henry (Junior) - shown in yellow in Figure 47. [216909 in [103]].

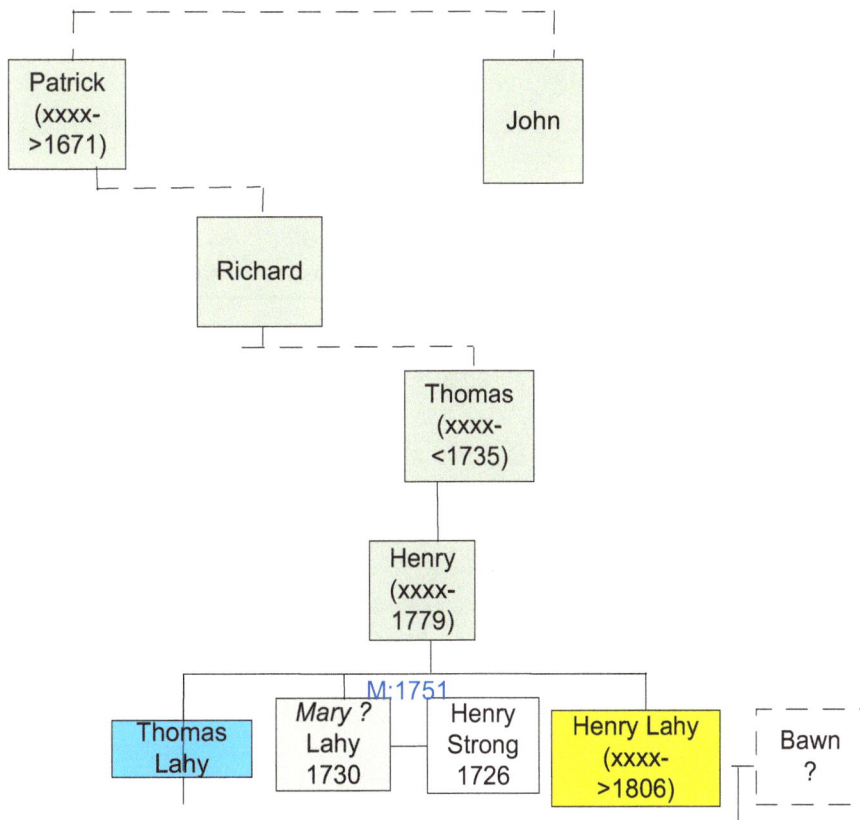

Figure 47 Location of Henry (Junior) in the Tree - In Yellow

Presumably Henry gave the other half of his lands to his eldest son Thomas (coloured in Blue in Figure 47). Both sons are mentioned in the Betham Abstracts Reference [129].

4.11 Joseph to Henry [Mortgage]

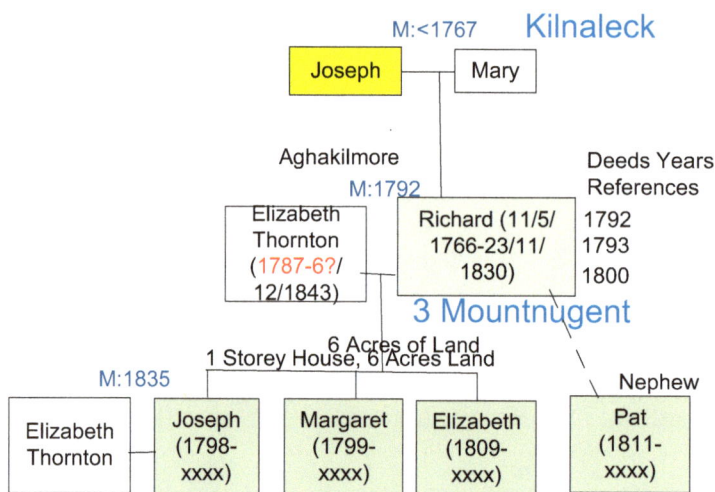

Figure 48 The Joseph Lahy Tree

In 1770 [183906 in [103]] Joseph Lahy of Kilnaleck (see Figure 48) was involved in a land deed with Henry Lahy for 70 Acres in Lower Aughakilmore. The sum of £120 was mentioned but it's a bit unclear who was selling / buying the land.

In 1780 Joseph was again involved in a land deal (this time with James Lahy of Lavagh – implying a family connection) selling land in Lavagh to John Bell [231422 in [103]]

In 1781 another deed [227527 in [103]] Joseph and Henry are again mentioned in a deed. An earlier deed / cheque is mentioned dated 1764 mentioning Henry the Elder (Henry's father) – presumably it was Henry the Elder who lent Joseph money to buy the land in Aughakilmore. This time the sum of £157 16s was mentioned along with a rent charge of £8 a year for lands in Aughakilmore known as 'The Cross'. Joseph's son Richard later had to 'give up' 'The Cross' to Henry Maxwell in part payment for a large debt in 1793 [103]. It's not known exactly how Joseph Lahy was related to Henry; however, he is probably a direct descendant of Joseph Lahy Quarter Master [Mentioned in [1]]. Joseph the Quarter Master's Will mentioned 'Joseph' his nephew – which could be this Joseph and also John 'a kinsman' – typically taken to mean cousin – which could be John of Upper or Lower Aughakilmore. Joseph is also mentioned in a deed in 1780 along with James Lahy of Lavagh [231422 in [103]] – who presumably is the James Lahy of Upper Aughakilmore who inherited the lands in Lavagh from his brother Thomas in 1766 [103]. They sold land together thus presumably were closely related.

4.12 William of Lavagh

William of Lavagh was involved in many land deeds from the mid to late 1700s (see Figure 49). In this diagram each line represents a land deed that William was mentioned in. People usually only listed their very close relatives in such deeds. Consequently, I've updated the 'Top of the Tree' to include William as a brother of Thomas and John (see Figure 50).

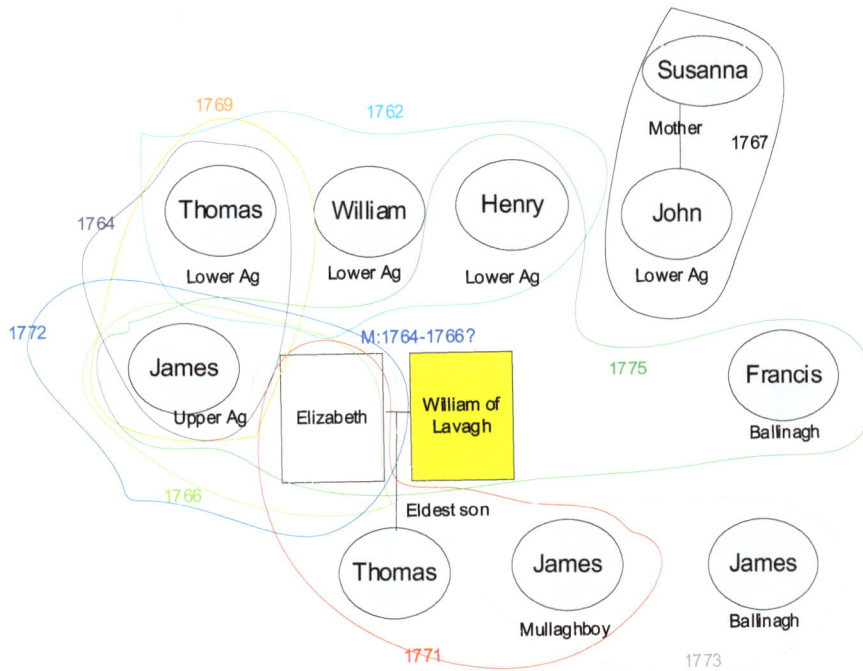

Figure 49 William of Lavagh, Land Deeds Personnel

A result of this analysis has led me to re-evaluate where William of Lavagh originated. I believe he originated in Upper Aughakilmore and have revised my theory of where he fits into the 'Top' of the tree, (see Figure 52).

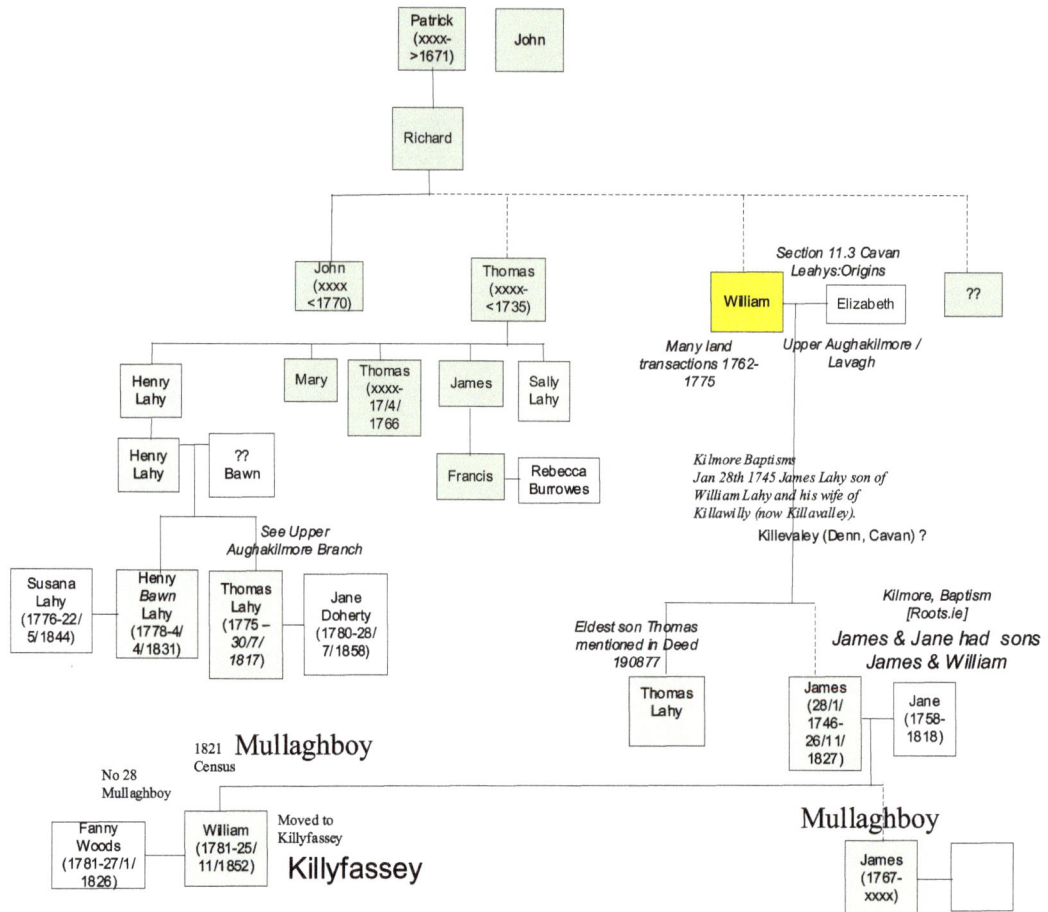

Figure 50 William of Lavagh, Position at the top of the Tree (based on land deeds)

4.13 Land Transfer in the 1700s & 1800s

As an exercise in visualisation – my thinking was – *follow the land and you can follow the family* - I put together a diagrammatic representation of ownership and transfer of land from the 1700s right up 1900. It was a difficult task and difficult to tell exactly who 'owned' the land as very often it was transferred to a 'lessor' for a term of 30 years or three lives (generations) after which it returned to the original owner. The reader should also bear in mind that typically the eldest son inherited the family 'homestead' and other sons given other portions of land or 'married into' land via dowries that accompanied their wives.

The Griffiths Valuation [57] information on Cavan is also included. I'm not sure exactly what we can learn from this representation, perhaps it needs more work or interpretation, but I thought best to include it in the hope that it may be of use to someone else – see Figure 51.

David Leahy M.Sc.

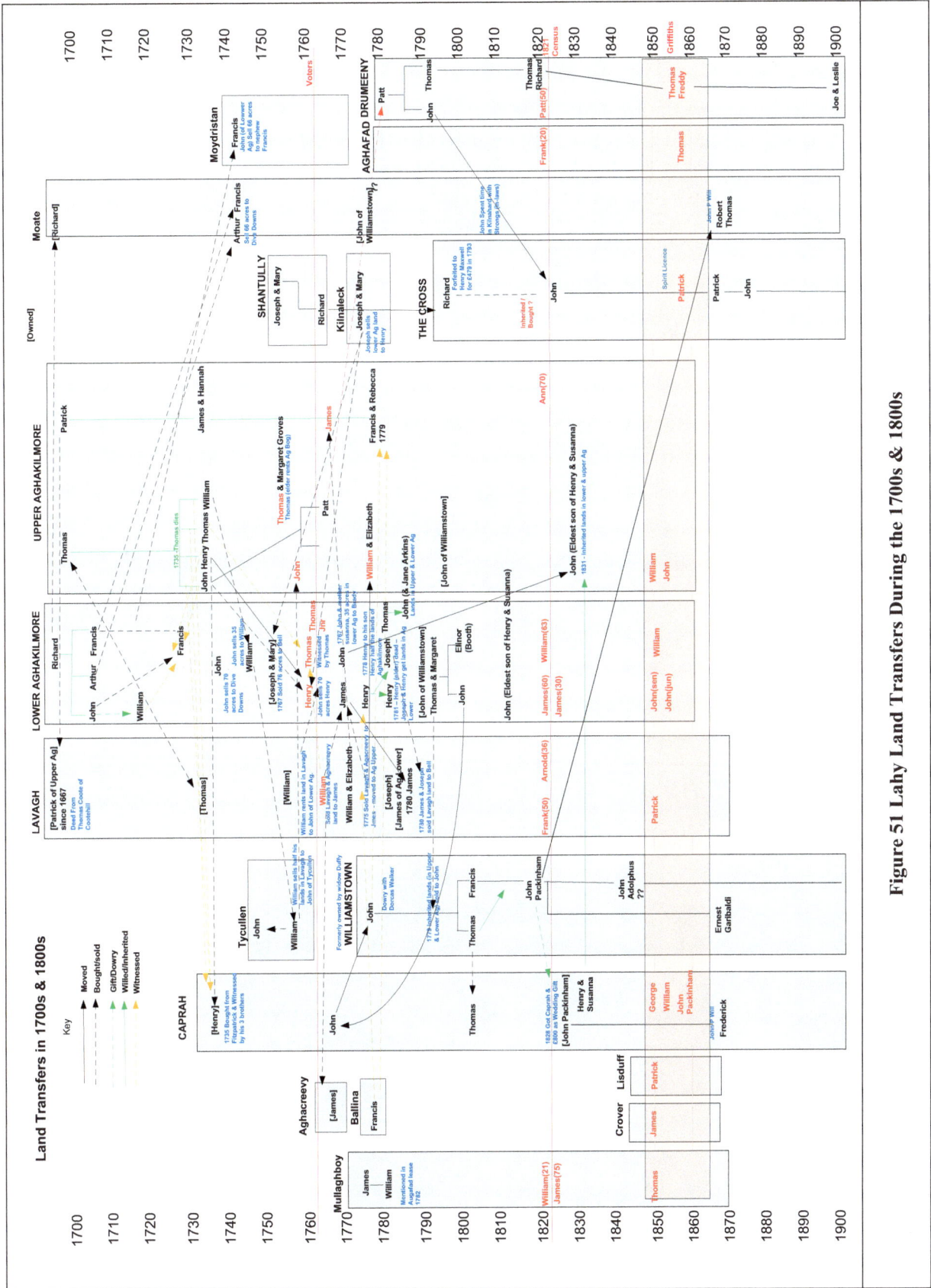

Figure 51 Lahy Land Transfers During the 1700s & 1800s

4.14 Books of Survey and Distribution

Books of Survey and Distribution were compiled around 1680 as the result of the wars of the mid-seventeenth century after the Cromwellian conquest of Ireland, when the English government needed reliable information on land ownership throughout Ireland to carry out its policy of land confiscation. They were used to impose the acreable rent called the Quit Rent, which was payable yearly on lands granted under terms of the Acts of Settlement and Explanation. It is possible to discover to whom, if anyone, the confiscated lands were granted so that we have a record of landowners for 1641 and 1680. As a result, it is possible to determine the amount of lands lost by the 1641 owners after the Irish Rebellion of 1641 and to discover the names of the new proprietors [Wikipedia]. (see [130])

4.15 Genealogical Abstracts

A few keen genealogists have made notes on the Wills and memorials that existed in the Four-Courts building in Dublin before it was burned down in 1922. Fortunately, their 'notes' survive (known as 'abstracts') – thus although they are not the original records, they are notes taken from the 'original' records and thus as close as we'll ever get to them (given that they were mostly completely destroyed). The Key Genealogists were:
- Sir William Betham (1779-1853) [129].
- Dr Francis Crossle and Philip Crossle [131]
- Gertrude Thrift [132]

4.16 Betham Abstracts [129].

Lahys / Leahys listed in the Betham Abstracts are shown in Figure 52. They all lived in Dublin, it's not known if they're connected to the 'Cavan' Leahys.

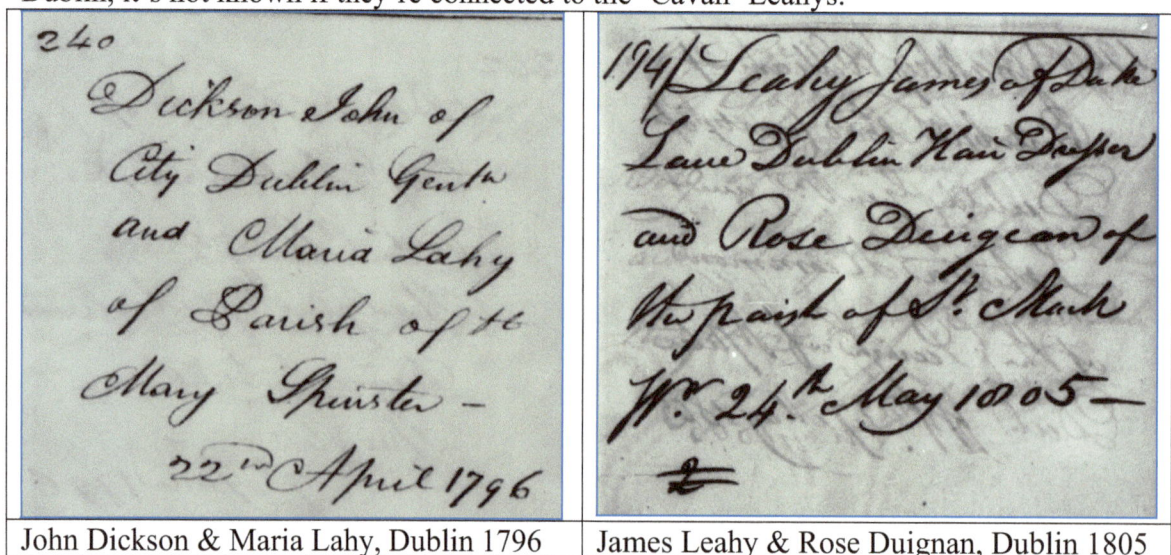

| John Dickson & Maria Lahy, Dublin 1796 | James Leahy & Rose Duignan, Dublin 1805 |

David Leahy M.Sc.

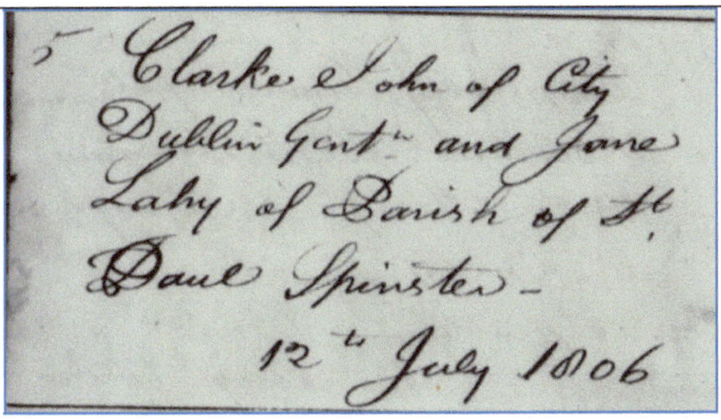 5 Clarke John of City Dublin Gentn and Jane Lahy of Parish of St. Paul Spinster – 12th July 1806	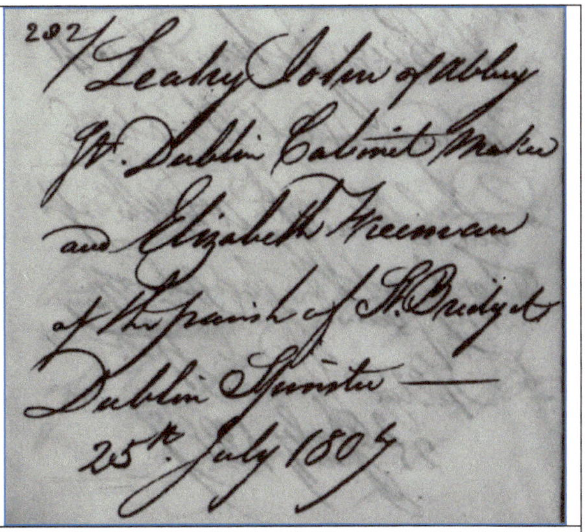 282 Leahy John of Abbey St. Dublin Cabinet Maker and Elizabeth Freeman of the parish of St. Bridget Dublin Spinster — 25th. July 1807
John Clarke & Jane Lahy, Dublin 1806	John Leahy & Elizabeth Freeman, Dublin 1807

Figure 52 Lahys / Leahys in the Betham Abstracts (Courtesy National Archives of Ireland)

4.17 Crossle Abstracts

A search of Lahys in the Crossle abstracts resulted in the following - Figure 53.

Date	Person / Notes	Image
1680	John Lahy of 'Clare' 1680?	
1738	John, William, Thomas & Henry Lahy & Hugh Flannigan, William Woods	
1746	William Wood, Kilnahard in Cavan & John Lahey	
	To my son John Wood a bond I have from John Lachy of £6 [Oliver Wood Will]	
1751	Oliver Wood, Kilnahard Will 1751 – 1762 Witnessed: Andrew Bell Tobias Lahy	

1759	Thomas Marlay of Dublin, Patt Lahy of Dublin, Gent	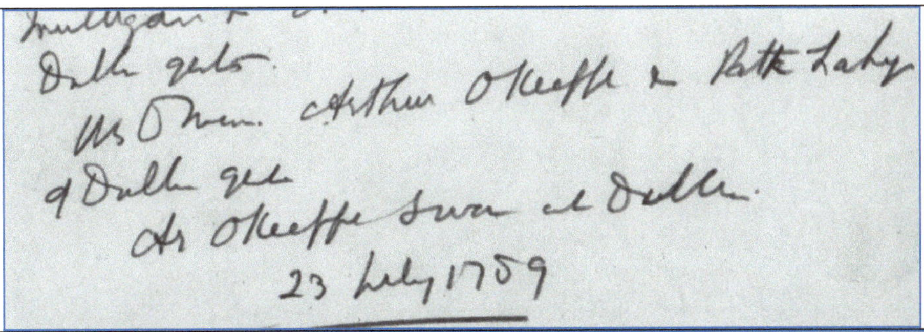 *[handwritten abstract]* ... Arthur O'Keeffe & Patt Lahy of Dublin ... Ar O'Keeffe sworn at Dublin. 23 July 1759
1765	Alex Brook V Thomas & Joseph Lahy	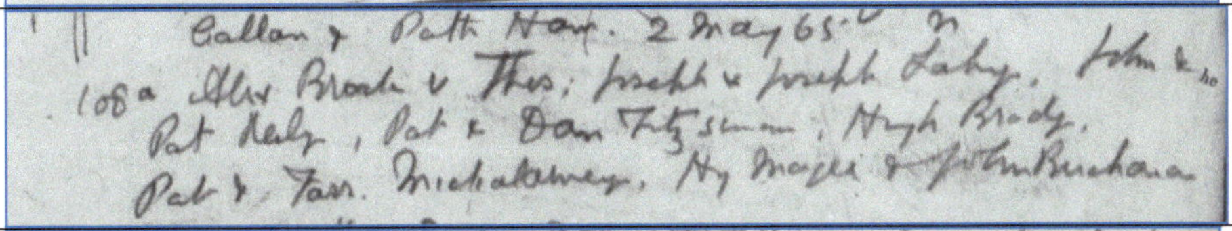 *[handwritten abstract]* Callan & Patt Hay. 2 May 65. Alex Brook v Thos; Joseph & Joseph Lahy, John & Pat Healy, Pat & Dan Fitzsimon; Hugh Brady, Pat & Fan. Michaluney, Hy Magee & John Buchan
1791	Pat Lahy (yeoman) & Mary Commons	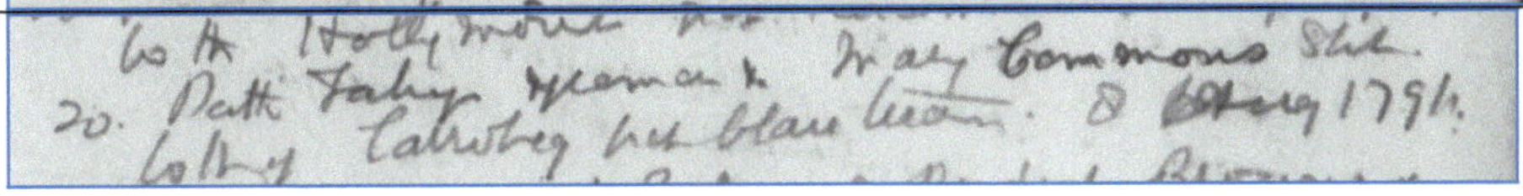 *[handwritten abstract]* ... Hollymount ... Mary Commons 20. Patt Lahy yeoman & Mary Commons ... Catherg his blance mean. 8 May 1791.
1805	William Lahy Witness [Orange Wood Will]	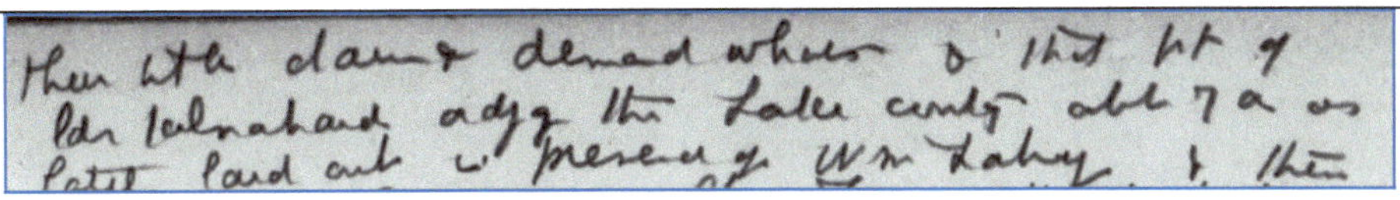 *[handwritten abstract]* Then with claim & demand where & that lot of ldr Culnahard adjg the Lake contg abt 7 a as Patt laid out w presence of Wm Lahy ... then
1809	James Lahy & William Lahy of Mullaghboy John Woods, Orange Woods	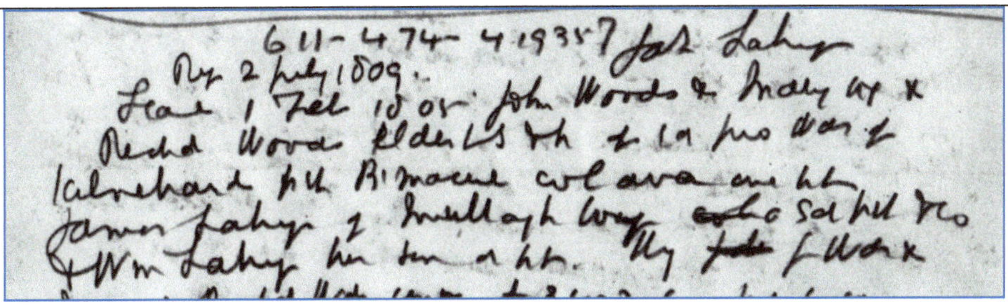 *[handwritten abstract]* 611-474-419357 Jas Lahy Np 2 July 1809. Lease 1 Feb 1805 John Woods & Mary ux & Rschd Woods eldest son & in pos war of Culnahard ... James Lahy & Mullagh boy ... & Wm Lahy his son a lot. ...
1815	Orange Wood, Francis Lahy	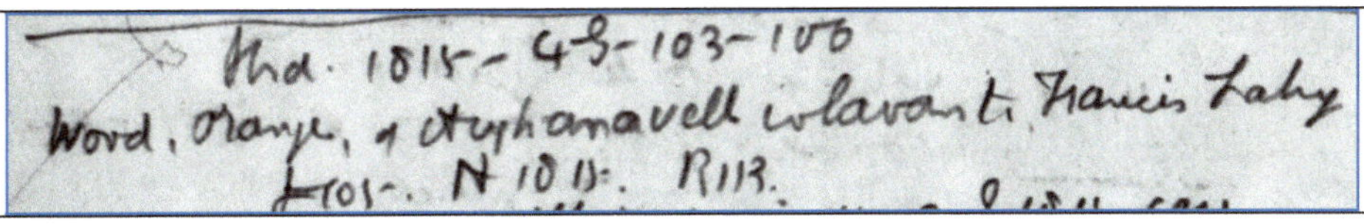 *[handwritten abstract]* Mld. 1815-43-103-106 Wood, Orange, & Aughanavell co Cavan Francis Lahy ... N 101. R113.

Figure 53 Lahys in the Crossle Abstracts (images Courtesy National Archives of Ireland)

The reference to Tobias Lahy witnessing a deed by Oliver Woods in 1751-1762 is interesting as it's the only other reference to 'Tobias Lahy' son of John of Upper Aughakilmore & Margaret Reed. He is only referenced in one other document – his uncle Thomas's Will of 1766 [103].

James and William Lahy of Mullaghboy are also mentioned. It is also interesting to note that the Wood family and Lahy family were quite close – witnessing each other's land deeds and Wills. The earliest 'Thomas' (who died before 1735) had a daughter Mary who married someone called 'Woods'.

Francis Lahy of Lavagh (who married Rebecca Burrowes) was involved in a 'fake news' controversy about his alleged conversion to Roman Catholicism in 1827 and Orange Wood stepped up to defend his reputation in the newspaper (Francis objected to be used as 'religious propaganda' by both Protestant and Catholic Churches). See [1] for more detail.

4.18 Thrift Abstracts [20]

A search of the 'Thift' abstracts resulted in just one result (Figure 54) John and Thomas Leahy involved in what looks like a court case against Daniel Callaghan in 1840

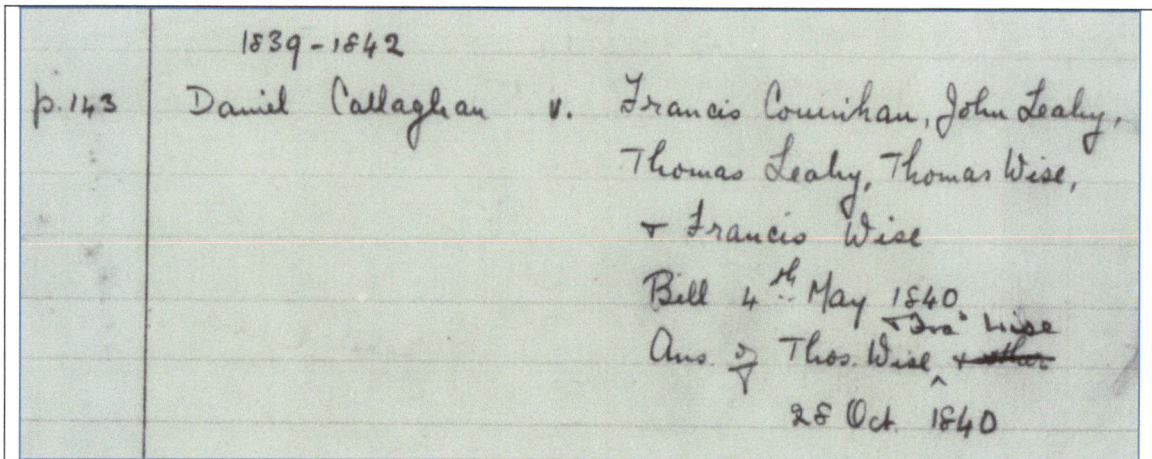

Figure 54 John and Thomas Leahy Court Case? - from Thift Abstracts (Courtesy National Archives of Ireland)

5 Early Court Cases 1600-1800

A few new court records sources [133 & 134] became available on *Ancestry* in 2020. The records just recorded the names of the plaintiffs and claimants (but no details on the case or locations). Searches based on **Lahy, Laughy, Laughey, Lachy, Lahey, Leaghy, Delahay, Lehy, Loughy.**

There were many '*Leahy*' matches, however Cavan Laheys didn't use the name 'Leahy' until at least 1850 (based Registry of Deeds Records). No locations were given and the assumption of 'Cavan' is just that – an assumption for most of the records. Nevertheless, some individuals can be identified due to cross-correlation with land deeds records at the same time. Below is a summary of some of the main disputes and who I believe the people involved to be (from land deeds evidence etc).

5.1 John, Thomas, William, Arthur & Richard, 1697:

John, Thomas, William and **Arthur** Laughey took **Richard Laughey** (their presumed father) to court, presumably over land – perhaps he wasn't prepared to Will it to them.

We know for sure that John's father was Richard [deed 63321, 1738], and that Thomas & James were brothers [Thomas, Will 1766] and that Arthur and Francis were direct descendants of Richard [deed 66435, 1739]

We also know that Francis was the nephew of John of Lower Aughakilmore [deed 66370, 1739].

We also know that Henry of Upper Aughakilmore is the nephew of John of Lower Aughakilmore [deed 66371, 1739] thus confirming John of Lower Ag to be the brother of Thomas (Henry's father) .

A number of other deeds [66369, 1739; 57842, 1735] list William in conjunction with John of Lower Ag in land deals. In one of them it states William is from Upper Aughakilmore. This leads me to believe that William is a 3rd brother.

It's possible that William is the father of Francis & Arthur, however this new court evidence (dated 1697) leads me to believe that 'Arthur' was a 4th brother, who was the father of Arthur and Francis (of Moate).

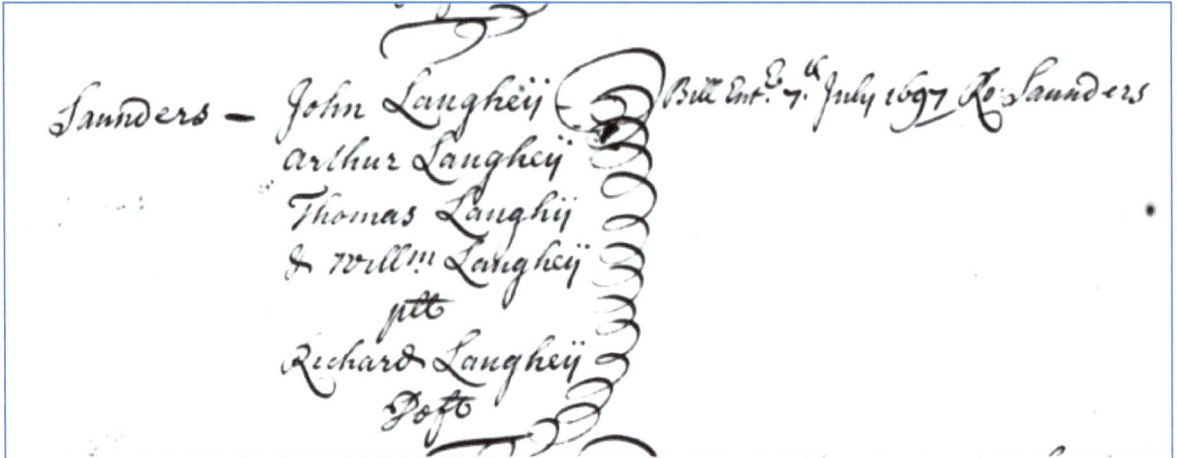

Figure 55 Names as they appear in the Court Case Document [133]

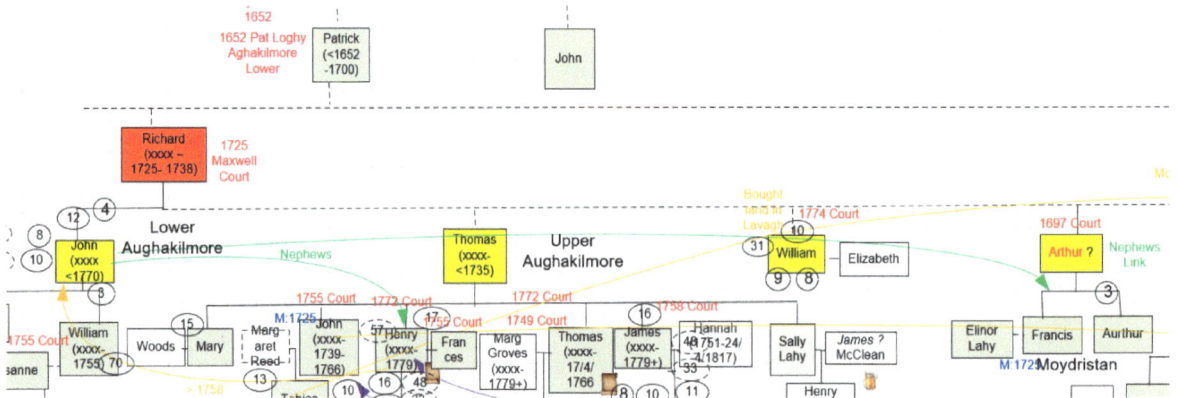

Figure 56 Richard (red) & 4 Sons (Yellow)

5.2 1725: Richard v Maxwell

Another record in Chancery Court

Date	Source	Name	Other Relevant Names on Court record	Likely Person on Tree	Justification / Notes
9/7/1725	Chancery	Richard Lachy	Robert Maxwell v John Coyne & Richard Lachy	Richard father of John of Lower Ag	Maxwell (biggest land owner in Cavan) & Richard still alive

This was probably Richard Lahy (who in 1697 was in a court action against his sons)–
Maxwell was the biggest landowner in the Ballymachugh area – he took Richard 'Lachy'
to court in 1725 for some reason.

5.3 1749 Thomas (son of Top Thomas) & wife Margaret:

I presume this to be Thomas (son of Thomas at the top) and his wife Margaret Groves.

Date	Source	Name	Other Relevant Names on Court record	Likely Person on Tree	Justification / Notes
13/1/1749	Exchequer X2	Thomas Laughy & Margaret his wife	Thomas Burrows,	Thomas and Margaret Groves (Top Thomas)	Thomas & Wife Marg. Spelling, Other Cavan names

5.4 1755 Henry (son of Top Thomas)

Date	Source	Name	Other Relevant Names on Court record	Likely Person on Tree	Justification / Notes
1/2/1755	Exchequer	Henry Lahy, & Frances his wife William Lahy John Lahy Susanna Lahy Francis Lahy	Woods, Maxwell, Heney, Bell, Edgeworth		Top of the tree bunch from Upper Aughakilmore. New Info – wife for Henry – Frances !

I presume this to be the earliest recorded Henry (son of Top Thomas). It no gives us his wife's name ' 'Frances'. There was a 'Susanna' mother of John in Lower Aughakilmore, I've suspected she was the wife of William (son of John of Lower Ag), this lends more weight to that theory. The John could be John of Lower Ag and the 'Francis' his nephew (son of Arthur) in Moate.

5.5 1758-1764 Thomas (son of Top Thomas) & James his brother

Date	Source	Name	Other Relevant Names on Court record	Likely Person on Tree	Justification / Notes
22/11/1758	Exchequer	James Lahy & wife Hannagh	Wood, Cootes	James & Hannagh Top of tree	James & Hannagh Top of tree
6/1/1759	Chancery	Thomas & James Lahy	Flood	2 brothers at top –	Thomas & James brothers

				Thomas & James	
6/4/1759	Chancery	Thomas & James Lahy		2 brothers at top – Thomas & James	Thomas & James brothers
3/2/1764	Exchequer	James Lahy & wife Hannagh	Thomas Lecky (another case)	James & Hannagh Top of tree	James & Hannagh Top of tree

These cases confirm James (son of Top Thomas) & Wife Hannagh as well as James his brother – (father of Francis who married Rebecca Burrowes).

5.6 1772 Thomas (son of Top Thomas) Vrs brother Henry

However, there must have been friction between Thomas (& Margaret) and his brother Henry as in 1772 Thomas took Henry Lahy & John Lahy (unclear which John) to court. I have a copy of This Thomas's will and he doesn't mention Henry (he left most land to James his brother).

Date	Source	Name	Other Relevant Names on Court record	Likely Person on Tree	Justification / Notes
24/7/1772	Exchequer	Thomas Lahy & Margaret his wife V Henry Lahy John Lahy James McClean Will Bell	Nugent, Gordon	Thomas & Marg Top of Tree (Thomas made will 1766, but doesn't mean he died same year) Henry Thomas's brother ? John his nephew?	Top of Tree Lahys

5.7 1774 James (son of Top Thomas) Vrs Uncle William

I presume this to be James (husband of Hannagh) versus William of Upper Aughakilmore (his uncle) & wife Elizabeth. The other Thomas in the defendants could be son of Henry (i.e. his nephew). It's unclear who the 2nd James could be.

Date	Source	Name	Other Relevant Names on Court record	Likely Person on Tree	Justification / Notes

19/3/1774	Exchequer	James Lahy 'Gent' V William Lahy, Eliz his wife Thomas Lahy James Lahy			Top of Tree Lahys

5.8 1800 – Jane Lahy v Henry of Capragh

A land deed (390529, dated 1805) between Henry Lahy and Jane Lahy alludes to her rights to enter premises in Upper and Lower Aughakilmore (and her children when they reach 21). This court action in 1800 probably is related. This is Henry (Bawn) Lahy of Capragh and wife Susanna. I presume the 'Jane' to be Jane's daughter of Thomas & Margaret, (thus continuing the feud from the earlier generations). However, Margaret's children are mentioned (Sydney & Margaret – minors). She possibly married another Lahy or kept her maiden's name or simply didn't get married. It is possible this is an entirely different Jane; however, it makes sense that Jane would have inherited a lot of land from her father Thomas, and there was 'history' of grievances between these family branches.

Date	Source	Name	Other Relevant Names on Court record	Likely Person on Tree	Justification / Notes
30/7/1800	Chancery	Jane Lahy & Sidney & Marg Lahy minors, by P. Jane their mother V Henry Lahy Susanna Heany Henry Heany	Woods, Bell		Other records of Jane Vrs Henry Jane (Atkins) Lahy ?

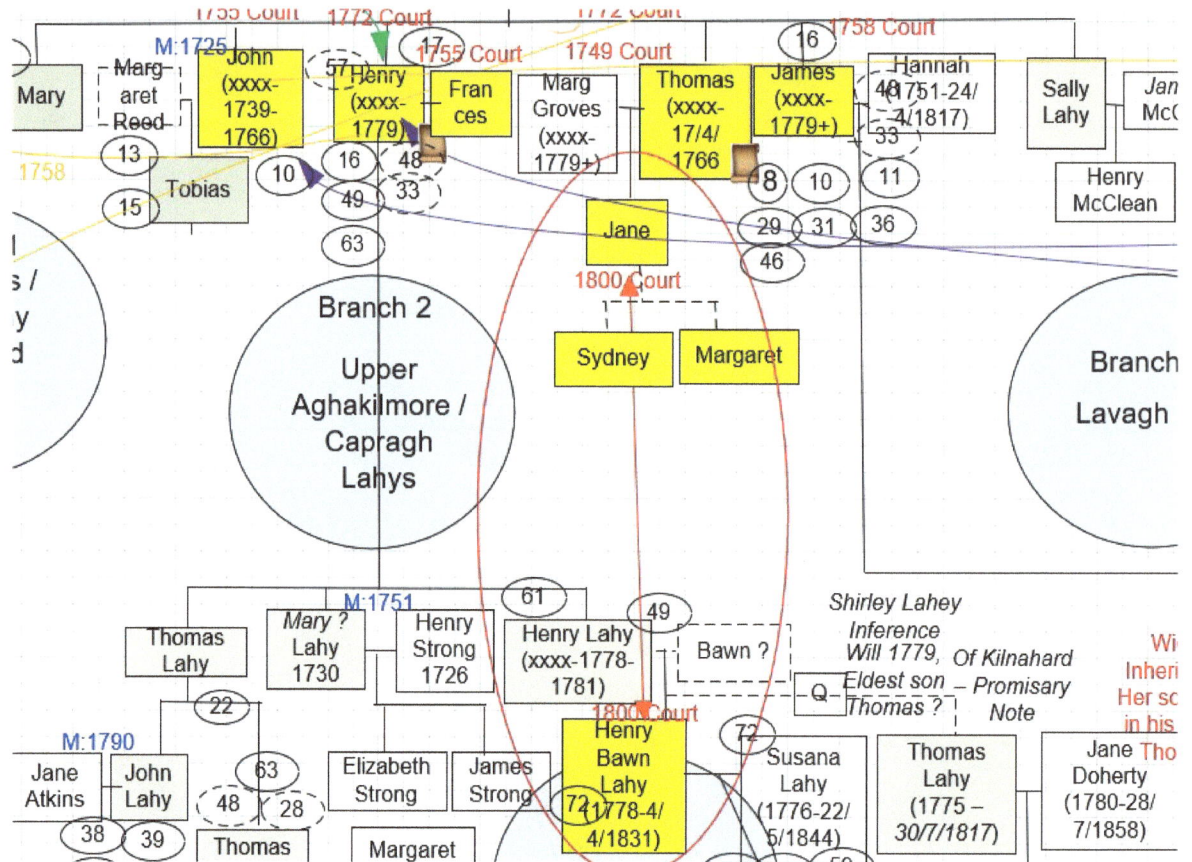

5.9 1800 – Maxwell v Richard Lahy

This court action is also listed in land deeds (348967, 1800). It concerns £1465 and 72 acres in Aughakilmore. I presume this to be Richard son of Joseph & Mary of Kilnaleck, who married Elizabeth Thornton and moved to Mount Nugent.

Date	Source	Name	Other Relevant Names on Court record	Likely Person on Tree	Justification / Notes
7/10/1800	Exchequer	Henry Maxwell v Richard Lahy			Known dispute (land deeds)

6 Ballymachugh

The location of County Cavan is shown in Figure 57 - coloured in red.

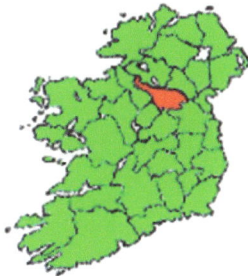

Figure 57 Location of County Cavan (red)

Ballymachugh Townlands

Ballymachugh is a parish in the barony of **Clonmahon** (see Figure 58 below). It borders the north and western shores of Lake Sheelin. A detailed description and history of Ballymachugh is given in [14].

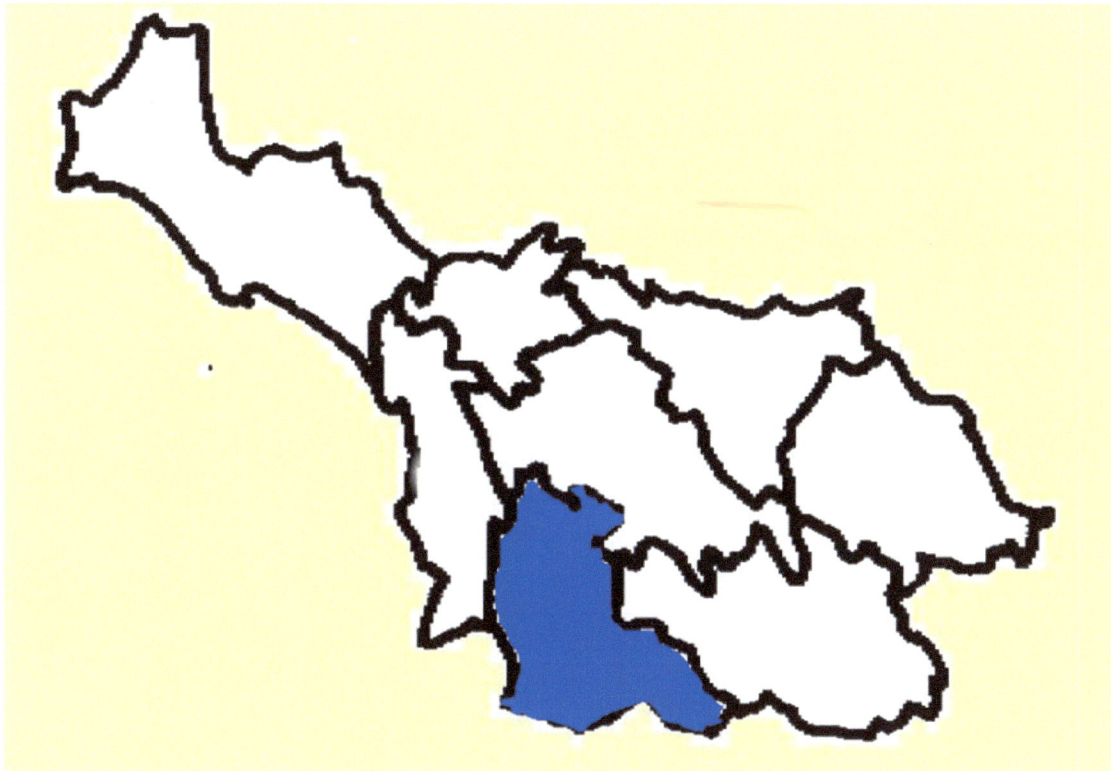

Figure 58 Barony of Clonmahaon (Blue)

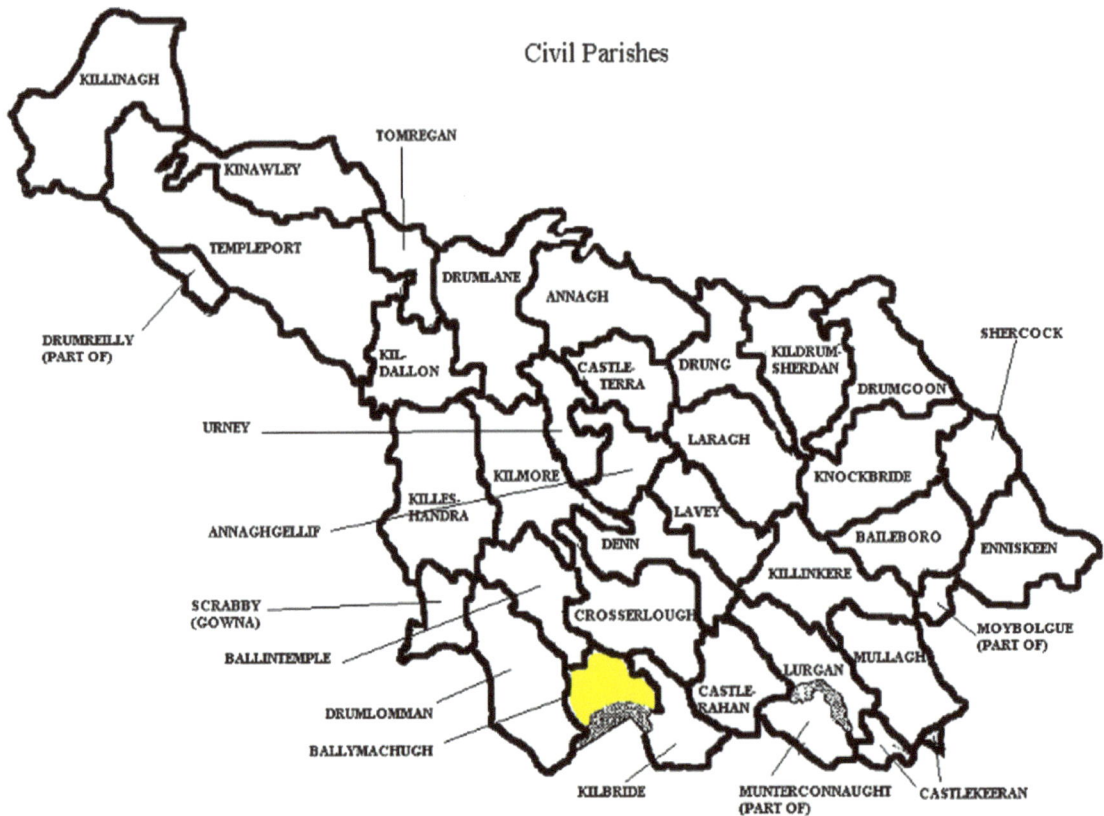

Figure 59 Ballymachugh highlighted (yellow)

Most of the Cavan Lahys lived in the parish of Ballymachugh situated along the north-west corner of Lough Sheelin (as shown in Figure 60), others moved to outlying areas such as Shantully / Derrin, Tircullen, Mullagh and Williamstown. I've included this townlands map as it helps to know what size the townlands were and where they were situated in relation to each other. Very often a 'townland' will consist of a piece of land with a single road / path and a single dwelling, although the larger townlands had many more dwellings and roads.

David Leahy M.Sc.

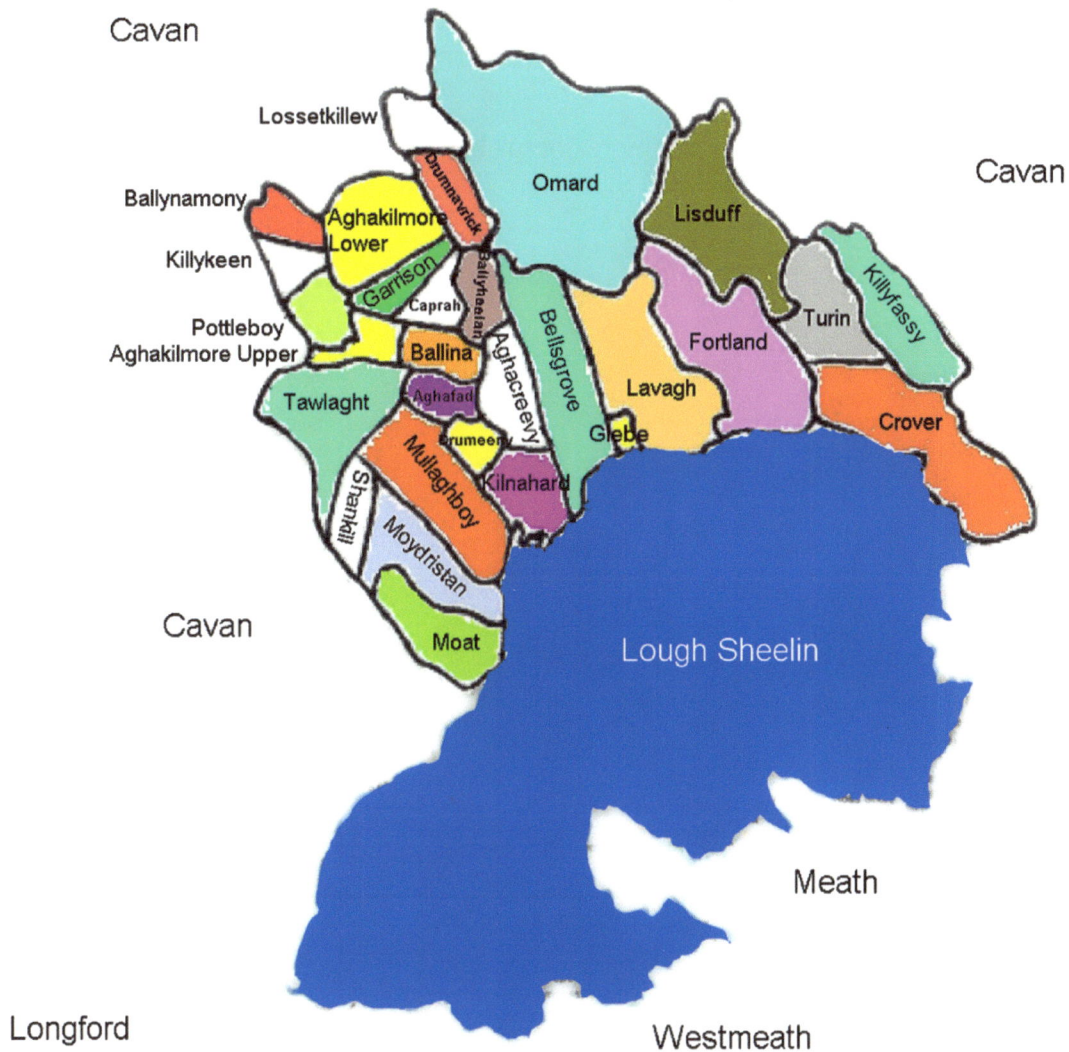

Figure 60 Townlands of Ballymachugh

Ballymachugh consists of 32 townlands:

Table 6 Townlands of Ballymachugh

Aghnahederney	Aghnahederney	Lavagh
Aughacreevy	Carragh	Lisduff or Foxfield
Aughafad	Crover	Moydristan
Aughakilmore Lower	Drumeany	Mullaghboy
Aughakilmore Upper	Fortland	Omard
Aughatereery	Gallonbane	Pottleboy
Ballina	Garrison	Shankill
Ballyhanna	Glebe	

Ballyheelin	Killyfassy	
Ballynamony	Killykeen Upper	
Bellsgrove	Kilnahard	

I should point out that Upper Aghakilmore doesn't have a lot of land, Lower Aghakilmore has much more and I'm sure that when men came of age they moved away from their homestead (apart from the eldest son) to stake their own claim of land.

Figure 61 Lough Sheelin Today

Figure 62 Sunset at Lough Sheelin

6.1 Place names

Place names in a lot of deeds are ambiguous. The most infuriating one is in Aghakilmore where a high concentration of Lahys lived. There are two sections of Aghakilmore (divided by a road). Aghakilmore is divided up into Lower (252 acres) and Upper (77 Acres). Usually the deed specifies which - however often it just says 'Aghakilmore'. I am making the assumption that because Lower Aghakilmore is more than three times the size of 'Upper' Aghakilmore that the term 'Aghakilmore' refers to Lower Aghakilmore. Incidentally there is also a 'Middle Aghakilmore' which is more commonly known as 'Capragh'.

6.2 Upper and Lower Aghakilmore

At this stage I should probably explain the difference between Upper and Lower Aghakilmore and a description of the townlands, as it is somewhat confusing.

Achadh-chille-moire (in Irish) is listed in the Four Masters [15] and means the field of the Great Wood. Mentioned in "Annals of the kingdom of Ireland" where there was a famous battle in 1429 between Teige O'Rourke (and the English of Meath) and Mahon O'Reilly (and the O'Neils, McMahons and Maguires). The Clan Mahon O'Reillys was defeated. One of the fields at 'The Cross' is known as the 'cross field', said locally to be where all the bodies from the battle were buried – although there is contradictory debate as to which field it is! - Questioning of locals in the area has led me to identify the battle 'Monument Field' and the burial 'Cross Field' as shown in Figure 63. Many locals still think that the top of the hill is known as 'The Cross' because of the main cross roads there - however I've been reliably informed that the name derives from the 'Cross Field' where the bodies from the battle were buried.

David Leahy M.Sc.

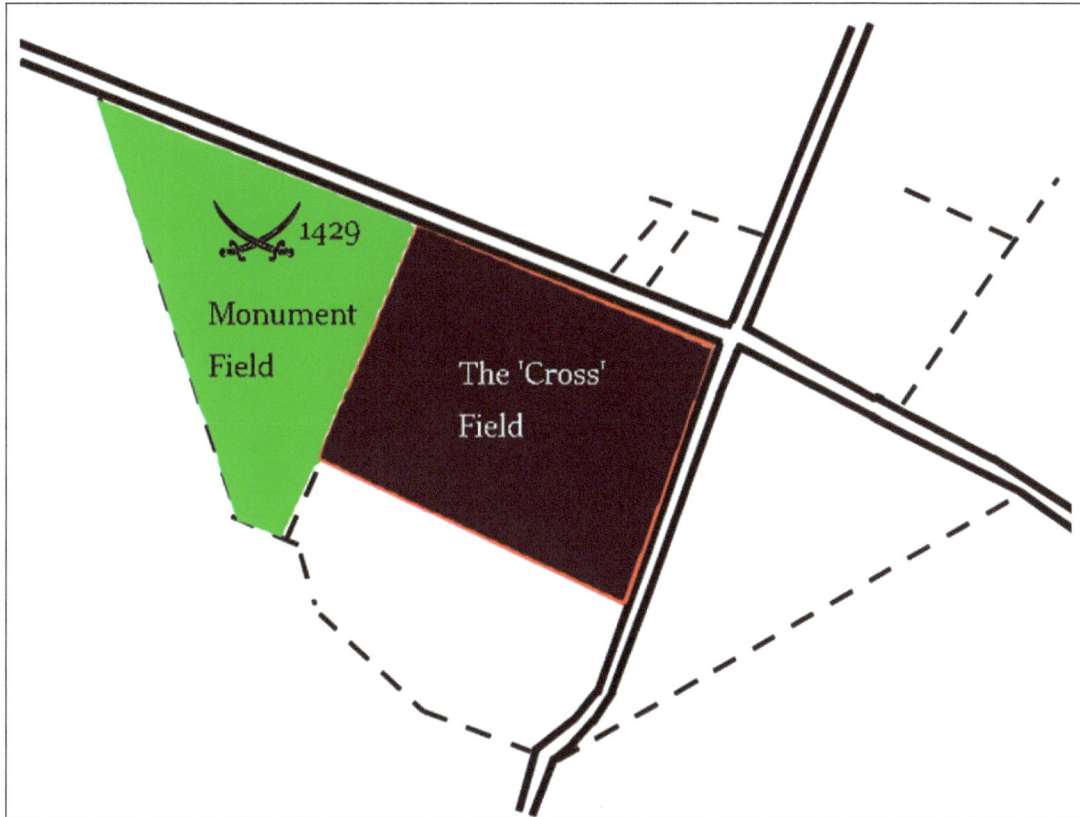

Figure 63 Location of the Battle of Aghakilmore and the 'burial' - Cross Field

Aghakilmore is divided up into Lower (252 acres) and Upper (77 Acres) as shown in Figure 64.

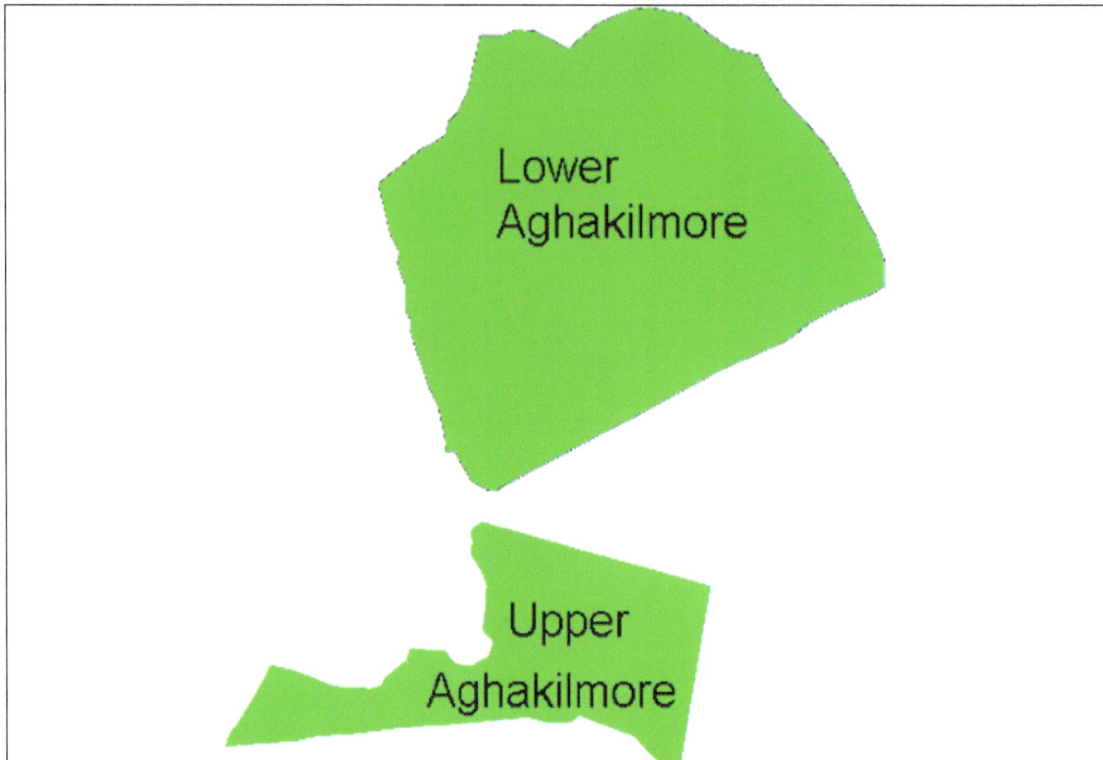

Figure 64 Relative sizes and positions of Lower and Upper Aghakilmore

A local historian from Ballymachugh told me that Aghakilmore had:

"Good arable land, which would have been clear of trees in the 1650s. For a pioneer community concerned about its security the site is ideal, with eyes on both hills the position offers a 365-degree view. You can see a very long way in all directions, into Meath, Westmeath, Longford, Leitrim, and Cavan, up to 40 miles away. If trouble started you would see the smoke rising a very long way off, you would have a lot of time to escape, and a good choice of escape routes, in all directions.

On a local level, the community would have been protected by the Bellsgrove River to the east (then a vast swamp), Lough Sheelin to the South, and the villages of Finea and Granard to the south and west. The local bandit base in the 1650s and 60s would have been the Erne Valley to the North West (modern Mullahoran and Ballintemple parishes), the northern approaches to Aghakilmore were also well protected by swamps and bogs. This would have been a very secure place to keep livestock safe from bandits.

This high ground is tactically the most important ground on the north shore of Lough Sheelin. In the 1650s the Bellsgrove River was a vast linear swamp running north from Lough Sheelin for about 3 miles. The only gap in this barrier was the ford at Ballyheelan, this was the choke point on the road north of Lough Sheelin. The ford is dominated by the high ground of Aghakilmore and Tawlaght, the western approach to the ford was at Ballina (the mouth of the ford) also a Lahy freehold. If I was the civil and military power

David Leahy M.Sc.

in Ballymachugh in the 1650s, I would be delighted to have this important terrain feature settled by a community of stout English yeomanry stock. In fact, I would probably do everything possible to facilitate it."

Upper Aghakilmore in the 1800s seemed to have two main settlements, one at the end of a lane from the main road, and the other along the side of the main road - as shown in Figure 65.

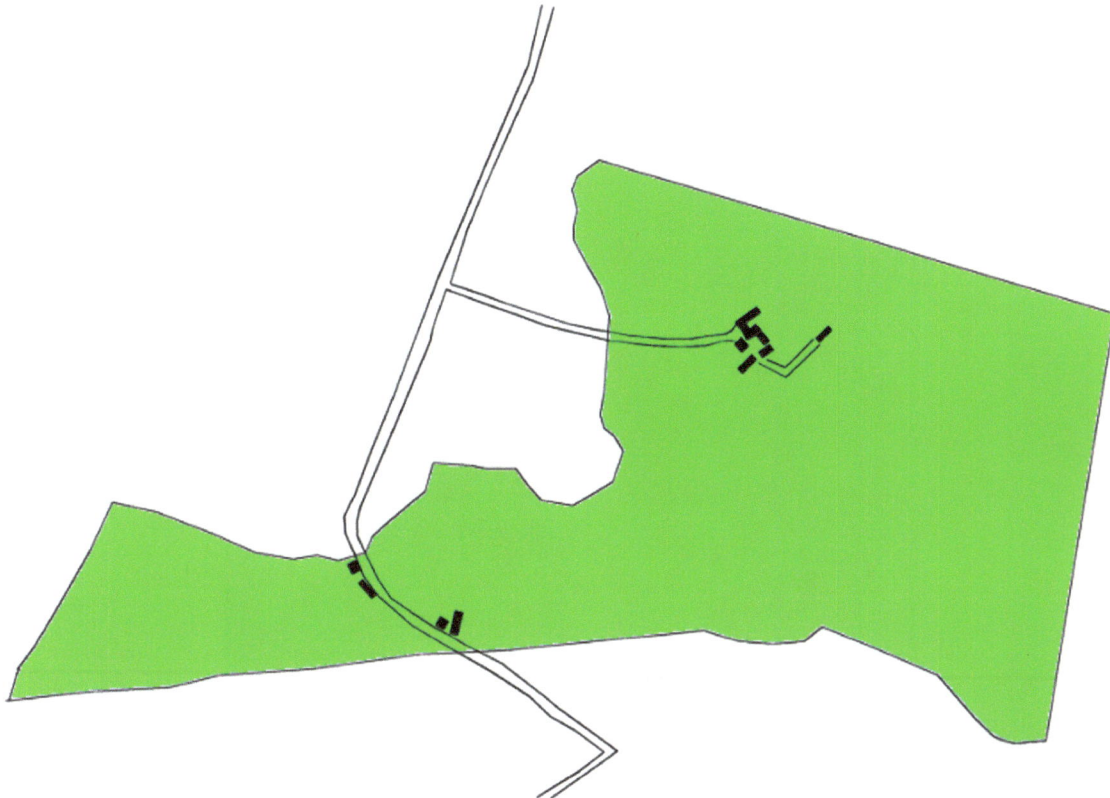

Figure 65 Upper Aghakilmore

Lower Aghakilmore in the 1800s on the other hand seemed to have a central 'hub of dwellings just off from a major intersection, another smaller 'hub' at the main road intersection known as 'The Cross' where there was (and still is) a pub and a collection of more widely dispersed dwellings - as shown in Figure 67.

Figure 66 The 'furry' road through Aughakilmore Upper Today

David Leahy M.Sc.

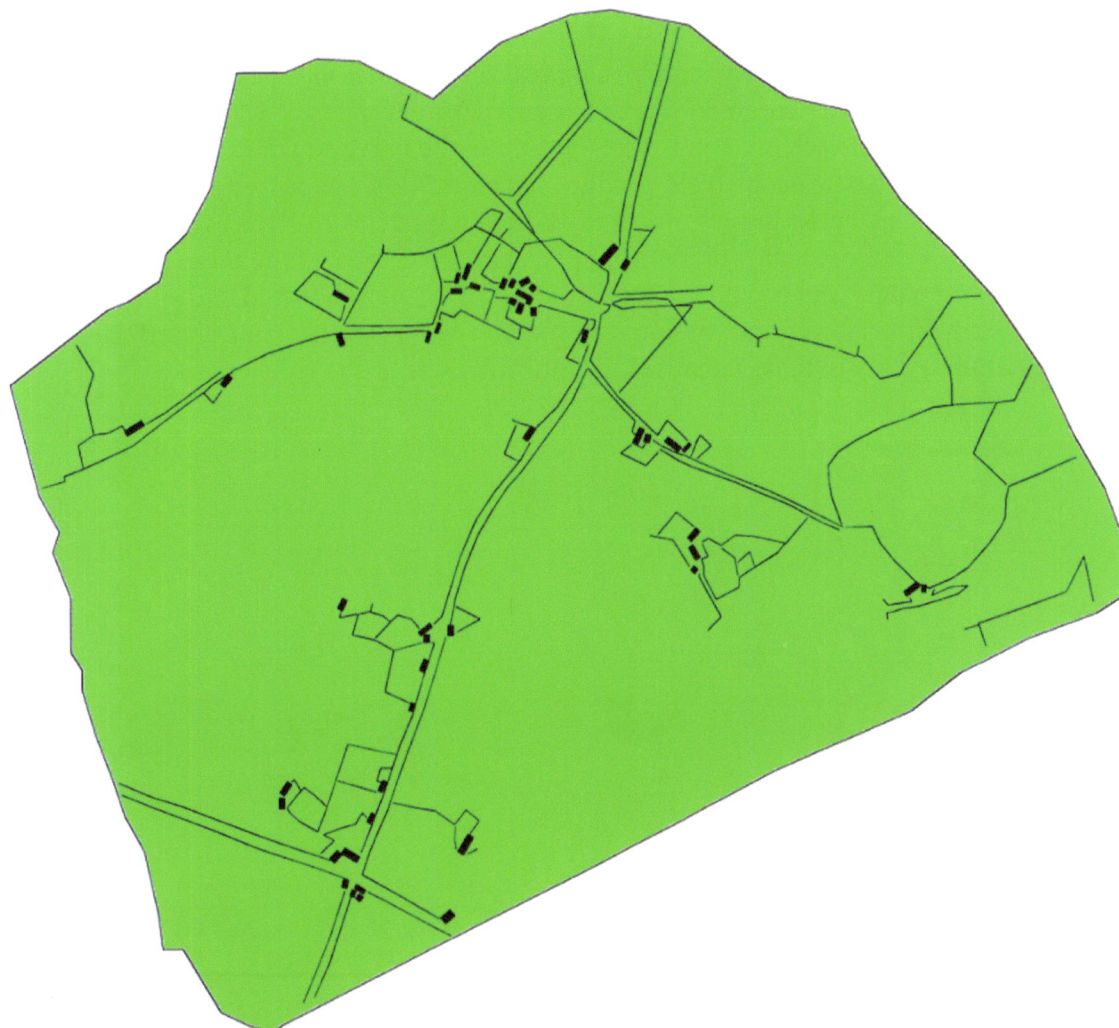

Figure 67 Lower Aghakilmore & Dwellings in the early 1800s

Life in County Cavan in the 1600s / 1700s

Living in County Cavan in the 17th and 18th centuries was not easy. Most of the population were poor, trying to scratch out a living on a small piece of land or working as labourers on other people's land. Money was scarce; often time's people paid their rent with a 'pig' rather than money. If you cut down trees you had to ask the landlord for permission to keep them (for firewood etc.) and half the time the landlord refused. Once can see how resentment might have grown between those who had and those who had not. If you had nothing and were destitute you went to the workhouse. These were not pleasant places to be but at least you got a little food. There was no social security and people relied on their immediate and extended families to support them. Quite often first cousins married in order to keep dowries (which took years to save), or acquired land within the family. In addition to that was the religious divide and if you chose to marry into the opposite religion you were often 'cut off' by your family and so it was a decision that wasn't taken lightly. Some changed religion for a few loaves of bread and a warm coat, and then changed back again the next week!

All of this took place in the Lahy family as with all of the other families in the area. Neighbours had disputes - commonly over land borders and rights of way etc. and at the same time they helped each other out when it came to the harvest and other labour-intensive activities. Some people held grudges for years and even passed them down to their children. Others chose to seek a better life and emigrate to Australia or America. These emigrants kept in touch with their families back in Cavan letting them know about life in the new country and encouraging them to follow. Some followed and some returned home for whatever reason. Some stayed and never returned and started the Lahy branches of the family in those countries that are still there today.

7 Other Lahys around Cavan in the 1700s

Little data exists for births of Lahys in the 1700s in Cavan. However, one renowned local historian - Bill Graham, did record some early Lahy births and some marriages (see Figure 68). I have yet to discover the source he used to obtain the records mentioned in this note. Incidentally local Leahys in the area who knew Bill Graham state that he was also convinced they were of Huguenot origin. Where possible I have tried to connect these people in the Top of the Tree diagram [ ] - otherwise they remain un-connected until more information comes to light.

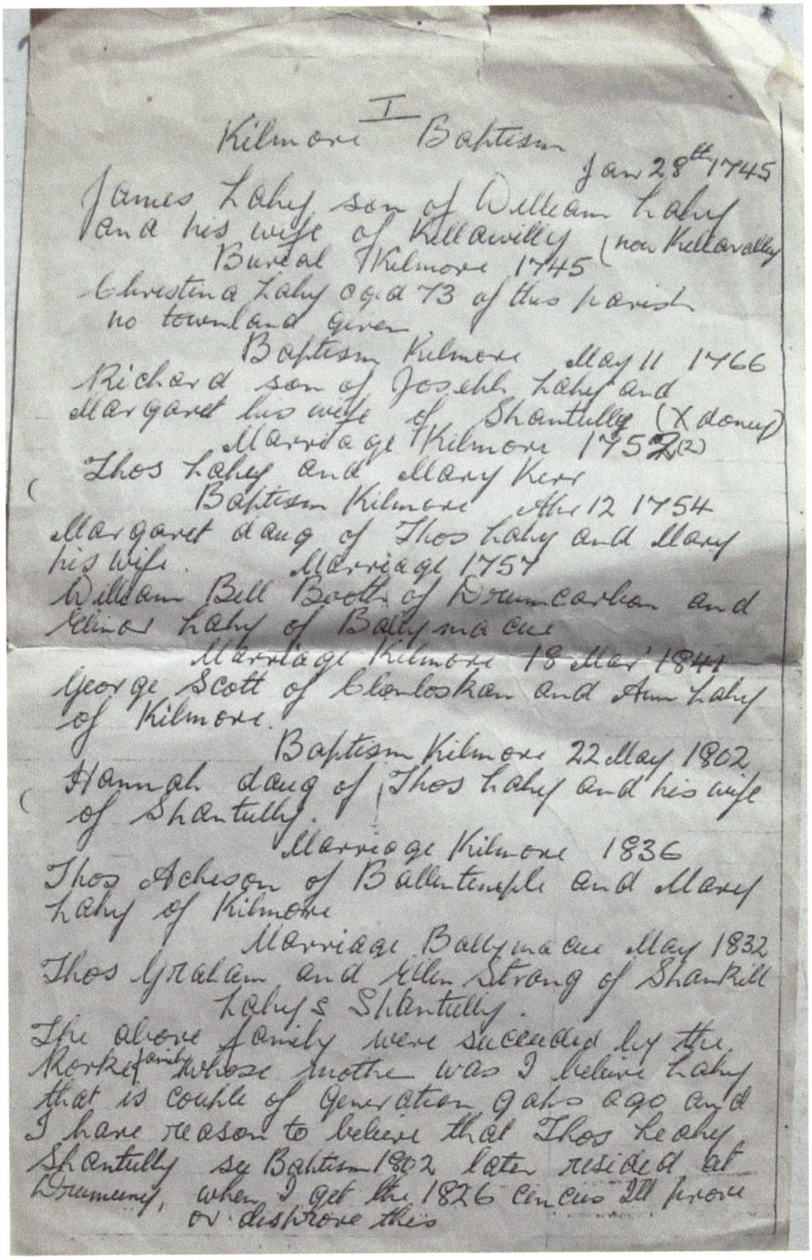

Figure 68 Notes on Early Lahys Provided by Bill Graham [Transcribed below] (Courtesy Pam Coote)

Transcription of the Bill Graham's Note [Figure 68].

Kilmore Baptisms
Jan 28th 1745 James Lahy son of William Lahy and his wife of Killawilly (now Killavalley).
Burial Kilmore 1745 - Christina Lahy of this parish, no townland given.
Baptism Kilmore May 11th 1766 Richard son of Joseph Lahy and Margaret his wife of Shantully (Crossdoney)
Marriage Kilmore 1752 Thomas Lahy and Mary Kerr
Baptism Kilmore Apr 12th 1754 Margaret daughter of Thomas Lahy and Mary his wife.
Marriage 1757 - William Bell Booth of Drumcarlow and Elinor Lahy of Ballymachugh.
Marriage Kilmore 18th March 1841 George Scott of Clonloskan and Ann Lahy of Kilmore.
Baptism Kilmore 22nd May 1802, Hannagh, daughter of Thomas and his wife of Shantully.
Marriage Kilmore 1836 Thomas Acheson of Ballintemple and Mary Lahy of Kilmore.
Marriage Ballymachugh 1832 Thomas Graham and Ellen Strong of Shankill.
Lahys Shantully:
The above family were succeeded by the Rorke family who's mother was I believe Lahy that is couple of generation gaps ago and I have reason to believe that Thomas Leahy of Shantully (re baptism 1802) later resided at Drumeeny. When I get the 1826 census I'll prove or disprove this.

I've had difficulty in tracing some of the births that Bill recorded. The closest I've come to locating Killawilly / Kilavalley – is *Killyvally* which is 5Km North West of Crossdoney on the shore of Lough Oughter or *Killawilly* located due East of Ballyconnell. I have not seen any evidence that Shantully Lahys later moved to Drumeeny. There was a Thomas Leahy in Drumeeny – however he was a direct descendant of the Lower Aghakilmore Leahys. I also haven't found any Rorke / Lahy connection.

7.1 Early Lahy Births

The following is a list of early Lahy baptisms obtained mainly by local historian Bill Graham [unknown from what source].

Table 7 Early Lahy Births

Name	Father	Mother	Place	Year	Source
James	William		Killawilly [Killavalley]	28/1/1745/6	Bill Graham
Margaret	Thomas	Mary		12/4/1754	Bill Graham
Richard	Joseph	Margaret	Shantully	11/5/1766	Bill Graham
Hannagh	Thomas		Shantully	22/5/1802	Bill Graham
John Laghy	William Laghy	Mary Morison	Kilmore (CoI)	16/11/1746	www.rootsireland.ie Note: Illegitimate - also entered as John Morison

Yellow shading indicates person is represented on the Top of the Tree diagram [ ].

7.2 Early Lahy Marriages

Source = National Archives of Ireland - Early Kilmore Marriages [32]

Table 8 Early Lahy marriages in Kilmore / Ardagh / Meath

Groom	Bride	Year	Source
Kilmore & Ardagh			
John Kirke	Ann Laughy	1712/13	National Archives of Ireland
Thomas Heslip	Sara Laghey	1718	National Archives of Ireland
Charles MClean	Anna Laughy	1721	National Archives of Ireland
John Loughy	Elinor Woods	1722	National Archives of Ireland
Francis Lahy	Elinor Lahy	1724/5	National Archives of Ireland
John Lahy	Margaret Reed	1725	National Archives of Ireland
Oliver Chivers	Ann Lahy	17??	National Archives of Ireland
Henry Strong	Mary Lahy	1751	National Archives of Ireland
William Lahy	Ann Lahy	1752	National Archives of Ireland
Thomas Lahy	Mary Kerr	1752	Bill Graham
John Lahy	Elizabeth Lahy	1752	National Archives of Ireland
William Booth	Elinor Lahy	1757	National Archives of Ireland
James Wilson	Elizabeth Lahy	1766	National Archives of Ireland
Mathew Edwards	Elizabeth Lahy	1771	National Archives of Ireland
Thomas Acheson [Ballintemple]	Mary Lahy [Kilmore]	1836	Bill Graham
James McArdle	Ann Lahy	1843	National Archives of Ireland
William Lahy	Isabella Chambers	1844	National Archives of Ireland
Meath			
Richard Lahey	Elizabeth Thornton	1792	National Archives of Ireland
James Walker	Elizabeth Lahey	1822	National Archives of Ireland
John Robinson	Anne Lahy	1828	National Archives of Ireland
John Lahy	Anne Stratford	1828	National Archives of Ireland
Thomas Leahy	Franes Lownds	1830	National Archives of Ireland
George Lahy	Mary Mathews	1833	National Archives of Ireland
Joseph Lahey	Elizabeth Thornton	1835	National Archives of Ireland
William Lahy	Elizabeth Price	1840	National Archives of Ireland
George Wilson	Elizabeth Lahy	1843	National Archives of Ireland

Yellow shading indicates person is represented on the Top of the Tree diagram [ ].
Non Yellow shaded individuals may be represented on subsequent (later) trees

7.3 Early Lahy Wills / Burials

Source = National Archives of Ireland [16].

Table 9 Early Lahy Wills in Kilmore / Ardagh

Name	Address	Year
Ardagh Wills Index & Prerogative Will Index & Testamentary - Ardagh Admin Bonds		
Christina Lahy [Burial at Kilmore] *	* Source = Bill Graham	1745
William Lahy	Aghakilmore Lower	1755
William Lahy	Aghakilmore Lower	1758
Francis Lahy	Aghakilmore	1757
John Lahy	Tircullen	1767
Jane Laghy	Aghakilmore Upper	1771
Joseph Lahy	14th Reg Dragoons	1771
Thomas Lahy	Aghakilmore	1772
Henry Lahy	Ahakellmore	1779
John Lahy	Ballymachugh	1795
John Lahy	Williamstown	1800
Thomas Lahy	Aghakilmore	1818
Patrick Lahy	Drumeeny	1842
James Lahy	Mullaghboy	1843
Thomas Lahy	Aghakilmore	1880

Yellow shading indicates person in represented on the Top of the Tree diagram [ ].
Non- Yellow shaded individuals may be represented on subsequent (later) trees

7.4 1761 Cavan Poll [17]

A list of the 1137 freeholders who had two votes at a County Court held in Cavan to elect knights to represent the county at a parliament held in Dublin on 19 May 1761.

Table 10 1761 Poll Cavan Lahys

Surname	Forename	Townland	Parish
Lacky	Joseph, [Quarter Master]	Aghakilmore	Ballymachugh
Laghy	William	Aghakilmore	Ballymachugh
Lahy	Henry	Aghakilmore Lower	Ballymachugh
Lahy	James	Aghakilmore Upper	Ballymachugh
Lahy	John	Aghakilmore Upper	Ballymachugh
Lahy	Thomas	Aghakilmore	Ballymachugh
Lahy	Thomas	Aghakilmore Upper	Ballymachugh
Lahy	William	Laragh, Laragh	Enniskeen
Lahy	Thomas, Jnr	Aghakilmore Lower	Ballymachugh

Of note is **William Lahy** of Laragh (Enniskeen). This is the only reference I can find to a Lahy being located at Laragh (Enniskeen parish). The relative location of Laragh to Ballymachugh is shown in Figure 69. Obviously, William was closer to the Mullagh / Bailieborough Lahys and so may have been related to them

Figure 69 Location of Laragh / Enniskeen (Courtesy Google Maps)

7.5 Other 17th and 18th Century Sources

Table 11 Other Early Sources

Resource	Year	Description	Lahys Listed?
Fiants	1584	Legal records listing the names of the principal people living in the various districts. Lurgan parish fiants edited by Dr O'Connell are in theBriefny Antiquarian Society Journal (B.A.S). Vol 1. and Crosserlough Parish also by Dr O'Connell are in B.A.S. Vol 2.	No Lahys / Leahys listed
Undertakers	1612	The Historical Manuscripts Commission Report, 4, (Hastings Mss) gives lists of English and Scottish large landlords granted land in the northern counties of Cavan, Donegal, and Fermanagh. These were known as undertakers	No Lahys / Leahys listed.
Muster roll	1630	Briefne 5(18) (1977-78(NLI P. 206	No Lahys / Leahys listed.
Book of Survey and Distribution	1641	These records show land owned in 1641 and who after forfeiture, owned it under the Cromwellian Act of Settlement. Edited articles also available in B.A.S Journal Vol 1-3 on Killinkere, Crosserlough, Munterconnaght, Castlerahan, Lurgan & Virginia Parishes	No Lahys / Leahys listed
Depositions	1641	These are eye-witness testimonies given mainly by Protestants, but also by some	No Lahys / Leahys listed

Resource	Year	Description	Lahys Listed?
		Catholics, from all social backgrounds, concerning their experiences of the 1641 Rebellion in Ireland. They provide vivid accounts of the events of that year and also list large numbers of people accused of participation in the rebellion or claiming to have suffered loss. Along with the victories of King William at the Boyne in 1690 and Aughrim in 1691, and the Battle of the Somme in 1916, the events they record have long been fundamental to the identity and culture of Unionist Protestants in Ireland, especially in Ulster. They are now all online at1641.tcd.ie.	
Civil Survey	1654-56	This too was a record of land ownership in 1640, compiled between 1655 and 1667, and fuller than the Books of Survey and Distribution. It contains a great deal of topographical and descriptive information, as well as details of wills and deeds relating to land title. It has survived for twelve counties only, Cork, Derry, Donegal, Dublin, Kildare, Kilkenny, Limerick, Meath, Tipperary, Tyrone, Waterford and Wexford. All of these have been published by the Irish Manuscripts Commission.	No Lahys / Leahys listed
Pender Census	1659	SLC film #924648 http://clanmaclochlainn.com/1659cen.htm	No Returns for Cavan
Subsidy Rolls	1662	These list the nobility, clergy and laity who paid a grant in aid to the King. They supply name and parish, and, sometimes, amount paid and occupation. They relate principally to counties in Ulster.	No Lahys / Leahys listed
Hearth Money Rolls	1664	A list of those who paid two shillings per hearth under the Hearth Money Act of 1662. They are important in being the only official, though incomplete, census prior to 1821. Edited articles include Parishes of Killeshandra, Kildallan, Templeport, Tomregan and Killinagh are in theBriefne Journal 1960. Killinkere, Lurgan and Mullagh are in B.A.S Journal, Vol 1. Castlerahan and Munterconnaght are in B.A.S Journal, Vol 2. Crosserlough is in B.A.S Journal, Vol, 3.	No Lahys / Leahys listed
Protestant Householders	1726	Lists of Protestant householders in parishes of BallyMcAleny (Scrabie), BallyMcHugh and Drumlumman, Edgeworth family papers	Anne Lahy (Widow) listed (no location)
Cavan Poll	1761	Proni T1522 Cavan Co. Library	Lahys present - See

Resource	Year	Description	Lahys Listed?
Book			Table 10
Flax Growers	1796	http://www.failteromhat.com/flax1796.php	No Lahys.
Census	1821	1821 Census	Lahys present - covered in next Volume.

7.6 Top of Shirley Lahey's Tree

According to Shirley Lahey [1],

> "On 28 January 1745 James son of William Lahy, was baptized in Co. Cavan. About the same time, or perhaps earlier, another Lahy was born but his first name is unknown to me though possibly Henry. This Lahy later became the father of Thomas who was a farmer. James and the father of Thomas, were thought to be brothers and so the grandfathers of Francis and Alicia, my great grandparent."

This would result in a 'Tree Top' as shown in Figure 70.

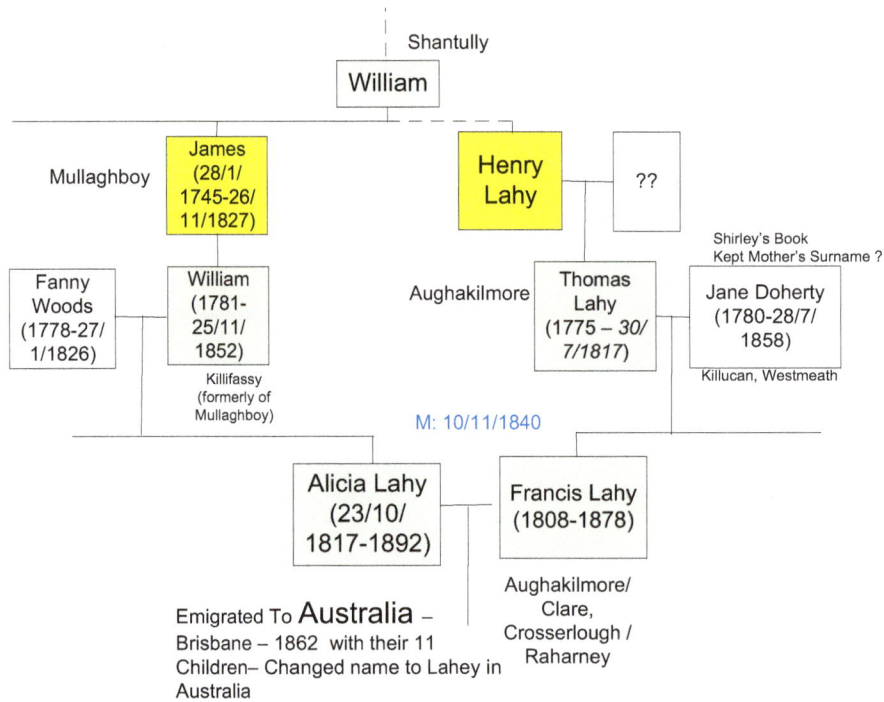

Figure 70 Top of Shirley Lahey's Australian Tree

The left side of the tree in Figure 70 has been populated from Church records and Census returns (1821). A key phrase in Shirley's statement is that **James** and **Henry** (yellow boxes) were 'thought to be brothers'. In a later section looking at the Upper Aughakilmore Lahys there is an inconsistency which leads me to believe that James and Henry were not brothers (see section 10.1.2 – Page 133). The inconsistency arises as the father of (Henry & Suzanna) is also a 'Henry' - not a William as shown in Shirley's tree (and also Henry (of Suzanna) didn't have a brother called James. The Henry & Suzanna in this tree did not have a son called Thomas thus it is most likely that Thomas was the brother of (Henry & Suzanna) - thus still the 'son' of a Henry [but not the brother of James]. The tree diagram in section 10.1.2 [Henry of Upper Aghakilmore] shows this. Thus I believe that the Australian branches are descendants of the Upper Aghakilmore Lahys.

David Leahy M.Sc.

8 Top of the Tree

8.1 Rationale

The very act of putting pen to paper to try and describe / explain what I perceive to be the top of the County Cavan Lahys structure has forced me to revisit evidence, re-evaluate assumptions and arguments which has thus made this a very useful exercise in itself!

8.2 Data

Parish registers of birth, deaths and marriages can get back to a certain date - typically mid-1800s. The 1821 census [18] is another good source to get back a little further. To go even further I was reliant on preserved Wills or descriptions of Wills (e.g. Betham abstracts). However, the best source to get back the furthest in time has been the Registry of Deeds land deeds, Wills and marriage articles [103] as well as privately held deeds.

8.3 Top of the Tree Structure

The top of the tree is very difficult to work out, especially with the knowledge that it is not actually the tree top - just the furthest back that I can directly go with the documentary evidence that is available. There is a tendency to 'join things up' as it makes a neater diagram, and no doubt I've fallen into that trap. This volume focuses on the earliest recorded Lahys in the area. A future volume will expand more details on Lahys / Leahys from about 1800 onwards. Other Lahys around in the early 1700s are listed in Table 7 Table 8 and Table 9.

I have tried to make it cater for all of the data available in the earliest available deeds and wills at my disposal; however, others may examine the same data / deeds/ Wills and come up with a different top of the tree model.

The top of the tree diagram gives the impression that these were the only Lahys around at the time which is obviously not the case, the wives, parents and children are not necessarily mentioned in legal documents and if you weren't involved in any land transactions or left a Will then there will be no evidence that you existed at this time (1600s and early 1700s).

There are many common names e.g. William, James, John, Thomas. When I first examined the land deeds I got the impression that these people were moving around the lake quite frequently. However, I believe now that is a wrong assumption. People did not 'move' about in the 1700s as easily and frequently as they do today. Typically, a couple would stay in their marriage house until death and then the eldest son would carry on there. All remaining sons would have to set up with a wife and dowry (or land given by the father) in another location, usually close by (to make use of family for labour, resources and child care etc.)

In   the solid lines represent documentary evidence whereas the dashed lined represent 'best guesses' based on the evidence. In my 'guestimation' there are at least eight main branches of Lahys / Leahys - circled in .

8.4 The Main Branches:

The main branches at the top of the Tree as I see it are as follows:

1. The 'Cross' / Drumeeny Branch - (descended from John of Lower Aghakilmore)
2. The Upper Aghakilmore / Capragh Branch
3. Williamstown branch (descended from Upper Aghakilmore / Capragh)
4. Clonlohan (probably descended from 1 or 2 above).
5. The Lavagh Branch (descended from James - father of Francis)
6. The Tircullen Branch (descended from John / Joseph of Tircullen)
7. Shantully Branch
8. Mullagh / Bailieborough Branch

These are illustrated in the following sections. .

There is also a tendency to assume that all of the Cavan Lahys are descended from Patrick (and it looks like that in the diagram) which is probably not the case, as Patrick may well have had brothers and cousins etc. from which other Lahy branches have sprung. However, to date we have no record of any of Patricks kin or other Lahys who were in County Cavan in the 1600s, so until other evidence comes to light for now Patrick, is the only known 'root' of the tree. I am however convinced that all the Cavan Lahys are connected - all the known evidence backs this up - you wouldn't let strangers from another family witness your daughter's marriage articles and your own land deeds, if they were not blood relations in some way.

The top of the tree as I view it is shown in . Overlaid on it are the numbered 'evidence circles' linking to justification notes for the existence of that person / link - shown in Table 12 page 106. I have made lines 'solid' when I have seen direct evidence of a relationship and dashed when I have no direct evidence, but is an educated guess based upon related evidence.

I will explain the rationale for the connections and structure in this diagram.

David Leahy M.Sc.

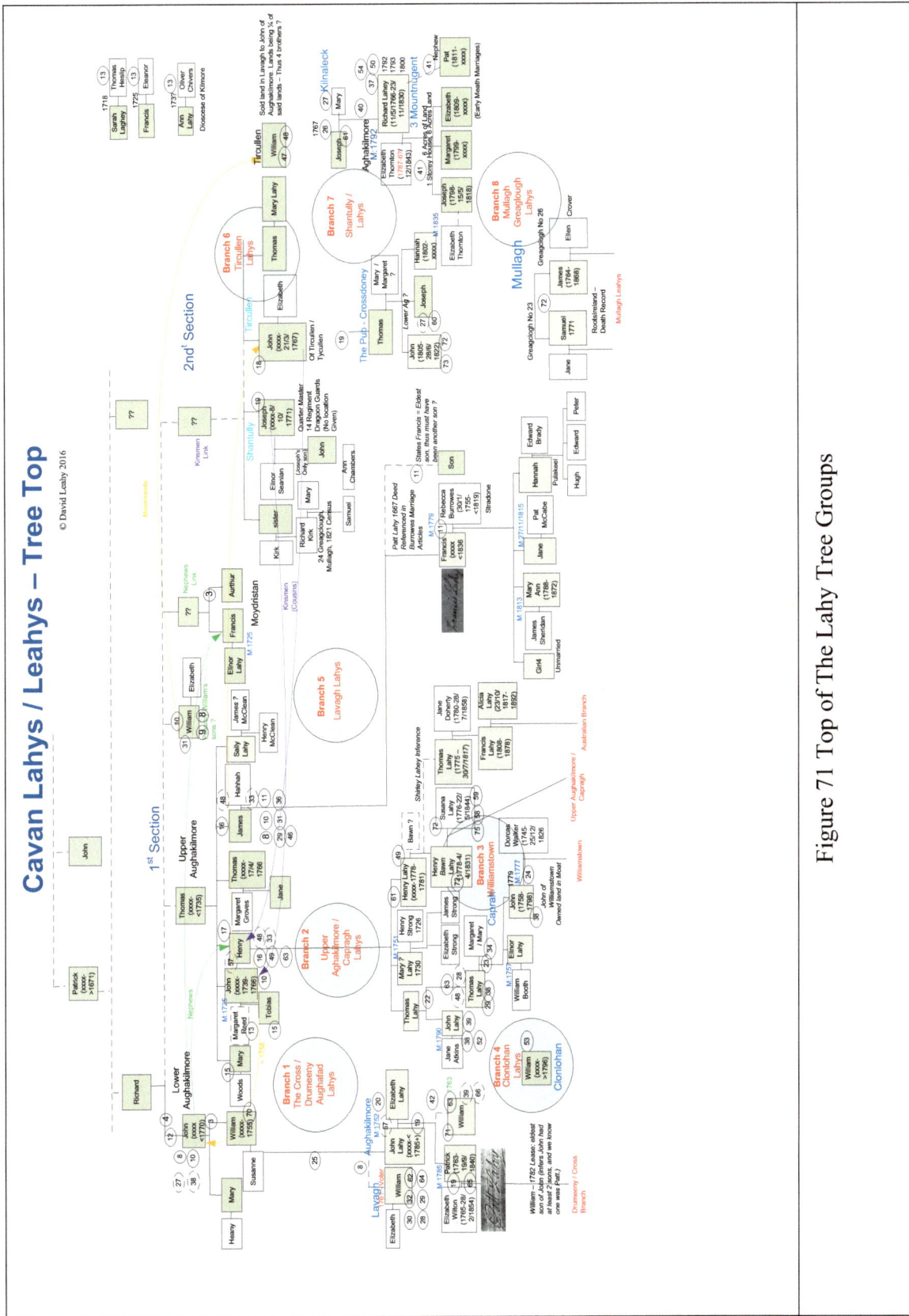

Figure 71 Top of The Lahy Tree Groups

Table 12 Sources for Top of The Tree Chart

1	1667 Patrick bought land in Aughakilmore from Thomas Coote and in Taulaught from Walter Ward – 2 deeds [1667] – Source = FS	15	1766 – Will Thomas Lahy of Upper Aughakilmore – Source = FS	29	Deed: 177801 – 1769. William Lahy of Lavagh. £240 paid by James Lahy of Aughakilmore Upper lands of Lavagh and Aghacreevy. Witnessed by Thomas Lahy of Aughakilmore Lower
2	Deed 11/1/1671 - 29th Year of Charles II Reign. Parties: 1. Walter Ward of Drogheda 2. Patrick Laghy of Aughakilmore Patrick gave Walter Ward £50 for 70 Acres in Aughakilmore – Source = FS	16	1779 Will Henry of Aughakilmore – Betham Abstracts	30	Deed: 190877 – 1772 - William Lahy and Wife Elizabeth of Lavagh. And James Lahy of Mullaghboy
3	1739 - Aurthur and Francis received part of the 'estate' of Richard (his grandsons ?) – Deed 66435 – 1739. Witnessed by Thomas – Uncle ?	17	John Lahy of Tycullen & Henry Lahy of Aughakilmore Lower (1760). 135902 Henry paid £60 for 70 Acres in Lower Aughakilmore. Witnessed by James McClean Innkeeper of Aughakilmore Middle, Henry Strong farmer and James Killroy, Schoolmaster and Thomas Lahy of Aughakilmore Lower.	31	Deed: 193166 – 1772. William and Elizabeth and James Lahy of Aughakilmore Upper
4	Richard the father of John of Lower Aughakilmore. Deed – 63321- 1738	18	1767 – John of Tircullen Will – Wife Elizabeth, brothers Joseph & Thomas – son of Thomas = Joseph. Sister in Law Mary, Kinsman Henry	32	Deed: 196816 – 1773. William Lahy of Lavagh and Elizabeth Lahy his wife and James Lahy of Mullaghboy and James Lahy of Ballina. Voluntary settlement
5	Francis is the nephew of John of Lower Aughakilmore [Deed: 66370 – 1739. John + Thomas of Upper Ag Witnessed	19	Deed:202256: - 1785 John Lahy & Elizabeth father & Mother of Patrick – marriage settlement 1785 – To Elizabeth Wilton from Derrin	33	Deed: 203250 – 1775. William Lahy and Elizabeth Lahy his wife of Aughakilmore Upper. James Lahy of Aghakilmore. £148 for land in Lavagh. Witnessed by Henry Lahy of Aghakilmore Lower, Francis Lahy of Ballina
6	Henry (of Upper Aghakilmore) is the nephew of John of Lower Aughakilmore [Deed: 66371 – 1739 – Witnessed by James + John of Upper Ag.	20	Kilmore Marriages – NLI – John Lahy of Aughakilmore & Elizabeth - 1752	34	Deed: 222030 – 1779 - Thomas Lahy of Lower Aughakilmore and Wife Mary, and John Lahy of Williamstown. 13/12/1779. Henry Lahy. 60 Acres of UPPER Aughakilmore 5 Schillings. Thomas sold land to John for 5 Schillings. Witnessed by William Lahy.
7	John, Henry and Thomas (of Upper Aughakilmore) sold 3/4 of the estate of Thomas Also owned land Lavagh (dec'd). Deed 55583 - 1735	21	1771 - Joseph Quarter Master 14th Dragoon Guards 27/8/1768 - 8/10/1771.Only son John, nephew Joseph, Brother John Lahy,Wife Elinor Lahy (Else Seanlan), Kinsman John Lahy,Nephew Richard Kirk	35	Deed: 250840 – 1786 James Lahy of Lavagh and Francis Lahy of Killcomell, Cavan and John Bell of Creevy, Longford. £567 2s, 8d Debt. Land in Lavagh

8	1738 – deed 66369: John Lahy of Lower Aghakilmore and William Lahy of Up Aghakilmore. 35 Acres in lower aghakilmore. Witnessed by William Blakely of Aughafad, Jam(es) Lahy and John Lahy of Upper Aghakilmore & Bxxx Delaney (Dublin Gent). 19 Acres in Lavagh and Aughacreevy.	22	Deed: 143581 – 1761. Mentions Thomas the Elder and Thomas the Junior of Aughakilmore	36	Deed: 250839 – 1786. James Lahy of Lavagh and Francis Lahy of Killcomell. 16 Acres and Lavagh lands in the possession of James Lahy
9	Thomas William & John all witnessed Deed 57842 – 1735 of Henry of Upper Aughakilmore – supports them being brothers	23	1779 – Deed 222030 - Thomas and Margaret Lahy of Aghakilmore. and Elinor Booth otherwise Lahy and John Lahy his son, both of Williamstown. Witnessed by Francis Lahy of Ballina.	37	Deed: 294154 – 1792. Richard Lahy of Aughakilmore and Francis Thornton of Larkhill to Marry
10	1738 – Deed 66369 – John Lahy of Lower Aghakilmore and William Lahy of Up Aghakilmore. 35 Acres in lower aghakilmore. Witnessed by William Blakely of Aughafad, Jam(es) Lahy and John Lahy of Upper Aghakilmore & Bxxx Delaney (Dublin Gent). 19 Acres in Lavagh and Aughacreevy.	24	Deed: 214253 - 1777 - John Lahy of Caprah. Marriage between John and Dorcas Walker.Lands of Williamstown formerly in the possession of widow duffy and half of lands in Togher in possession of Alex Walker. The said John Lahy in possession of lands of Moat and Middle Aghakilmore.	38	Deed: 296468 – 1790. Thomas and John Lahy of Lower Aghkilmore and Thomas Atkins of Killgolough, Cavan and Jane Atkins (daughter).£150 dowery and lands in upper and lower Aughakilmore. Witnessed by John Lahy of Williamstown, John Married Jane Arkins
11	Rebecca Burrows Marriage Articles 1779 - NLI	25	Deed 174157 - 1767-1769 William of Lavagh to John of Aughakilmore & his mother Suzanna.	39	Deed: 299871 – 1790. Thomas Lahy – and Son John Lahy of Lower Aghakilmore and Thomas Atkins of Kilgolough and Jane Atkins daughter of said Thomas Atkins lands in Upper Aghakilmore in possession of William Heaney. Witnessed by John Lahy of Williamstown,
12	1709 – Deed Richard Lahy to John Lahy – 70 Acres Aughakilmore & 38 Acres in Lavagh [Rev Peter Brady Notes on Deeds] - FS	26	Deed 166410 – 1767 Joseph & Wife Mary of Kilnaleck sold 76 Acres in Lower Ag to Andrew Bell of Bellsgrove	40	Baptism Records – Rootsireland.ie
13	Kilmore Marriages – NLI – John Lahy & Margaret Reed - 1725	27	Deed: 183906 – 1770. Joseph of Kilnaleck 70 Acres in Aughakilmore to Henry Lahy. Executed by John Lahy (Late) of Aughakilmore. Witnessed by James Lahy of Upper Aughakilmore.	41	1821 Census
14	Kilmore Marriages – NLI – Francis & Elinor	28	Deed: 160734 – 1766. William of Lavagh sold land to James of Aghakilmore Upper. Witnessed by Thomas of Ag Lower.	42	1782 Aughafad Deed [Farnham Papers]] - Royalties Turf Bogs reserved lives of Patt Lahy Lessee, William Lahy eldest son of John Lahy Lessee and William Lahy eldest son of James Lahy of Mullaghboy

Table 13 Sources for Top of The Tree Chart (Continued)

43	Baptism Records – Rootsireland.ie	54	Deed:348967 -1800. Rick (Richard) Lahy of Aughakilmore and the late Henry Maxwell. £1465 lands in Aughakilmore	65	Deed: 1789 (FS) - Henry (Lord Bishop of Meath) granted 12 Acres of Lavagh to Pat Lahy For the lives of:P at Lahy & Wife Elizabeth and 2yr old daughter Cathereine Witnesses: Joseph Duncan in the presence of Henry Maxwell
44	Farham papers 1769 Lease – James Lahy of Mullaghboy – Thomas & John Chambers – Scored out	55	Deed:443664 – 1799 - Francis Lahy of Lavagh to James Strong of Taulaght	66	Paper: 1806 – (FS) Farm book of Sheridans [of Ballinagh], records William Lahy of the Cross in the account book
45	Farnham Papers:1789 Lavagh to Pat Lahy For the lives of: Pat Lahy & Wife Elizabeth and 2yr old daughter Cathereine	56	Notes on Deeds – Rev Peter Brady from 1800s.William to James – 16 Acres in Lavagh & Aghacreevy	67	1803 – Deed 391569 – Ann Married to Robert Stratford. Father = John of Williamstown (deceased). She has £250 Dowery and £30 / year from Father's Will. Witnessed by Patt Lahy
46	1769 Will Dispute – Margaret (Wife) and James (Brother) challenge will of Thomas - Morman Records	57	Notes on Deeds – Rev Peter Brady from 1800s.- 1738 – John to Henry 35 Acres Aughakilmore & 19 Acres in Lavagh	68	Farnham Papers: 1808 - Deed – Pat Lahy – Derrin. 19 Acres, 5 Perches. Patrick Lahy lessee, James Lahy, forth son of lessee aged six years and Thomas Lahy sixth son of lessee aged two years.
47	William in Tircullen Deed 135904 – 1760 – Transferred to John of Lower Ag – half his lands in Lavagh. Being ¼ of said premesis (land divided between 4 brothers ?) Witness: Thomas of Aughakilmore	58	There is a Susan Lahy who died May 22, 1844, of Caprah, widow of Henry Bawn Lahy, aged 68.	69	From Patt Laghy 1667 Deed: Latin: *Protus in offir totulorum Cancellar Hibernie decimo septimodie Novembr duo terti septio Caroli Stdi Vitesimo Testio Et Exctminatur per* First in offer of the title of councillor of Ireland 17th November [?2 3 7 Charles? Reference to date during Charles' reign?] Witnessed and Executed by . . ?Ralph
48	Deed: 146370 – 1763. William Lahy of Tycullen and John Lahy of Aughakilmore – William released and granted onto said John all part of the town and lands of Aughakilmore wheron the John then Lived & agreed for fee £5 Sterling. Witnessed by Thomas, Henry & James of Lower Aghakilmore	59	[Susanna Articles 1831: Memorial: Book 10, Pg 155]	70	Prerogative Wills of Ireland – William of Aughakilmore Lower 1755
49	Deed: 216909 – 1778. Henry Lahy of Aghakilmore and Henry Lahy his son. One half of the lands of Aghakilmore.	60	Deed: - 1780- 231422 - James Lahy of Lavagh and Joseph Lahy of Aghakilmore (Brothers ?) and John Bell from Creevy, Longford. Sold lands in Lavagh (in	71	William Lahy of 'the Cross' purchase of flax seed from Cornelius Sheridan– 1806 Sheridan's Farm Book (FS)

			possession of tenants James Smyth and Henry Gallaghan) and lands in Aghakilmore in possession of Patrick and Lawrence Reilly		
50	Deed 300648 – 1793 - Richard Lahy of Aughakilmore and Henry Maxwell of Crover, cavan £479 for Lands in Aughakilmore known as the 'Cross'.	61	Deed: 227627 - 1781 – Joseph Lahy of Aughakilmore and Henry Lahy great second son and heir at law of Henry Lahy late of Aughkilmore. 20/7/1764 - £ 120	72	Death Records – Rootsireland.ie
51	Deed: 332001 – 1797:Thomas Lahy of Aughakilmore and Terence Joey of Aughakilmore (Publican). 10 Acres in Aughakilmore for 41 years yearly rent of £1 8s 31/2 d	62	Deed 143827 1762 - William Lahy of Lavagh to Thomas Cheevers and Thomas Heaney both of Aghakilmore half of all his lands in Lavagh being the one forth part of the said premesis to hold during the term of 21 years from 1s May next – yearly rent 15 s per acre.	73	'Remembering the Dead' Book – James Plunkett Coyle – Has Parents as *John* & Mary
52	Deed:319919 – 1793 - Thomas Lahy and John Lahy of Aughakilmore – fell behind in rent to Pat Kilroy of Killeadrean	63	Deed 143828 – 1762 - Thomas Lahy of Lower Aghakilmore sold to Thomas Cheevers of Upper Aghakilmore half of Upper Aghakilmore for the term of 21 years. Lease commencing 1st May 1763 at yearly rent of £14 5s 6d. Witnessed by Richard Cheevers of Lis Nugent & Oliver Cheevers his son & William Lahy and Henry Lahy of Lower Aghakilmore.	74	New YorkEmigrant Savings Bank, John Leahey & Wife Jane. – Westmeath. Labourer – 7 Caroline St
53	Deed:345139 – 1796. William Lahy of Clonlohan, parish of Drumhsman on behalf of his daughter Margaret Lahy. James strong took his wife Pillarg Lahy	64	Deed 149470 – 1764 - William Lahy of Lavagh sell onto Thomas Cheevers of Aughakilmore all that half of the said William Lahys undivided moiety or half part of the lands of Lavagh and Aghacreevy now in the possession of the said William, Lahy, Thomas Lahy and James Lahy as the same is now held by the said Thomas Cheevers the said part undivided thereby demised to the said Thomas Cheevers containing 16 acres to hold for 30 years. Witnessed Robert Cordner, Robert Acheson	75	The Laheys: Pioneer settlers and sawmillers – Shirley Lahey ISBN: 0646427644
				76	Kilmore Marriages – NLI – John Kirk & Ann Laughy – 1712/13

8.5 Tree Description Rationale

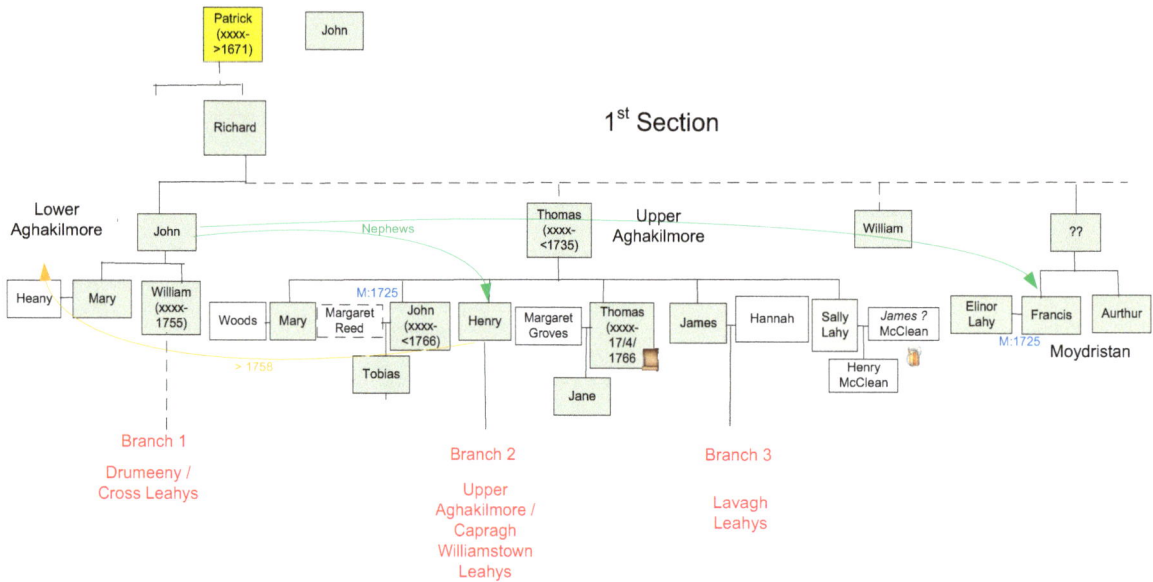

Figure 72 Tree Top 1st Section

I propose to describe what I know about the individuals in the top of the tree in a row- by-row fashion proceeding down each branch as shown in Figure 73.

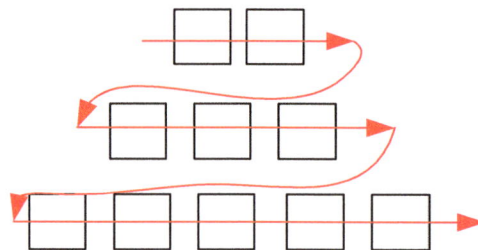

Figure 73 Description Pattern

9 Branch 1 - Lower Aghakilmore

The Upper and Lower Aughakilmore Lahys were inexorably linked and often times the generic 'Aughakilmore' term was used to describe the area where they lived. Thus, although for clarity and structure I have separated the two branches here, in reality I believe they were very closely related'.

The Lower Aughakilmore Lahys were the most numerous as can be seen by the number of dwellings in Figure 67 (not all dwellings were Lahys). I am directly descended from the Lower Aughakilmore Lahys who later on lived at the pub known as 'The Cross' (see Figure 88 on page 125).

9.1 Top - Patrick

How we discovered Patrick

At the National Library of Ireland, I discovered the Francis Lahy / Rebecca Burrows articles and within them I discovered a reference to an earlier deed dated 1667 in which a **Patrick Lahy** bought land from Thomas Coote. As the records at the Registry of Deeds only go back as far as 1708, I thought there would be no chance of ever finding a copy of this deed. It is not at the Registry of Deeds or the National Archives, and all local solicitors' records have been long destroyed. However, one morning whilst staying at Ross House near the lake, a little robin came and chirped at my window, and I thought maybe that's a sign? Sure enough, later that day during a visit to Cavan's Ballymachugh Church of Ireland Graveyard I noticed a man cleaning a 'Sheridan' grave. I thought maybe he worked at the Church so I walked up to him and asked him if he knew the Sheridans as we'd heard they were related to the Lahys but weren't sure how. He introduced himself as Francis Sheridan and told me that he was a direct descendant of the Sheridan line and that *yes* the Lahys and Sheridans were connected a few times. In fact, he said they are buried beside each other. He pointed to an illegible gravestone next to the Sheridan grave he was cleaning as stated that his family had passed down knowledge that Francis Lahy and Rebecca Burrows were buried there. My cousin had learned of a tip to read illegible gravestones - by spraying them with shaving foam and rubbing a sponge over the surface. So sure enough we tried that, and low and behold the text Francis and Rebecca Lahy was revealed. I also mentioned to Francis that I'd heard the Lahys had been in the area since at least 1667, as I'd seen a reference to a land deed of that date. He agreed and then declared that he had the 1667 land deed in his loft! I was astonished and wondered why it would be in his loft. Francis declared that it was probably the Sheridan's family purpose to be able to show an 'audit trial' of how they had come into possession of the land they owned as the family were Roman Catholic and hundreds of years ago Roman Catholics were prohibited from owning land.

I was delighted to hear the news and later met up with Francis in Dublin to get a copy of the deed - which had two versions; a short and a longer version.

Pat Laghy

Thus, at the top of the Cavan tree lies Patrick, there were obviously Lahys before him, however currently no currently available documentary evidence place Lahys here before Patrick. The 1652 Commenwealth Census [121] places Pat Loghy in Lower Aughakilmore as a land owner in 1652, thus this is the earliest documentary record of a Lahy in Cavan.

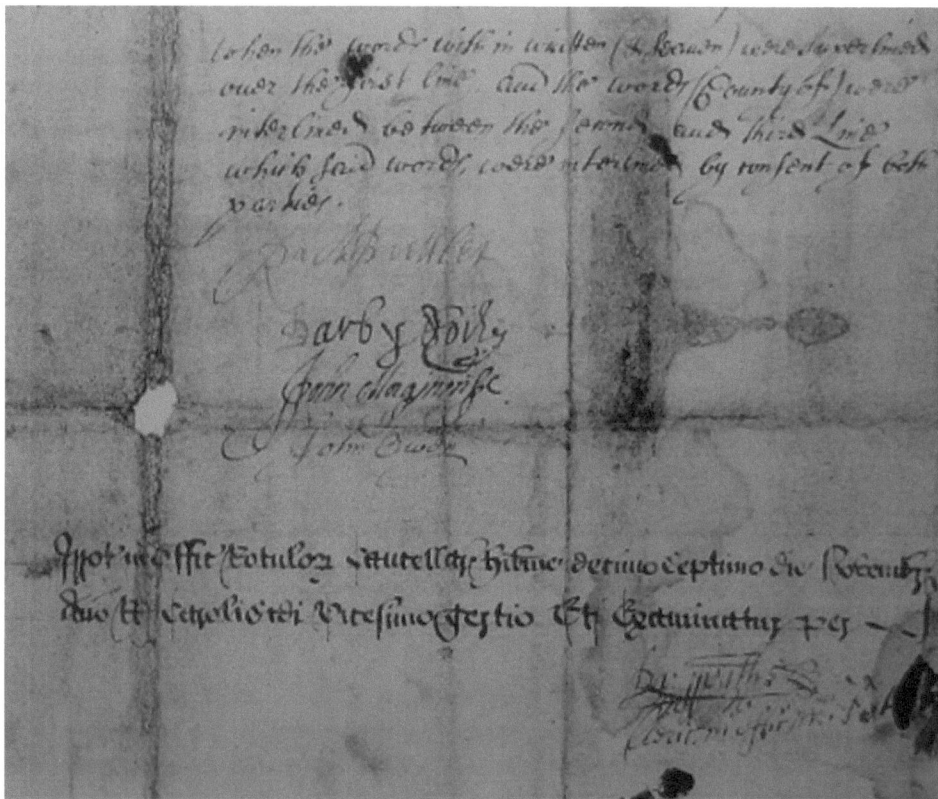

Figure 74 Latin inscribed cover of the small 1667 Deed [12]

The latin reads:

Protus in offir totulorum Cancellar Hibernie decimo septimodie Novembr

duo terti septio Caroli Stdi Vitesimo Testio Et Exctminatur per

This translates roughly as:

First in offer of the title of councillor of Ireland 17th November

David Leahy M.Sc.

[?2 3 7 Charles? Reference to date during Charles' reign?] Witnessed and Executed by . . . ?Ralph [*unclear!*]

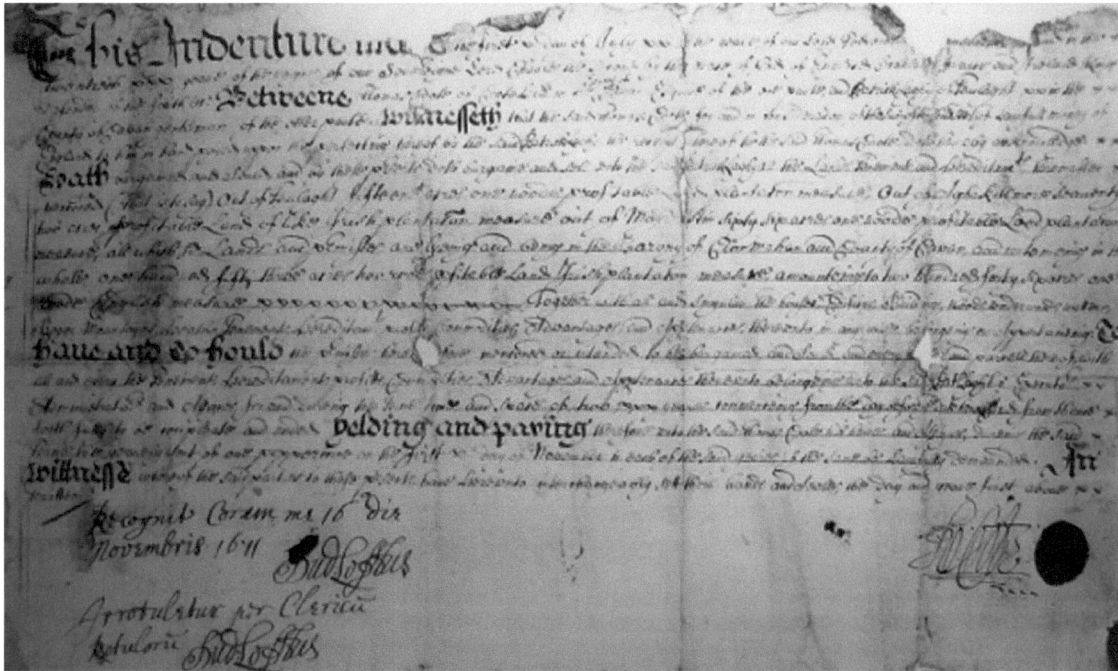

Figure 75 Small version of the 1667 Pat Laghy Land Deed [12]

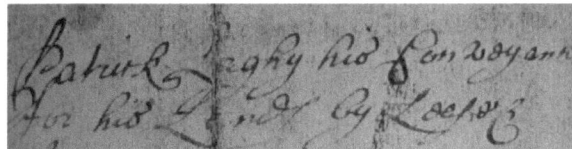

Figure 76 Pat Lahy in Cavan - *Patrick Laghy*

Signatories on the Deed Cover Include:

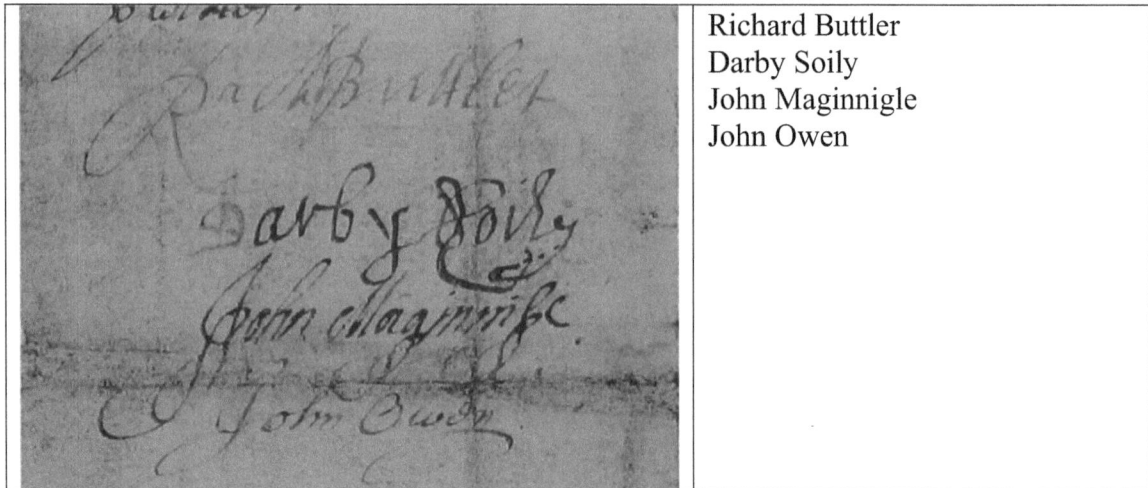

	Richard Buttler Darby Soily John Maginnigle John Owen

Figure 77 Signatories of the 1671 Deed

What the 1667 Deed Tells Us

Essentially this deed tells us that Patrick Laghy lived in Tawlaght (in Upper Aghakilmore) and bought land from Thomas Coote of Cootehill. Thomas Coote's father Charles Coote [19] was given land by the crown in lieu of his family's service to the crown during the 1600s upheaval in the area (and no doubt 'taken' from the incumbent Roman Catholics). Patrick bought:

- 15 Acres in Tawlaught
- 72 Acres in Aghakilmore
- 66 Acres in Moydristan

The acres are in Irish Measure, which equates to 246 English Measure Acres.
Various small sums of money (e.g., 10 shillings and £10) are mentioned throughout the deed which may be rent values due, however no large sum of money is mentioned. The deed it has to be said is difficult to read both in terms of legibility and semantics due to the convoluted 'legal' jargon of the day.

The difficulty with a deed like this is that it doesn't say where exactly the land was or the boundaries. Patrick probably purchased even more land (judging by what was inherited later on) but the records unfortunately aren't accessible at present. The Lahys owned land all around Lake Sheelin, so it could be that Patrick's ancestors had made those purchases. Another deed dated 11/1/1671 has Patrick Laghy (this time of Aghakilmore) buying 70 Acres in Aghakilmore from Walter Ward of Drogheda.

All in all, it seems that Patrick was quite wealthy to enable him to purchase such an amount of land. Also note the surname spelling 'Laghy' this spelling is rarely used after this time period.

Francis Lahy Marriage Articles 1779

David Leahy M.Sc.

To jump ahead a little (about 100 years) the Francis Lahy and Rebecca Burrowes marriage articles [20] make reference to Francis's father - James:

> *"said James Lahy is now seized and possessed of the several denominations of land herein after mentioned by deed bearing date the second day of July one thousand six hundred and sixty-seven, and made by Thos. Coote late of Cootehill in the county of Cavan Esg. Deceased to* **Patrick Lahy** *deceased at the yearly rent of one peppercorn in consideration of the sum of sixty pounds sterl. That is to say sixty acres or thereabouts in the townland of* **Upper** *Aghakilmore as the same is now possessed by the said James Lahy or his under tenants"*

This provides us a little more information in that it looks like Patrick paid £60 for 60 acres. It also reaffirms the direct ancestry (through inheritance) from Patrick through eventually to James and to Francis. This deed also mentions land in the townland of Lavagh and seeks to assure the pension of Margaret Groves (widow of Thomas Lahy - who I presume to be a brother of James). It was quite common in 'Wedding Articles' to mention 'pensions' for female members of the family. As it wasn't cheap to produce such long drawn-out legal documents it made sense to lay down in a legal document and provide for the future for the older females of the family. I will expand more on this Thomas later.

Update on Patrick:
Since first publication, new information has come to light on Patrick – see section 4.3 on page 49.

9.2 Top - Richard

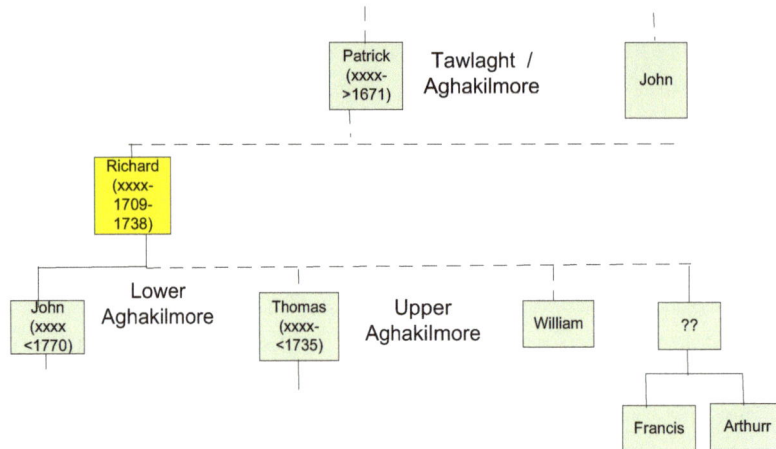

Figure 78 Richard Lahy

Richard is first mentioned in Notes from a Deed dated 1709 [21] where he rented or sold 70 Acres of Land in Lower Aghakilmore and 38 Acres on Lavagh to John Lahy (presumably his son).

He is next mentioned in a Deed dated 1738 [22] as being the father of John of Lower Aghakilmore and also as being deceased - thus he must have died between 1709-1738.

Richard Lahy seems to be of the generation before the top level of brothers (see Figure 78) and so possibly is a son or brother of Patrick. The name 'Richard' does continue down through some of the family branches although interestingly not through his named son John's line.

Another deed dated 1739 [23] has Arthur and Francis selling land in Moate, mayabrasten [Moydristan?], clonmahon) *"formerly the Estate of Richard Lahy"* - they are probably Richard's grandsons, but it is not known who their father (one of Richard's sons) was. It is not known what became of this Francis and Arthur. However, Ardagh Wills [16] does list aWill of a Francis of Aghakilmore dying in 1757.

Richard son of Patrick Laghy?
According to [21], Richard was selling / giving lands to his son John in 1709. He must have been at least 40 to be giving / selling lands to a son who must have been at least 20 years old by then. That would put Richard's birth at about 1670 - around the time that Patrick Laghy is first recorded in the area.

Richard's son John's daughter Mary is recorded as getting married in a deed dated 1719 [24]. She was probably at least 19 and born around 1700. If John got married around then, then he was probably born around 1680 thus his father [Richard] would have been born potentially 1660.

David Leahy M.Sc.

9.2.1 1st Generation - 4 Brothers Evidence

The following details evidence for the existence of four brothers; John, Thomas, William and a possible 4th brother as shown in Figure 79.

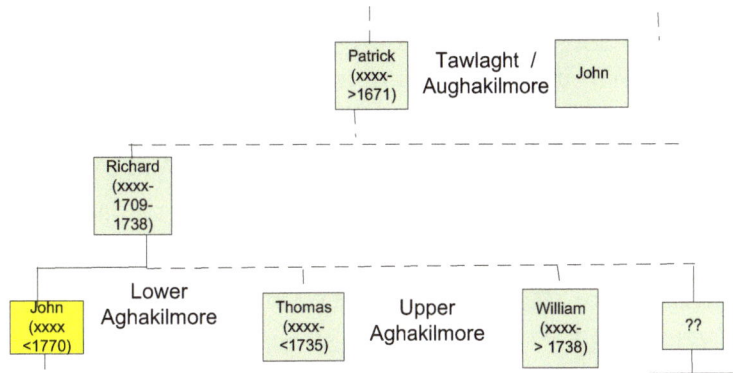

Figure 79 John of Lower Aghakilmore - Brother 1

9.2.2 John (of Lower Aghakilmore) [Root]

On the left of Figure 79 is John (of Lower Aghakilmore). John is mentioned in the marriage articles of his daughter Mary in a deed dated 1719 [24]. He is also confirmed as a son of Richard in a deed dated 1709 [21] and in another dated 1738 [22].

In a deed dated 1709, Richard [21] gives 70 acres in Aghakilmore and 38 acres in Lavagh to John Lahy. In a later deed dated 1738 [22] John (of Lower Aghakilmore) sells 70 acres in Aghakilmore which is confirmed as being part of the estate of the Richard Lahy, and it also confirms John as being his son. From this we can conclude that Richard died between 1709 and 1738.

In the early 1700s, John of Lower Aghakilmore is mentioned in *nine* separate land deeds from 1719-1769, giving weight to the proposition that he was quite a distinguished land owner and respected by many other 'Lahys' in the area as he witnessed their land transactions. The earliest mention of him is in the marriage articles drawn up for his daughter Mary in 1719 [24] - who married William Heany / Heaney. His own son William was also mentioned - 60 acres were to go to him unless he produced no heirs (in which case son in law William Heany would get the land in Aghakilmore). His son William was probably younger (unmarried) as no partner was mentioned in 1719.

If Mary's marriage articles were drawn up in 1719 then she was probably in her early 20s. Thus, her father probably married 1690-1700. Given that most were in early 20s when married her father John was probably born 1660-1670. This means that John her father could have been a direct son of Patrick (who we know was still around in 1667). But it is probably more likely that he's a grandson of Patrick - as there is a deed [22] - 1738 mentioning a John as son of Richard, also notes from a deed dated 1709 which has Richard gives 70 Acres in Aghakilmore and 38 Acres in Lavagh to John.

Ardagh Wills [16] lists aWill of a John of Lower Aghakilmore in 1770. A land deed dated 1770 [25] mentions the 'late John Lahy of Aghakilmore thus I presume John to have died around 1769 / 1770. Unfortunately, no copy of his Will exists to date.

As well as giving land to his son William in 1719, John also gave land to his nephew Henry [26] and nephew Francis [27]. He obviously owned quite a lot of land and was quite generous with it. Figure 80 shows John of Lower Aghakilmore's signature from the 1760 Tircullen deed [47]. The 1738 deed [22] mentions John of Lower Aghakilmore but is also witnessed by John of Upper Aghakilmore. Figure 81 shows this signature. It is impossible to be sure which John signed the document but it looks very similar to the signature in Figure 80.

Some private notes on land deeds taken in the 1800s by the Rev Peter Brady [21] show that Richard sold / gave 70 Acres in Aughakilmore and 38 Acres in Lavagh to John Lahy (Richard had a son John - this must be him). In the same notes [21] in 1738 John Lahy sold / gave what appears to be the same land (70 Acres in Aughakilmore and 38 Acres in Lavagh) to Thomas Lahy. One of John's brothers was Thomas but he was dead by 1735 so it must have been his nephew Thomas (Thomas 'Junior' son of Thomas) who received the land.

David Leahy M.Sc.

Figure 80 John [of Lower Aghakilmore]'s signature from 1760 Tircullen deed [47]

[Registry of Deeds (Property Registration Authority) retains the copyright]

Figure 81 John [of Upper Aghakilmore] Signature [22] - 1738 Deed

[Registry of Deeds (Property Registration Authority) retains the copyright]

9.2.3 Thomas senior (of Upper Aghakilmore) [Root]

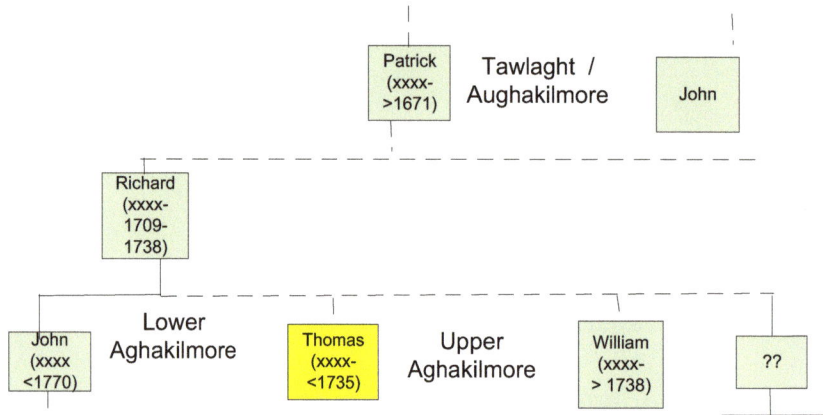

Figure 82 Thomas of Upper Aghakilmore - Brother 2

The first mention of this (earliest) Thomas is in a deed [48] which states that John, Henry and Thomas of Aghakilmore Upper sold land in Lavagh in 1734, which was 3/4 of the estate of **Thomas Lahy (deceased).** These were presumably Thomas senior's sons. It would also imply that he had four sons - the fourth being James - see section 10.1. In 1739, a land deed (involving Lavagh and Aghacreevy - [26]) links John Lahy of Lower Aghakilmore and Henry Lahy of Upper Aghakilmore his nephew. This provides more evidence that John of Lower Aghakilmore and Thomas were brothers (Thomas had a son called Henry).

9.2.4 William (of Upper Aghakilmore) [Root]

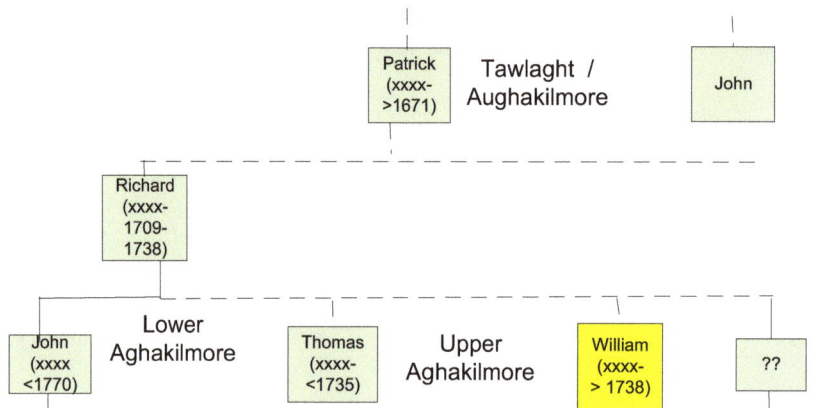

83 William of Upper Aghakilmore - Brother 3

In a 1735 deed [49] Henry [son of Thomas (Senior)] (of Upper Aghakilmore) bought land in Middle Aghakilmore (Capragh) from Richard Fitzpatrick and the deed is witnessed by Thomas Lahy, William **Lahy** and John Lahy (probably Henry's uncles as his father is deceased by 1735). This land in Capragh passed all the way down through Henry's ancestors and is still in possession of Leahys living there today.

In 1738, a land deed [50] lists John Lahy of Lower Aghakilmore and William Lahy of Upper Aghakilmore were involved a transaction involving 35 Acres in lower Aghakilmore. It is most likely that brothers would sell land together. The deed is witnessed by James & John of Upper Aghakilmore (probably William and John's nephews) - which really does tie in this close-knit family. Thus, I believe this William was the third brother - son of Richard and lived until at least 1738.

9.2.5 4th Brother? [Root]

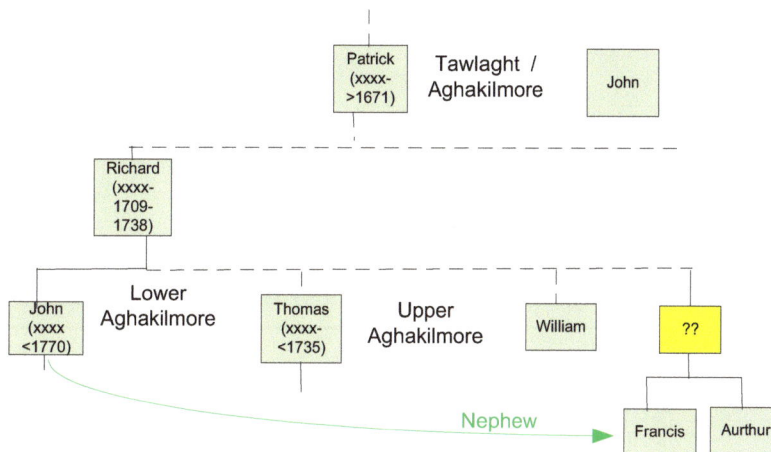

Figure 84 Possible 4th Brother?

In 1739 **John Lahy** of Lower Aghakilmore was involved in a land transaction with his **'nephew' Francis** (of Upper Moydristan) [27]. This suggests the existence of a fourth brother (father of Francis and Arthur). Another deed dated 1739 [23] mentions Arthur and Francis Lahy (of Moate and Moydristan) in a land transaction of land on Moate and Moydristan which is *formerly the estate of Richard Lahy* of Aghakilmore (deceased). This also connects them to this direct line. Richard was probably the father or Grandfather of Francis and Arthur (for them to be direct inheritors). It is possible that there were two individuals named Richard (their father and Grandfather), however I believe Richard was their Grandfather.

The father of Arthur and Francis may well have been William (mentioned above) suggesting only 3 brothers, or even Thomas (suggesting just 2 brothers) but I have no evidence of this. Given the traditional naming convention the father may have been a 'Francis'. However, I'll keep a 'place-holder' for a fourth brother until other evidence becomes available - see Figure 84.

9.2.6 2nd Generation - [Lower Aghakilmore]

1.1.1 William of Lower Aghakilmore

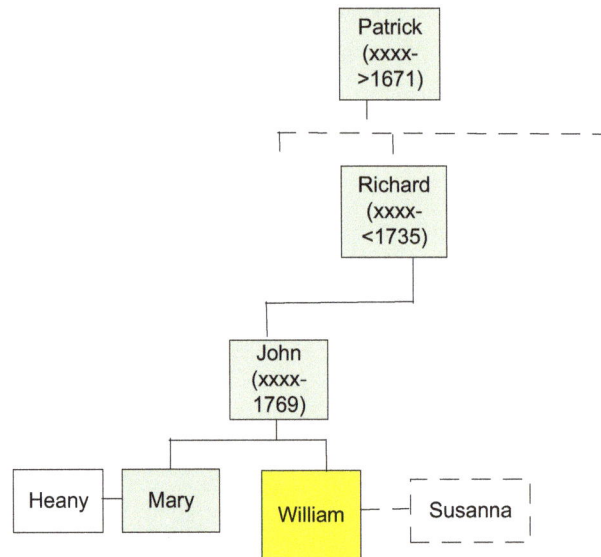

Figure 85 William of Lower Aghakilmore

William of Lower Aghakilmore is mentioned for the first time in his sister (Mary)'s wedding articles in 1719 [24].

It is not known whether William, the son of John produced an heir to qualify him to the lands in Aghakilmore; however, there is a record in Ardagh Wills [16] of a Will of a William Lahy of Lower Aghakilmore in 1755. Another source (Testamentary - Ardagh Admin Bonds - [51] records William Lahy of Aghakilmore Lower as having a Testamentary in 1758 - I presume this to be the same William.

A William (of Lower Aghakilmore) also witnessed a deed (alongside John of Upper Aghakilmore - probably his uncle) involving his father John and Francis of Upper Moydristan [John's nephew] - in 1739 [27].

The presence of a Will suggests that he had land to leave as an inheritance (and thus must have married and produced an heir?) - presuming that it is the same William. A deed dated 1767 [52] mentions John (of Lower Aghakilmore) and his mother Susanne [in 1767 it is unlikely that William's father John was alive alongside his mother!] which could indicate that William was married to a woman named Susanna (see Figure 85). William is

David Leahy M.Sc.

notable by his *absence* from the land deeds in the early 1700s; perhaps he died at a young age.

9.2.7 3rd Generation [John of Lower Aghakilmore] John and Elizabeth and their son Patrick

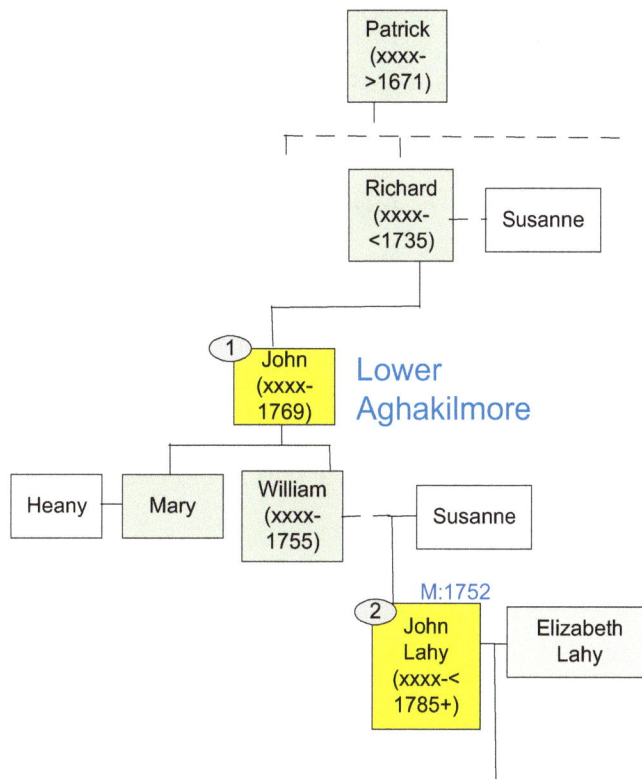

Figure 86 John of Lower Aghakilmore [Options]

In a deed dated 1767 [52] a *second* John Lahy of Lower Aghakilmore is mentioned along with his mother Susanne]. This *second* John of Lower Aghakilmore could either be:

1. Son of Richard [thus Richard's wife was Susanne] (No 1 in Figure 86)
2. Son of William [thus William's wife was Susanne] (No 2 in Figure 86)

I'm inclined to believe No 2 mainly because Richard had died before 1735 and his wife probably did not last another 40 years after his death. The 1st John of Lower Aghakilmore could still have been alive (he is mentioned as deceased in 1770 – [25]) however it is very unlikely his mother would still be alive! John's signature in 1767 is shown in Figure 87 - quite unlike the 1st John of Lower Aghakilmore's signature in Figure 80 and Figure 81.

Figure 87 John's signature from 1767 Deed [52], with mother Susanne

[Registry of Deeds (Property Registration Authority) retains the copyright]

Given the naming convention of naming 1st born son after your own father, it's likely that any such 'son' of William was named 'John' or 'William'. In [32], (Kilmore Marriages) there is a record of a **John Lahy** and **Elizabeth Lahy** having married in 1752. The fact that they were both Lahys does suggest a 1st or 2nd cousin marriage (as this was common at the time - to keep dowry / land within the family). It is purely conjecture that John was the son of William, however given the lack of evidence from this period I think it is a logical assumption to make from the available data. It is not known which Lahy family Elizabeth came from.

Another data source [53] confirms John and Elizabeth as the parents of Patrick Lahy who married Elizabeth Wilton in 1785. Naming their son Patrick again lends weight to the descent from the 1667 Patrick. The names Patrick and John are used for alternate generations down this 'line' all the way to my father's brother John Charles. I have thus expanded the previous tree to include these data and assumptions - as shown in Figure 89.

In the Marriage articles of Patrick and Elizabeth Wilton (1885) [53] John Lahy senior gave half the lands in Aghakilmore to his son Patrick and half to his - 'yet to be born' grandson. This confirms that John 2 [as shown in Figure 89] owned substantial lands in Aghakilmore and also gives us evidence that John 2 was still alive in 1785.

In Prerogative Wills [119] there is a **John Lahy of Ballymachugh** listed in **1795**. Although there may have been a few other John Lahys around at the time, I think that it is quite likely that this is the same John. We know he was alive in 1785 at the marriage of his son Patrick, he could well have died 10 years later in 1795 and being a substantial land owner left a Will as recorded in [119].

The Lahys in this line eventually purchased a pub in Lower Aughakilmore (possibly from McCleans) known as the 'Cross' and owned it up until the late 1940s - Figure 88.

David Leahy M.Sc.

Figure 88 The 'Cross' Pub [1940s]

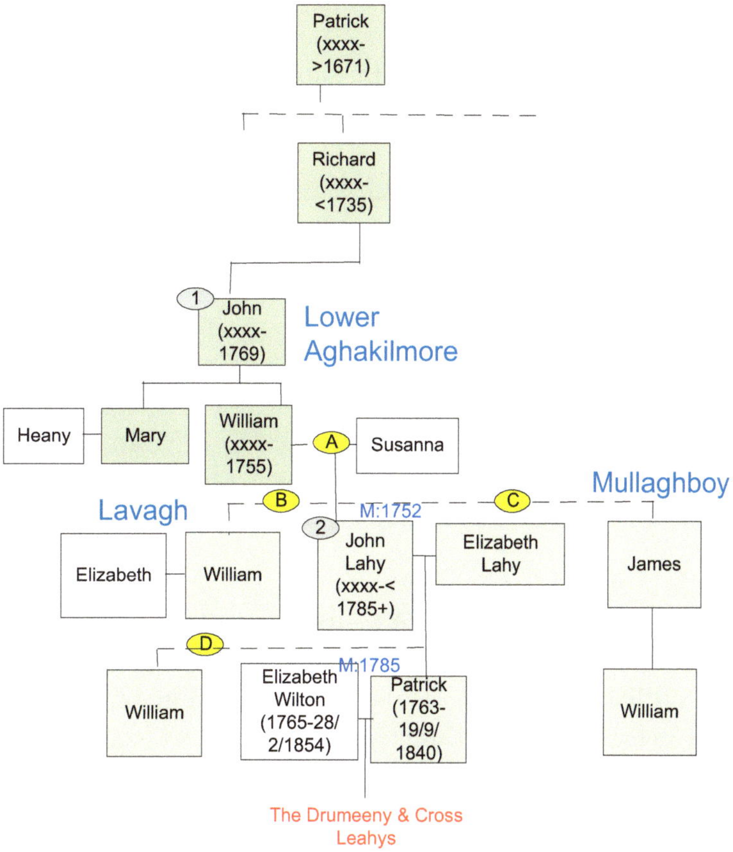

Figure 89 Patrick & John of Lower Aghakilmore (and possible extensions)

(Dashed line indicates conjecture)

I believe the following signature - Figure 90 (from a Land Deed dated 1785 involving Francis Lahy and Connor Sheridan [54] is that of Patrick Lahy, son of John and again in 1798 (Figure 91) as a witness to John of Williamstown's daughter's marriage articles [43].

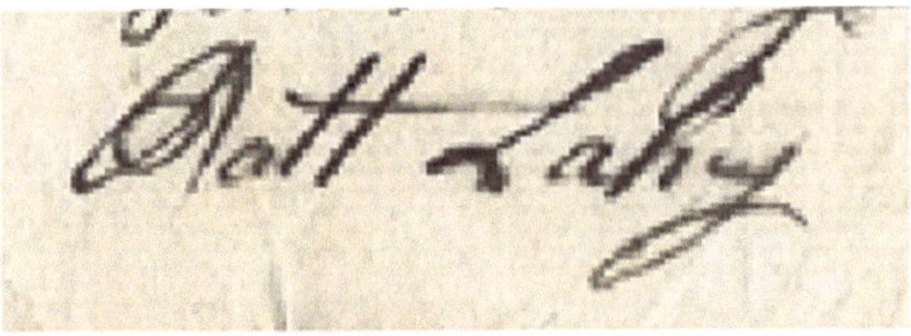

Figure 90 Patrick Lahy signature 1785 Francis Lahy / Sheridan Deed [54]

Figure 91 Patrick Lahy's Signature from 1803 Deed Involving John of Williamstown's daughter Ann – [46]

[Registry of Deeds (Property Registration Authority) retains the copyright]

The dashed lines in Figure 89 are assumed connections. The evidence and reasoning behind these assumptions (labelled in yellow A-D) are described below.

A - William father of John and husband of Susanne

In a deed dated 1767 [52] John Lahy of Lower Aghakilmore is mentioned along with his mother Susanne. This is very unlikely to be the 1st John of Lower Aghakilmore as by this time he would be quite old - and unlikely to have his mother still alive too! I think I can assume that this John is the son of William and grandson of the 1st John. That being the case his mother was Susanne and therefore likely to be the wife of William. I believe that William isn't mentioned because by this time he has died. In Ardagh Wills [16] there is a record of a William of Aghakilmore Lower having died in 1755. In addition, John named his eldest son William [1782 Lease document [55]] as per Irish naming convention (Table 21 Page 197) after his own father - further supporting the premise that William was John's father.

B - William of Lavagh son of William and brother of John?

In the deed dated 1767 [52] John Lahy and his mother Susanne are mentioned alongside William of Lavagh. William of Lavagh seems to be involved in quite a few land transactions (1762, 1764, 1766, 1767, 1769, 1772, 1773 and 1775). Thus, he must have inherited quite a bit of land - mostly in Lavagh and Aghacreevy [where his grandfather had land]. It is a possibility that he was the eldest son (hence being named William) of William (son of John of Lower Aghakilmore). As such he would have inherited the most land. It is a tenuous link, but families back then tended to have many children so I think it is a credible link.

We know from earlier deeds that Richard had left 70 Acres in Aghakilmore to his son John and 38 Acres in Lavagh. This presumably would have been inherited by his son William - and thence John through to Patrick (land in Aghakilmore) and William (land in Lavagh). Alternatively, William of Lavagh may belong to the Lavagh branch of the family - see section 13.

C - James of Mullaghboy, brother of John and William

James of Mullaghboy is mentioned together with William of Lavagh in 2 deeds dated 1772 and 1773. That alone would give me suspicion that they were brothers, however in the 1782 Lease document [55] there is a William mentioned as 'son' of James of Mullaghboy (alongside Pat and his father John) which gives me even more confidence that James is a brother of John and possibly William (of Lavagh). James of Mullaghboy is recorded in the Farnham papers renting land in 1769 [69].

D - William brother of Patrick

In a 1782 Lease document [55] Pat and John are mentioned together - this probably refers to father and son. It goes on to mention Pat as Lessee and *William Lahy eldest son of John Lahy Lessee.* To me this indicates that John had at least 2 sons (otherwise it would have said *'only'* son). We know one was Patrick [53] - so the other could have been William. The eldest son typically got most of the inheritance and in this case the land deeds do show this. In the 1761 Cavan Poll [17] there is a record of William of Aghakilmore.

Lahys presence in Lower Aghakilmore by Land Deed

The assumption is that if neither Upper or Lower is mentioned then it is probably Lower Aghakilmore, given its much larger area and population.

Table 14 Land Deeds evidence of other Lahys in Lower Agakilmore in the 1700s

Year	Person(s)	Deed	Reference
1719	John & William (son)	58573	Ref 24
1738	John	63321	Ref 22
1739	John	63370	Ref 27
1758	Henry Thomas	135902	Ref 30
1760	John Thomas	135904	Ref 47
1761	Thomas (Elder) Thomas (Junior)	143581	Ref 43
1762	Thomas William Henry	143828	Ref 38
1763	John Thomas	146370	Ref 39

	Henry James		
1766	Thomas	160734	Ref 40
1767	John & Susanne [mother]	174157	Ref 52
1769	Thomas	177801	Ref 41
1770	Henry John [Late]	183906	Ref 25
1771	Thomas	187079	Ref 93
1775	James Henry	203250	Ref 82
1778	Henry & Henry [Son]	216909	Ref 85
1780	Joseph	231422	Ref 89
1781	Joseph Henry [2nd son of Late Henry]	227627	Ref 35
1779	Thomas & Margaret [Wife] William	222029	Ref 92
1790	Thomas John	296468	Ref 42
1792	Richard & Elizabeth Thornton [Wife]	294154	Ref 66
1793	Richard	300648	Ref 67
1793	Thomas John	319919	Ref 44
1797	Thomas	332001	Ref 86

10 Branch 2 - Upper Aghakilmore / Capragh

Thomas (mentioned in 9.2.3) is the root of this branch (see Figure 92) and will henceforth be known as *Thomas Senior*.

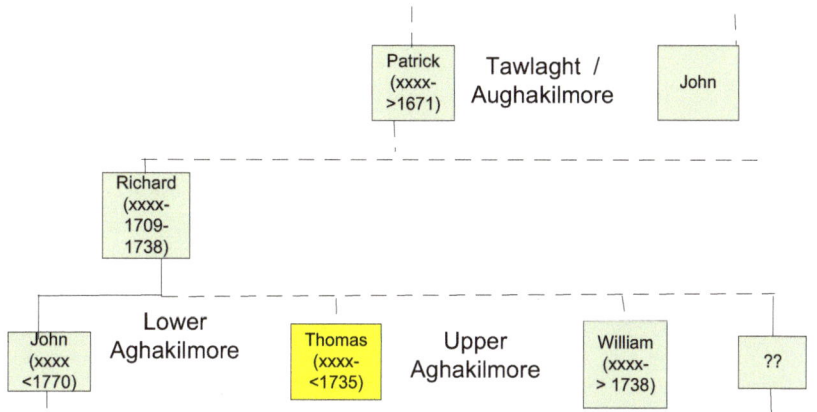

Figure 92 Thomas Senior of Upper Aghakilmore - Brother 2

10.1 2nd Generation [Thomas] - Thomas (Junior) of Upper Aghakilmore

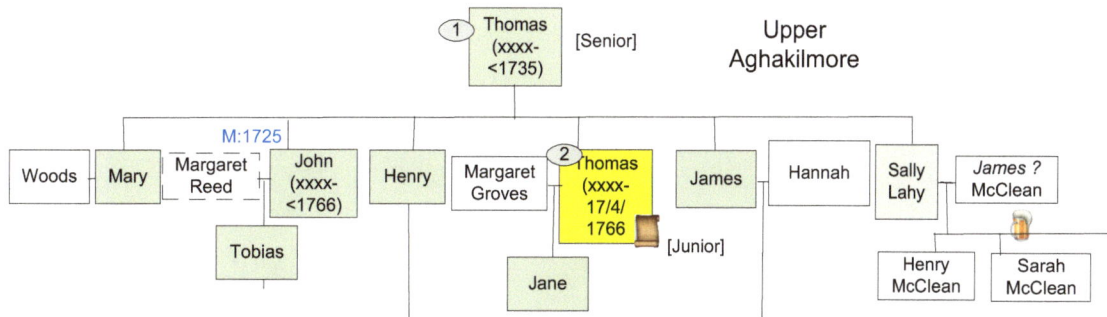

Figure 93 Thomas (Junior) of Upper Aghakilmore

Nothing is known about Thomas (senior) (No 1 in Figure 93) of Upper Aghakilmore apart from the fact that he died before 1734 (mentioned as deceased in deed [48]).

A deed dated 1735 [49] lists **Thomas**, William & John all witnessing a land transaction involving of Henry of Upper Aughakilmore [their presumed brother]. Thomas's signature is on this deed and shown in Figure 94 and compares very well with the signature on the Thomas Lahy on the 1758 John of Tycullen deed [30] see Figure 95 and Thomas's own Will of 1766 [28] [Figure 96]. Thomas (Junior) also witnessed (although no signature on deed) a deed between John of Lower Aghakilmore and Francis of Upper Moydristan. I presume it to be Thomas Junior, as his father was dead by 1735.

Thomas appears to have received quite a bit of land from his Uncle - John of Lower Aughakilmore - 70 Acres in Aughakilmore and 38 Acres in Lavagh [21]. This could imply that John of Lower Aghakilmore's own son William was dead - and thus his closest male heirs - his nephews.

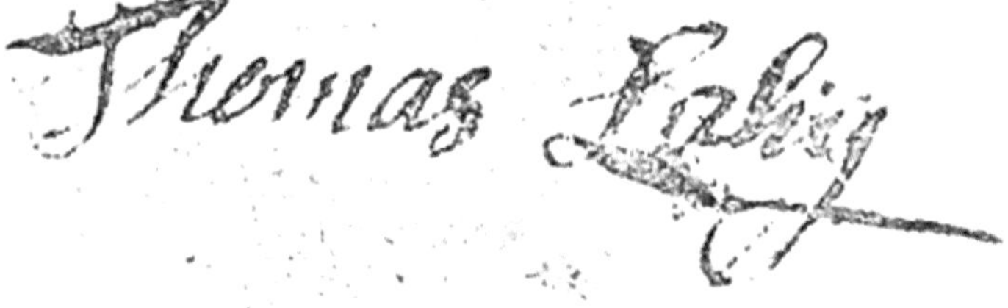

Figure 94 Thomas (Junior)'s Signature from 1735 Deed

[Registry of Deeds (Property Registration Authority) retains the copyright]

Figure 95 Thomas's signature on 1758 John of Tycullen Deed

[Registry of Deeds (Property Registration Authority) retains the copyright]

Figure 96 Thomas's Signature from his Will in 1766

[Registry of Deeds (Property Registration Authority) retains the copyright]

The discovery of a Will of Thomas (No 2 in Figure 93) who died in 1766 has greatly expanded our knowledge about this section of the family [28]. The tree laid out in Figure 93 is put together from a combination of **Thomas (Junior)'s** Will [28] and the Will of **Henry** (his presumed brother [dated 1777-1779] [29]). Although neither one mentions the other in their respective wills, I presume them to be brothers and it's often the case that brothers wouldn't for example leave goods / land to other brothers who have already

David Leahy M.Sc.

received an inheritance or have made their own living independently. The reader should bear in mind these presumptions and if further evidence comes to light in future then these assumptions may need to be revisited.

Thomas (Junior) left half his land in Upper Aghakilmore and Lavagh to his wife Margaret Groves. The maiden name 'Groves' is obtained from a later document - Francis & Rebecca Marriage Articles [20] in which Margaret Groves - the widow of Thomas is catered for). He also leaves £50 to his daughter Jean/Jane Lahy and £5 to his nephew Tobias (son to his late brother John). He leaves £5 also to his sister Mary Woods - thus she obviously married a man named Woods. John's son 'Tobias' may have died young as his name never crops up again in legal documents, deeds or marriage articles.

In the Ardagh Wills Index (see Table 9) a Jane Laghy's (of Aghakilmore Upper) Will is recorded in 1771 - this may be Thomas's daughter Jane.

Thomas also leaves to **Sarah McClean** youngest daughter **to James McClean** of Ballachulan five pounds - this is most likely a niece - and is highly significant in 'joining' thisWill with that of his presumed brother Henry.

Another Lahy land deed dated 1758 [30] involving Henry Lahy and John of Tircullen is witnessed by **James McClean** - **Innkeeper** of Aghakilmore Middle. Not only does this link John of Tircullen with Henry (probably cousins) but also James McClean - a brother-in-law, and also the first mention of a pub in the area known as 'The Cross' - very close to 'Middle Aghakilmore' or Capragh. This pub or 'Inn' was eventually acquired by the Leahys and is the place my father was born and grew up in - see **Figure 88**. The McCleans and Lahys have also intermarried earlier (see **Table 8**) Charles McClean and Anna Laughy married in 1721.

The main benefactor of Thomas (junior) other than his wife was his brother James - who was given my sole right to the lands of Upper Aghakilmore, Lavagh, Aughafad, Moate, Aghakilmore Middle [Capragh] all lying and being in Ballymachugh- together with all arrears of rent due on any of them. These are the lands that transferred down eventually to James's son Francis who married Rebecca Burrowes [see section 13.2].

A legal dispute regarding Thomas's Will was registered in 1769 [31] involving Acheson against Lahy. Margaret and James (wife and brother of Thomas) are mentioned. On 3 March 1769 Margaret and James were to:

> *"appear before us [The court] – In the house of the Rt Hon Philip Tindall Esq situate in Leinster, Dublin on 11 April next – To deposit in the registry of this court the said will"*

Later on that year (14 July 1769) it was recorded that Margaret and James:

> *"have neglected to introduce said original will of said Thomas Lahy dead – Philip Tindall Esq Doctor of Laws – further proceeding in said business did at the petition of the proctor of said Robert Acheson decree a citation to issue against*

said Margaret Lahy and James Lahy in this case why they shall not be exonerated for their manifest contempt in not appearing."

Margaret and James were subsequently ordered to:

"appear before us [The Court] on 4th Nov next – there to show cause why should not be exonerated for their manifest contempt in not appearing at the time and place specified (and their effects) in said citation"

It is not known whether or not they subsequently attended the November 4th meeting and so the outcome of the dispute is not known.

10.1.1   2nd Generation [Thomas] - John of Upper Aghakilmore

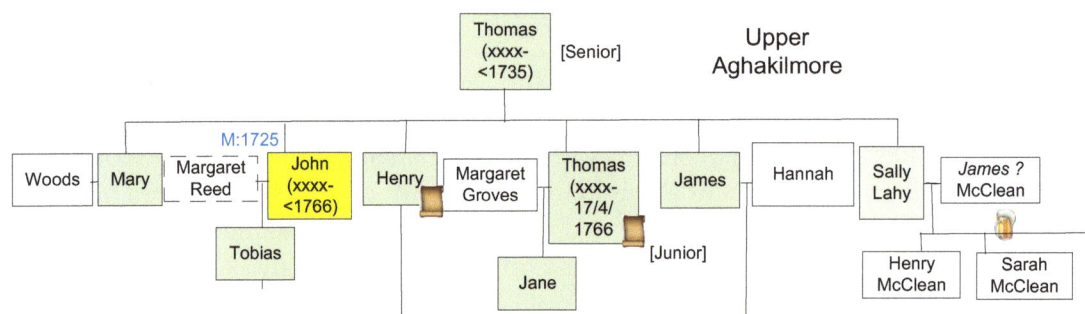

Figure 97 John of Upper Aghakilmore

John Lahy of Upper Aghakilmore witnessed / was involved in land deeds from 1719 to 1739. In 1719, he witnessed the Wedding articles of John of Lower Aghakilmore's daughter [24]. John of Upper Aghakilmore witnessed a land deed dated 1739 [27] between John of Lower Aghakilmore and Francis of Upper Moydristan (John of Lower Aghakilmore's nephew). Thomas Lahy of Upper Aghakilmore (probable brother) witnessed the same deed.

The 1766 Will of Thomas (junior) of Upper Aghakilmore [28] mentions a brother John (and nephew Tobias). However, John is recorded in this Will as being deceased by 1766. I take this to be **John of Upper Aghakilmore.** In the 1761 Cavan Poll [17] there is a record of John of Aghakilmore Upper. He is mentioned in no more deeds after 1739 so I presume he died between 1761 and 1766. This John would most likely have been the nephew to *John of Lower Aghakilmore*. There is a record in Early Kilmore Marriages [32] of a John Lahy having married a **Margaret Reed** in 1725 it likely that this was John of Upper Aghakilmore as his uncle John of Lower Aghakilmore was already married years before (marriage articles of his daughter in 1719 [24].

It is possible that John of Upper Aghakilmore was a cousin of John of Lower Aghakilmore (rather than the nephew). The limited number of deeds and detail in the deeds makes it difficult to tell. According to the 1766 Thomas Will [28] John had a son called Tobias, however I can find no further reference to Tobias therefore I presume him to have died young.

John of Upper Aghakilmore witnessed two deeds in 1738 [26 & 27] involving John of Lower Aghakilmore [his uncle?]. The signature is shown in Figure 98, but it is unclear as to which John's signature this is (Upper or Lower).

Figure 98 John of Upper Aghakilmore's Signature from 1738 Deed [27]

[Registry of Deeds (Property Registration Authority) retains the copyright]

10.1.2   **3rd Generation [Thomas]** - Henry of Upper Aghakilmore

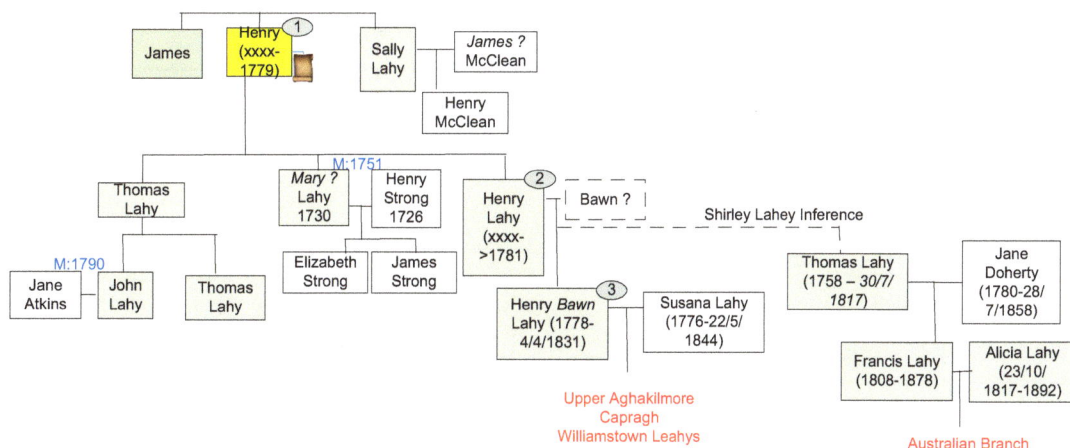

Figure 99 Henry Lahy Will Tree Output

This is Henry 1 (as shown in Figure 99), presumed son of Thomas (Junior). His eldest son is named after his father - as per established Irish naming convention.

I am convinced that this is Henry's signature (as he would have been at least 30 years old and managing deeds etc. by now) (see Figure 100) - as co-signatory with his brother Thomas in the John of Tycullen 1758 Deed [30].

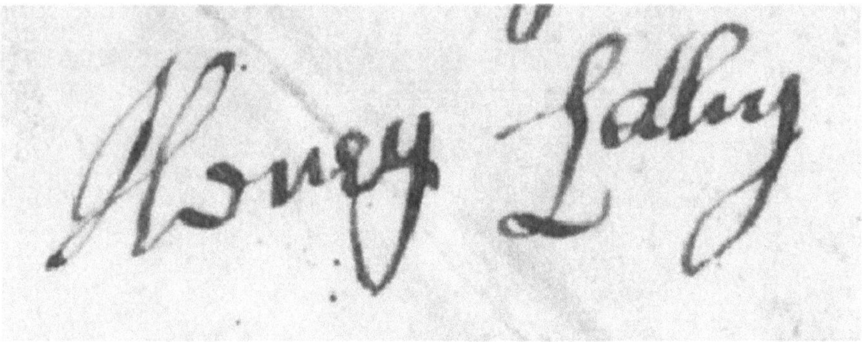

Figure 100 Henry's Signature from John of Tycullen Deed (1758) - [30]

[Registry of Deeds (Property Registration Authority) retains the copyright]

The following is a transcription of notes on Irish Will made by Sir William Betham [Betham Will Abstracts No 321], [29].

> *Lahy Henry, Ahakilmore,*
> *Cavan Gent 30th July 1777 - 23rd December 1779*
> *Eldest son Thomas Lahy*
> *Grandson John Lahy, son of same - Thomas, Brother of same*
> *Brother James Lahy*
> *Son Henry Lahy*
> *Granddaughter Elizabeth Strong*
> *Grandson James Strong*
> *Grandson Henry Lahy*
> *Sister Sally Lahy - Henry McClean, son of same*
> *Son in Law Henry Strong*

Of special note **connecting the Henry to the Thomas** mentioned above are brother *James* and a nephew named *McClean*.

Henry 1 mentions a son Henry 2 and also a grandson 'Henry 3'. He also mentions a son Thomas and his 2 sons (John and Thomas). Thus, we can assume that the 'grandson' was Henry 2 (the son)'s boy - otherwise they would have been mentioned along with Thomas's other 2 sons. This makes sense from the current owners of the Upper Aghakilmore land today - they are Leahys who are directly descended from this grandson 'Henry Bawn Lahy' who married Susanna [88]. The 'Bawn' middle name could be the maiden name of his mother (or a place name e.g. townland Bawn in Kilcogy).

I have added data to Figure 99 from other sources to show linkages for example Shirley Lahey from the Australian branch of the Leahys [1] maintained that the 'Thomas' at the top of her tree was the son of a 'Henry', so he may well have been a brother of Henry Bawn Lahy as the dates coincide. There were not many Henrys around at the time who owned land, so I think I can make an educated guess that Shirley's Thomas was a son of Henry 2 (who married Bawn?) or Henry of Capragh and the brother of Henry who married Susanna (see Figure 99). Shirley's Thomas may well be the Thomas & Jane of Kilnahard – who later moved to Killucan, as the date of Thomas's death coincides – (see section 17.1).

David Leahy M.Sc.

10.1.3 4th Generation onwards [Thomas Root]

Capragh is another townland in between Upper and Lower Aughakilmore - because of that it was sometimes known as Middle Aughakilmore. The townland map from the 1800s (Figure 101) shows two main dwellings in Capragh. John (of Williamstown) lived in Capragh before moving to Williamstown, this is the first reference we have for Lahys in Capragh (in deed [33] dated 1777). John of Williamstown is a close relative of Henry and it is said that his son (Captain Francis) had a stone with his name on it on the edge of the road next to the dwelling on the lower part of Figure 101.

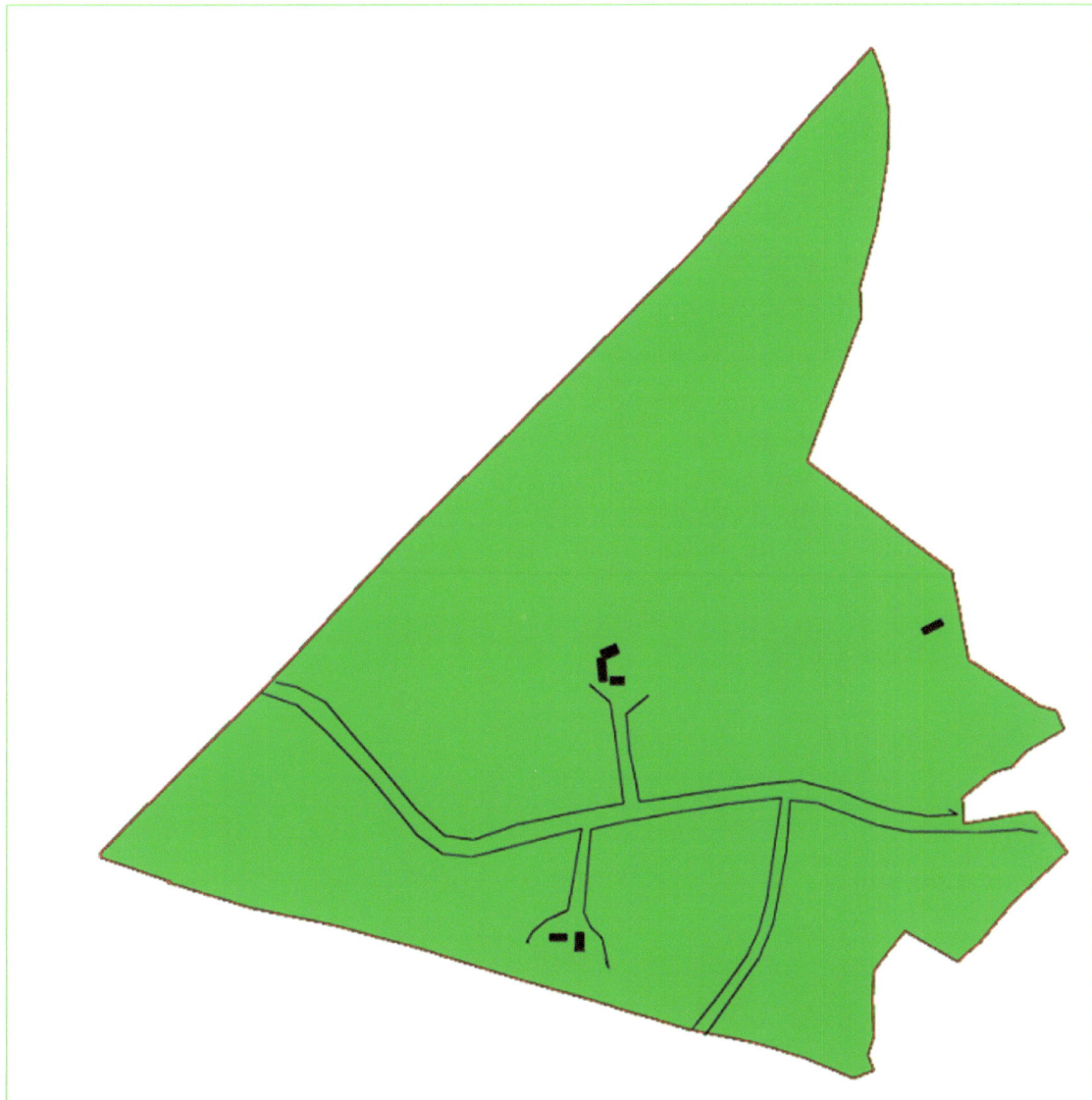

Figure 101 Capragh Townland showing dwellings in mid 1800s

Figure 102 The Old House in Capragh (Later in late 1800s) (Courtesy Lewis Leahy)

The people in the picture are unknown, but through a process of elimination I can make an educated guess that this may be *John William Lahy* and *Harriet Lahy* (13 years older than him) - who were married and were 2nd cousins (both of the Upper Aghakilmore line). The photograph was originally black and white and probably taken in the late 1800s or early 1900s. The house still stands but now only holds old farm equipment.

1.1.2 Henry of Capragh

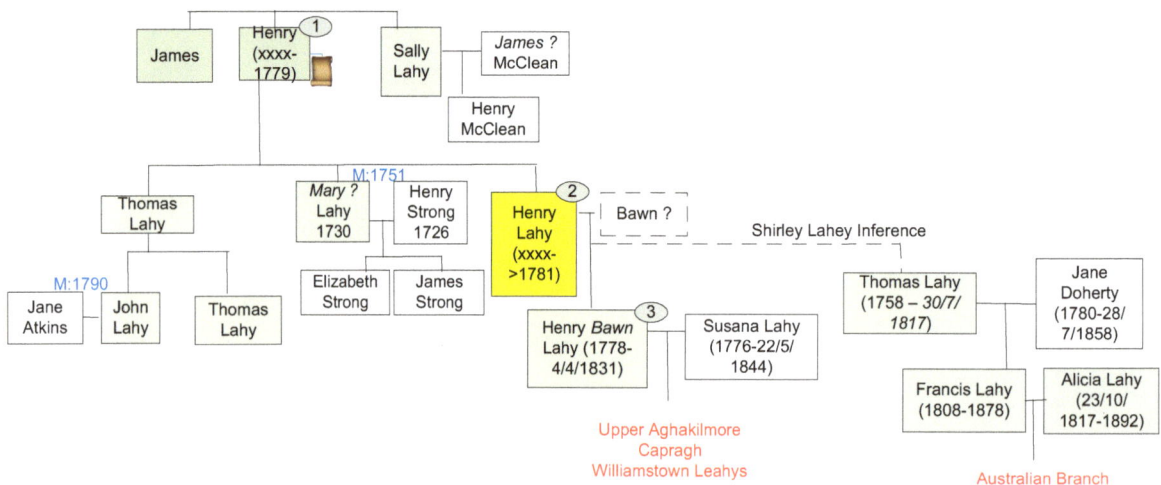

Figure 103 Henry of Capragh

David Leahy M.Sc.

In reviewing the deeds records, I can only be sure that it is Henry 1's son mentioned after 1777 - when the father died. Any Henry mentioned after 1777 must be either Henry 1's son 'Henry 2' or grandson, 'Henry 3'.

In 1779, a deed [34] mentions land in Upper Aghakilmore belonging to Henry and Thomas (brothers). This is most likely Henry 2 - as there is no record of 'Henry 3' having a brother Thomas. In 1781, there was a deed [35] in which – *Joseph Lahy of Aghakilmore and Henry Lahy great second son and heir at law of Henry Lahy late of Aghakilmore* is mentioned. As 'Henry 1' only had two sons and this being only a few years after Henry 1's death, this must surely be Henry 2. In the 1761 Cavan Poll [17] there is a record of Henry of Aghakilmore Lower.

There are deeds dated 1805 [36] mentioning Henry of Capragh and F. Gilroy and in 1806 [37] in which a Henry Lahy of Capragh (Yeoman) and Jane Lahy of Aghakilmore exchange land. It is possible that this was 'Henry 3', but I suspect it was 'Henry 2' the elder, and interesting to note his occupation as a Yeoman!

A Yeoman and/or Husbandman was a common English term for a farmer who had his own smallholding. A yeoman was generally one more step up the social scale than a husbandman and farmed more land (a husbandman usually grew enough for him and his family and rented his land from a landlord, but a yeoman would have some surplus and was generally more prosperous and had the freehold of his land himself rather than answering to a landlord), Yeomen may also have been called to do military service and thus were often armed.

It also begs the question of who was Jane Lahy, and which family did she belong to?

1.1.3 Jane Lahys

It's worth looking in a bit more detail at one of these deeds [37] dated 1805 involving Jane:

> Henry Lahy of Capragh (Yeoman) and Jane Lahy of Aughakilmore in said County, Widow of the other part reciting articles entered into by the said Henry and Jane Lahy bearing date 4th day of June last and consisting of several covenants and agreements....concerning town and lands of Upper Aughakilmore and Lower Aughakilmore....shall be lawful for said Jane and her children to enter into premises and use half part of the lands of Upper and Lower Aughakilmore and the rent and profits etc.. to which said Henry Lahy is entitled, should be subject to the payment of half such debts.... Contracted or created by the different persons of the name of Lahy (and Jane's children which when reach age of 21 will also be subject to this agreement).Witnessed by Andrew Bell Esq and Owen Keogh.

Jane was obviously a 'woman of 'means' married to or daughter of a prominent Lahy. She appeared to possess substantial lands in Upper and Lower Aghakilmore - possibly Henry's nephew John's wife [2]- Jane Atkins, but it sounds more like an older woman (widow) - so it may well be Thomas (Junior)'s daughter Jane [103] or even a wife of Henry at the top [1]. The deed also mentions Jane's children, but frustratingly doesn't name them! More evidence is needed to pin this Jane down! Figure 104 illustrates these 'possible' Janes.

In Prerogative Wills [119] there is a **Jane Laghy of Upper Aughakilmore** listed as having a Will in 1771. This is obviously not the Jane mentioned in the 1805 [37] deed, so it must be either Jane 1 [Henry's Widow] or Jane 3 [daughter of Thomas]. Obviously, Thomas's daughter could have married another Lahy [quite common practice] however my gut feeling is that this Jane who died in 1771 leaving a Will was probably Henry's wife [at the top of Figure 104].

It is also worth noting the existence of a marriage licence listed in the National Archives of Jane Lahy and John Clarke in 1806 (no location given).

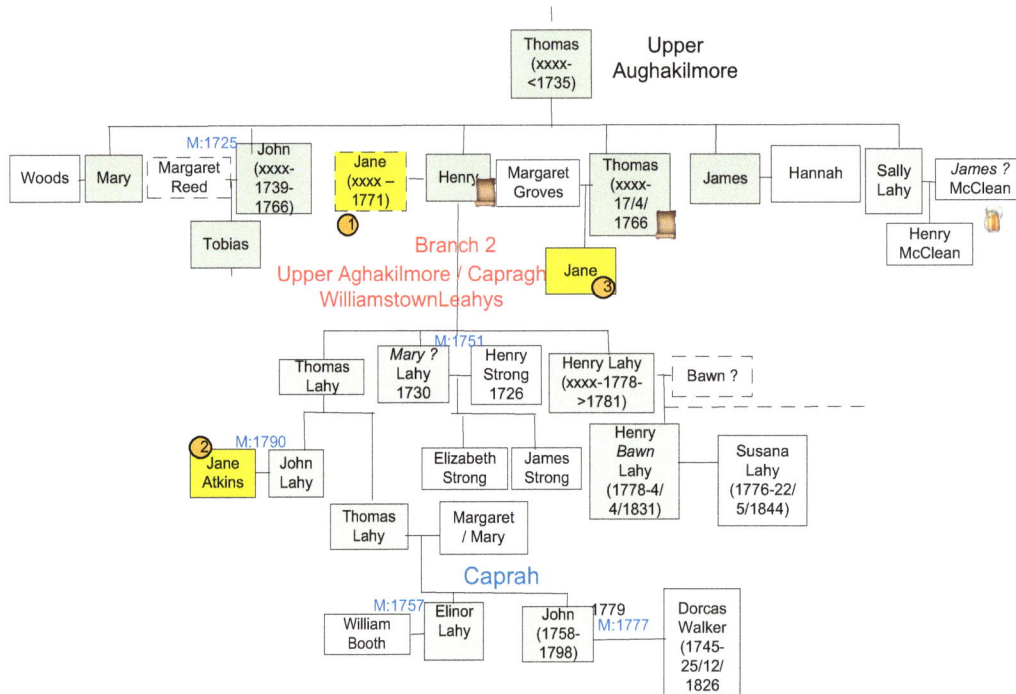

Figure 104 Possible Jane's (of Deed [37])

David Leahy M.Sc.

1.1.4 Thomas of Lower Aghakilmore

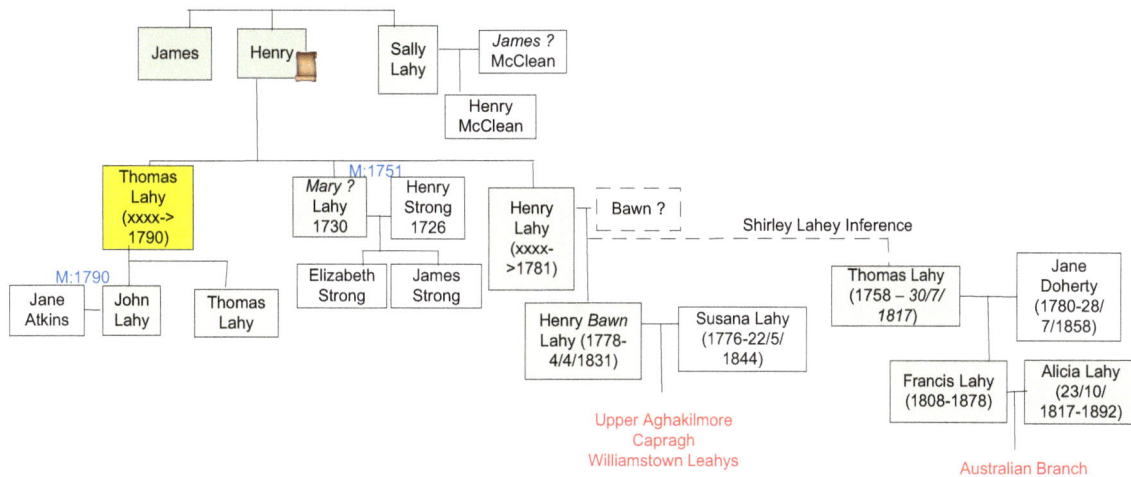

Figure 105 Thomas of Lower Aghakilmore

In a land deed [38] dated 1762 - Thomas Lahy of Lower Aghakilmore sold to Thomas Cheevers of Upper Aghakilmore half of Upper Aghakilmore for the term of 21 years. Thomas's father Henry lived in **Upper** Aghakilmore, however I presume that at some stage Henry gave his son Thomas land in **Lower** Aghakilmore as this is where is recorded as living in the mid-1700s.

Thomas witnessed another deed in 1763 [39] another in 1766 [40] and yet another in 1769 [41]. Thomas is also mentioned in his son John's marriage articles [42] in 1790 thus we can presume he was alive until at least 1790.

Thomas of Lower Aghakilmore seemed to be a close friend / relation to William of Lavagh [section 13.3 – page 157] as he is a signatory on several of his land deeds.

That is all I know about this Thomas Lahy.

1.1.5 Thomas Junior of Lower Aghakilmore

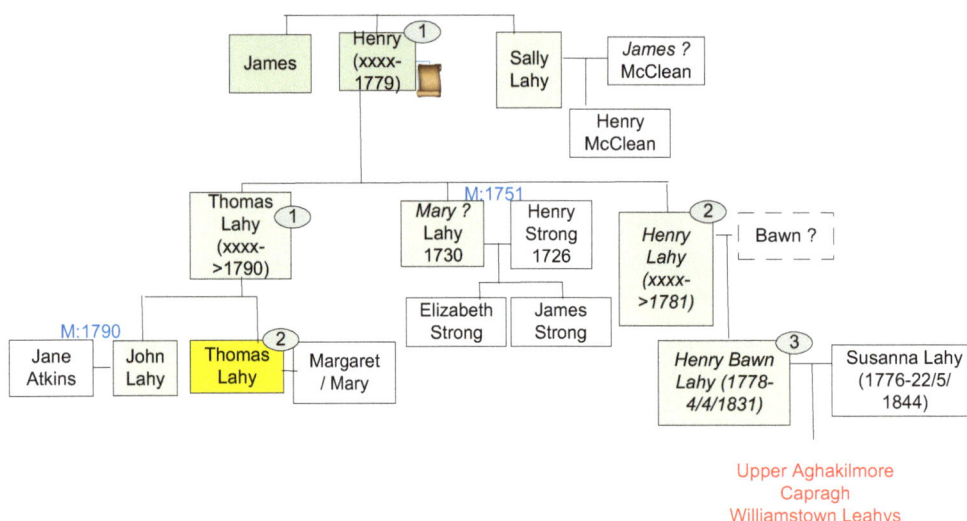

Figure 106 Thomas Junior of Lower Aghakilmore

In 1761, a land deed [43] mentions Thomas the Elder (1) and Thomas the Junior (2) of Aghakilmore which gives additional evidence to Henry 1's Will of the existence of this Thomas (2). In the 1761 Cavan Poll book [17] there are also two Thomas Lahys mentioned (one from Upper Aughakilmore and one from Lower). There is also evidence that Thomas of Lower Aughakilmore was married to a Margaret or Mary. Sometimes women called Margaret are known by 'Mary':

In 1779 – Deed [34] mentions Thomas and Margaret Lahy of Aghakilmore and Elinor Booth [otherwise Lahy] and John Lahy his son; both of Williamstown (see section 11). Thus, John and Elinor (brother and sister) must have moved to Williamstown by 1779. Indeed, there exists a deed in 1777 [33] in which John received land in Williamstown as part of a marriage gift [marrying Dorcas Walker] the lands purportedly formerly belonging to the widow 'Duffy'.

1.1.6 John married to Jane Atkins

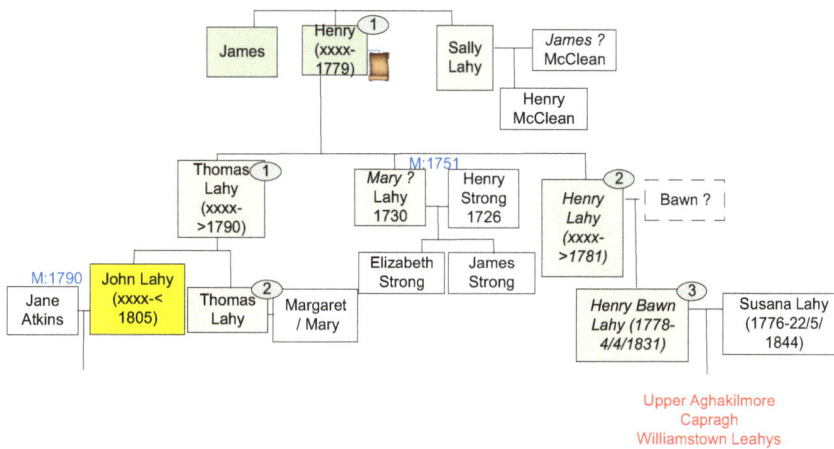

Figure 107 John of Lower Aghakilmore married Jane Atkins

Thomas 1,'s other son John married Jane Atkins / Arkins (from Killgolough) in 1790. The marriage articles [42] describe a £150 dowry along with land in Upper and Lower Aghakilmore. They are also witnessed by John of Williamstown (son of his brother Thomas).

Not much else is known about this John other than in 1793 [44] John and Thomas (either his father or brother) fell behind in rent to Pat Kilroy of Killeadrean.

There is a deed [37] dated 1805 mentioning Henry of Capragh along with Jane Lahy (Widow) mentioning Lands in Upper and Lower Aghakilmore. This to me sounds like it could be John's wife (Jane Atkins) - suggesting that John died young before 1805. Henry was from the same family branch so it would make sense for him to enter into land agreements with Jane, the widow of John.

1.1.7 Henry Bawn Lahy

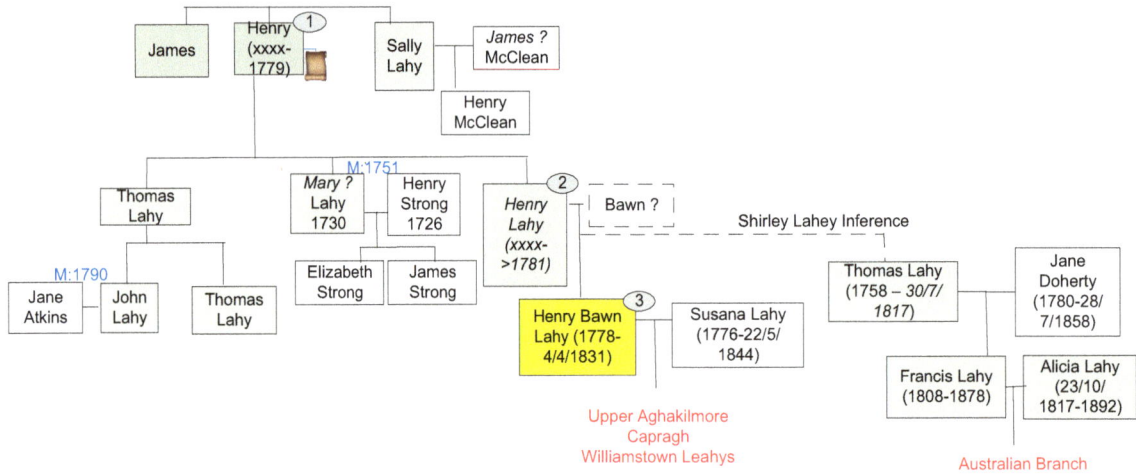

Figure 108 Henry Bawn Lahy

Henry Bawn Lahy (or Henry 3 as shown in Figure 108) is the root of the Upper Aghakilmore and Capragh Lahys that still live in the area today. As mentioned previously it is possible that this Henry was mentioned in deeds dated 1805 and 1806.

A deed dated 1831 [45] mentions a Henry (sen) of Capragh and his sons George and William. Henry [103] died in 1831 aged 57 and is buried along with most of the other Lahys in Ballymachugh Church of Ireland graveyard.

When 'Henry [103]'s wife Susanna died in 1844 she was listed as the widow of 'Henry Bawn Lahy' this middle name 'Bawn' could be the maiden name of his mother (or a place name e.g. townland of Bawn in Kilcogy).

Lahys living in Upper Aghakilmore and Capragh in the 1700s from the Deeds evidence are shown in Table 15.

The assumption is that if neither Upper or Lower is mentioned then it is probably Lower Aghakilmore, given its much larger area and population.

Table 15 Land Deeds evidence of other Lahys in Upper Aghakilmore & Capragh in the 1700s

Year of Deed	Townland [Living In]	Person(s)	Deed	Reference
1719	Upper Agakilmore	John	58573	Ref 24
1734	Upper Agakilmore	John Henry Thomas	55583	Ref 48
1735	Upper Agakilmore	Henry	57842	Ref 49
1738	Upper Agakilmore	William James John	66369	Ref 50
1739	Upper Agakilmore	Thomas John	66370	Ref 27
1739	Upper Agakilmore	Henry [nephew of John of Lower Ag] James John	66371	Ref 26
1769		James	160734	Ref 28
1770		James	183906	Ref 25
1772		James	177801	Ref 41
1777	Capragh	John	214253	Ref 33

11 Branch 3 - Williamstown

The Williamstown Lahys from my understanding are a branch off the Capragh / Upper Aghakilmore Lahys. They chose to live on the opposite side of Lake Sheelin near the South-East corner of the lake (see Figure 109) – principally 'married in' to the area.

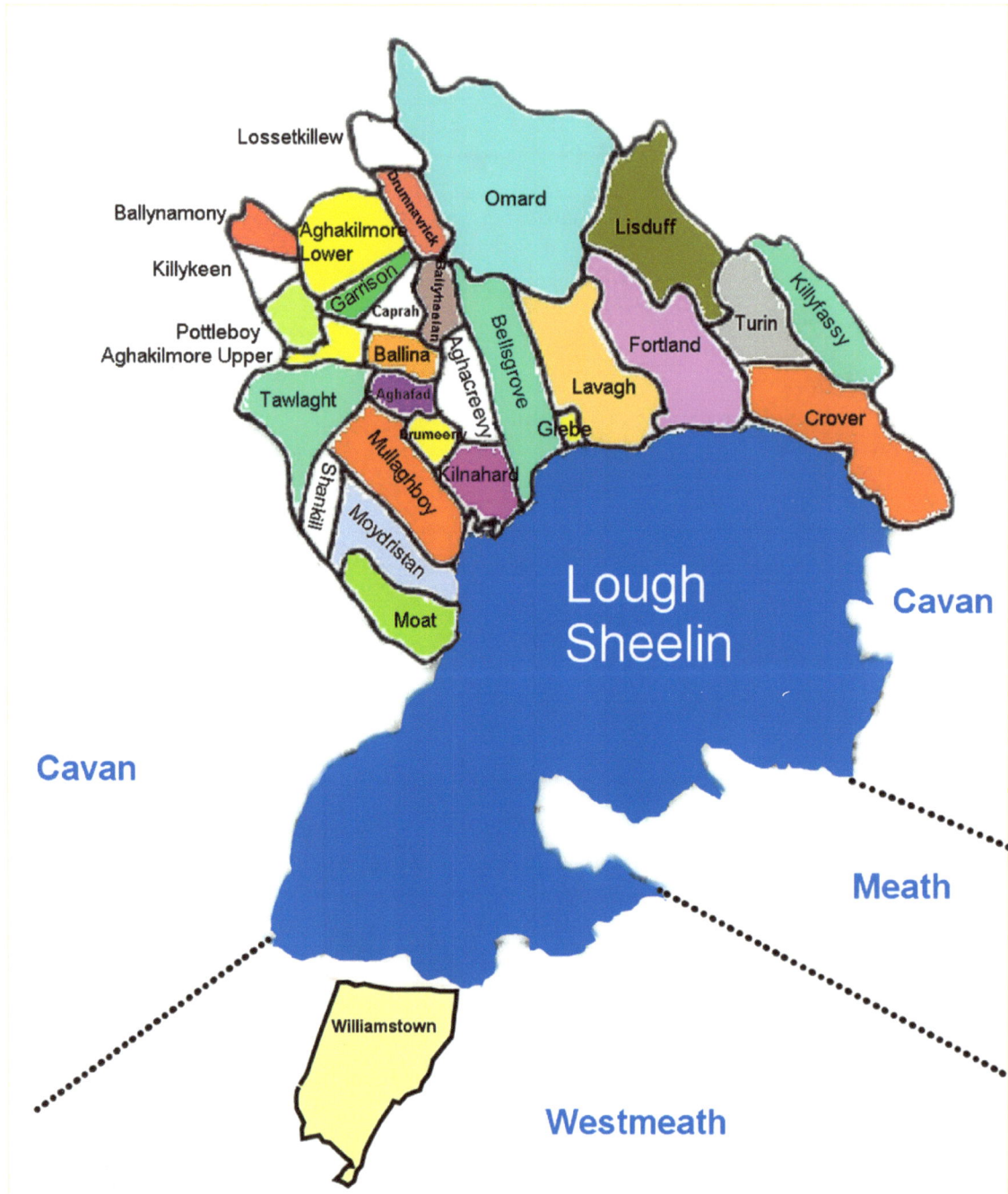

Figure 109 Location of Williamstown (Westmeath)

David Leahy M.Sc.

11.1 John of Williamstown

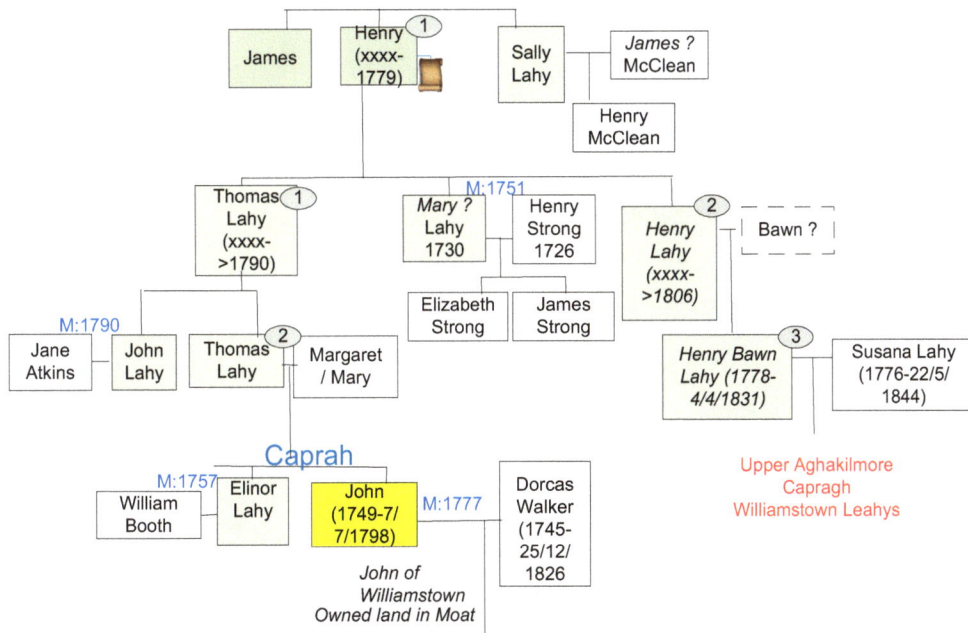

Figure 110 John of Williamstown's position in the Tree

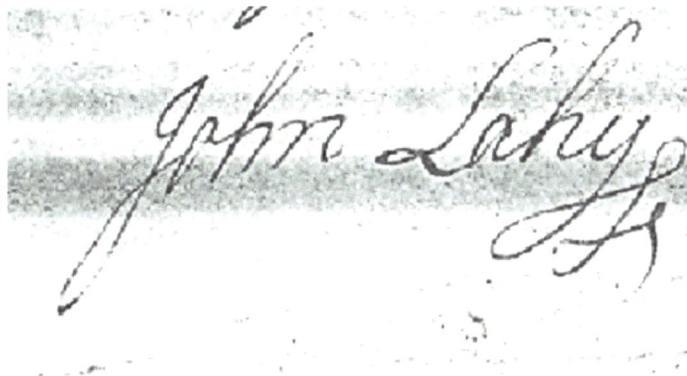

Figure 111 John of Williamstown's Signature from 1779 Deed [34]

John of Williamstown originated in Capragh - and probably lived in the dwelling on the lower part of Figure 101 - before getting married and moving to Williamstown.

In 1779 – Deed [34] mentions Thomas and Margaret Lahy of Aghakilmore and Elinor Booth otherwise Lahy and **John Lahy his son, both of Williamstown**. Thus, proving that John of Williamstown was Thomas [2]'s son.

If we step back a few years there is another land deed [33] dated 1777 which are John's marriage articles to Dorcas Walker. John is listed as being from Capragh and in possession of lands of Moat and Middle Aghakilmore (Capragh). As part of the dowry, ***John received lands of Williamstown formerly in the possession of Widow Duffy*** and half of lands in Togher in possession of Alex Walker. This must be how the Lahys came into possession of the townlands of Williamstown. John's uncle (John of Aghakilmore, married to Jane Atkins) also witnessed the articles.

John of Williamstown is also a significant mention in the 1779 Francis Lahy & Rebecca Marriage Articles [20] he was probably a 3rd or 4th cousin to Francis.

In a land deed dated 1803 [46] Dorcas Lahy - widow of John Lahy of Williamstown is mentioned [marriage articles of their daughter Ann to Robert Stafford]. Prerogative Wills of Ireland [104] show a John of Williamstown's Will registered in 1800.

Figure 112 Williamstown House today

Figure 112 shows how Williamstown house looks today. The old house was probably in the back portion.

John of Williamstown must have been quite influential as he is a signature on many other deeds around this period. He had two sons – Francis and Thomas. One presumes Francis to be the older brother, as when Thomas died in 1812 in his will, he left his brother Francis the lands of Capragh and Togher – but not Williamstown as it was probably earmarked to go to Francis (the eldest brother).

David Leahy M.Sc.

12 Branch 4 - Clonlohan / Clonloaghan

This may not be a distinct 'branch' as such, it's probably more of an off-shoot from either the Williamstown / Upper Aughakilmore branch or the 'Cross' / Drumeeny branch, however I felt it worth including as a distinct branch as I can't for definite attach them to either of these two branches and data may come to light in future which shows their origins as being further back in the tree. The relative location of Clonloaghan is shown in Figure 113.

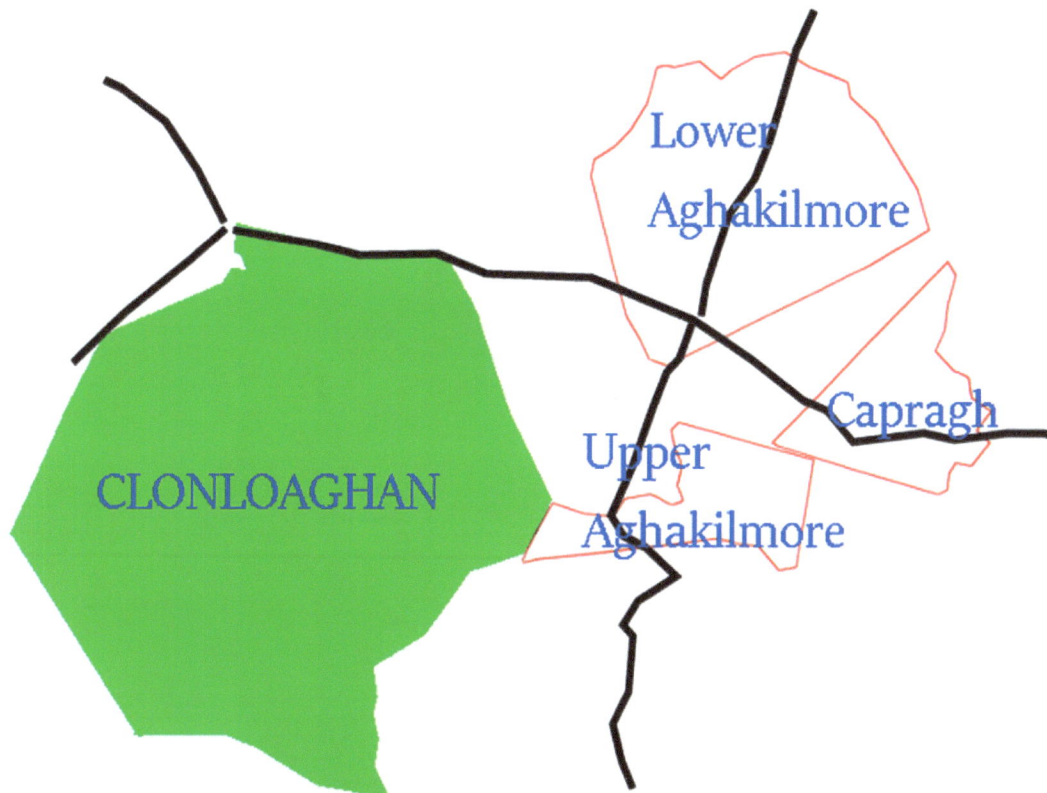

Figure 113 Relative location of Clonloaghan

The earliest reference I can find to Lahys in Clonlohan is Deed [56] dated 1796 - Marriage articles for Margaret Lahy daughter of **William**. She was to marry James Strong and was given a portion of land in Clonlohan (part of her father's farm). It is not known which 'William' this was (Upper or Lower Aughakilmore origin). Later in 1830 a John Lahy sold a farm in Clonloaghan to Lord Farnham - the area marked by dark and light blue in Figure 114. Thus, this must have been his father William's farm in 1796. Later in the 1800s the Griffiths Valuation of Ireland in the mid-1800s [57] there is a William Lahys farm - shown as the light blue area in Figure 114. In the early 1830s there is also a record of a John and later Henry having rented a farm in Clonloaghan [58] - also shown (in yellow) in Figure 114. In August 1832 Henry Lahy requested a reduction in rent (from Lord Farnham) due to some of the land being 'mountain' (presumably rocky) [59]. His request was denied.

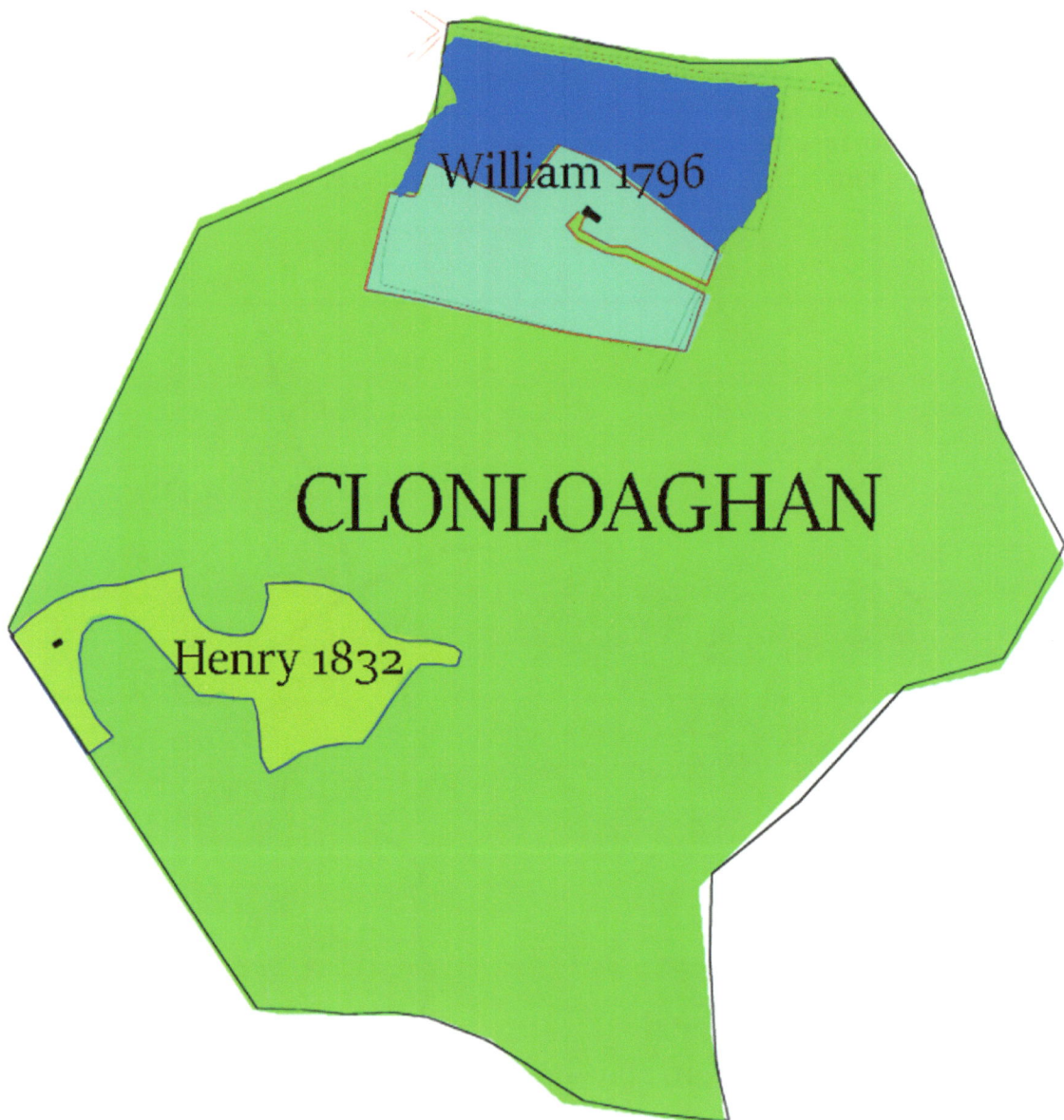

Figure 114 Clonloaghan Lahy Farms

In the 1821 Census [18] only John and Anne are listed as living in No 12 Clonlohan.

Henry of Clonloaghan witnessed a deed by Henry (sen) of Capragh in 1831 [105].
A later deed - [60] dated 1886 mentions William Lahy of Mullaghboy and Henry Lahy of Clonlohan and the RIC Barracks in Capragh. The lands of Capragh were owned by the Upper Aughakilmore Lahys thus giving a clue as to William and Henry of Clonlohan's origins - i.e., probably descendants of the Upper Aghakilmore Lahys.

As mentioned in section 2.8 Mary 'Lahy' Walker who was documented in her obituary of 1895 as being descended from De La Hayes - Huguenots was most likely the Mary listed in the 1821 census as being the daughter of John of Clonloaghan (see Table 16), As Clonloaghan Lahys undoubtedly were connected to the Upper Aghakilmore Lahys we can conclude that this is another piece of evidence towards the Huguenot origins of the Cavan Lahys.

Table 16 Mary of Clonlohan in 1821 Census

Name	Age
John	36
Anne	36
William	13
Margaret	10
James	8
David	6
Mary	**4**

13 Branch 5 - Lavagh

The earliest mention of Lahys in the townland of Lavagh is a land deed dated **1734** [48] in which John Henry & Thomas sell on 11 acres – *"being 3/4 of the estate of Thomas Lahy (deceased)"*. Later in 1738 [50] John of Lower Aghakilmore, William, James and John of Upper Aghakilmore are mentioned in a deed selling land in Lower Aghakilmore (35 acres) and Lavagh and Aughacreevy (19 acres).

It is my opinion that there were individuals from a few branches who inhabited Lavagh:

1. **James Lahy** [of Upper Aghakilmore] Descendants [see next section 13.1 on page 151]

2. **John Lahy** (of Lower Aghakilmore) Descendants [see section 9.2.2 on page 117]

Figure 115 The Townland of Lavagh

David Leahy M.Sc.

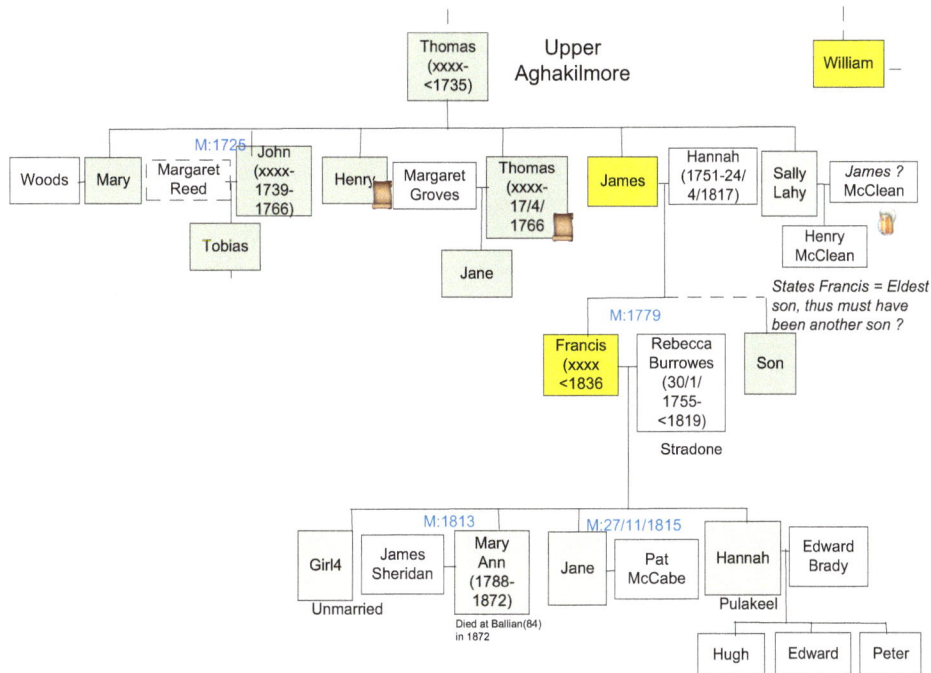

Figure 116 Top of the Lavagh Lahys

13.1 James of Lavagh / Upper Aghakilmore

Most of what we know of James Lahy comes from his eldest son Francis's marriage articles to Rebecca Burrowes - dated 1779 [20]. In this key document James gives over part of the lands of Lavagh to his eldest son Francis as part of a marriage present. It is worth noting that this particular deed relates these lands as the same lands sold to Patrick Laghy by Thomas Coote in a deed dated 1667 (see 9.1). This James is also probably the same James (and main executor) mentioned in Henry's 1766 Will (see 10.1). The Francis / Rebecca Burrowes articles also mention James's wife Hannah. James Lahy of Upper Aghakilmore is mentioned in land deeds dated (1739,1763,1764,1766,1769,1770, 1772, 1775 & 1779). There are a few deeds dated 1780 and 1786 bearing the name James Lahy of Lavagh. This may be the same person who has moved e.g. to live with a child in retirement. There is a William of Lavagh who is possibly a second son of James and it may be he went to live with William in his old age (see Figure 116).

13.2 Francis of Lavagh

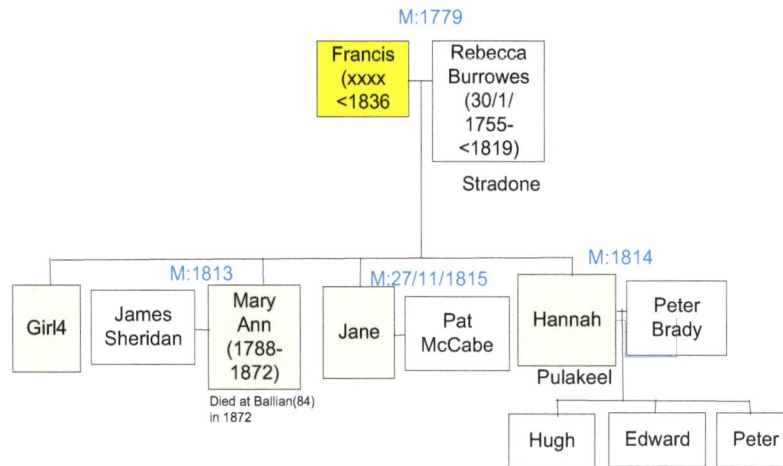

Figure 117 Francis Lahy of Lavagh

The first mention of this Francis is in his wedding articles [20] when he married Rebecca Burrowes of Killiconan (daughter of Alexander Burrowes of Stradone). Francis is stated as the *'Eldest son and heir at law'*. This implies there was a younger son - possibly William (Of Lavagh) see below. Francis's father James on his wedding day gave him 60 acres of land in Upper Aghakilmore and there is also mention of land in Lavagh to go to Francis upon his father's death (and provision made for a pension for James's wife Hannah, and his [brother] Thomas's wife Margaret Groves. The wedding articles [20] refer to land sold by Thomas Coote to Pat Laghy in 1667 - confirming a direct descendancy from Pat Laghy. It is also interesting to note that John Lahy of Williamstown is one of the main parties mentioned in the extremely long marriage articles. John would have been a distant cousin of Francis.

Francis and Rebecca had four daughters three of whom got married to Roman Catholics and subsequently had sons who went on to become priests. Locals thought this ironic as two major Protestant families had married [to keep this land within Protestant hands it was said] and the result was that all of the land ended up in Roman Catholic offspring's hands.

Their daughter Hannagh married Peter Brady of Pullakell in 1814. A John Brady and Hugh Brady are also mentioned in the marriage articles [61] but it is not clear what relation they were to Peter. Seventy acres in Lavagh are mentioned and 200 acres in Killymullen and Corsumalla.

In 1815, another document - the marriage articles of their 4th daughter Jane are detailed [62]. The text in the deed states:

"Pat Mc Cabe and Francis Lahy of Lavagh and Wife (Rebecca Burrows) and Jane Lahy 4th daughter of Francis and Rebecca, spinster"

This is where we get the evidence of 4 daughters from (although only 3 married). Jane married Pat McCabe, and 70 acres in Lavagh are also mentioned. Arnold Lahy of Knocknaheen Co Cavan is a witness, presumably being a close relation.

Francis abode?

Francis obviously started out in Upper Aghakilmore at his parent's abode and I presume this is where he lived when he got married (his father gave him 60 acres there as a wedding gift). Table 17 lists records of Francis Lahys in the late 1700s, they may all be the same person who owned land in different places or some of them may be different people.

Table 17 Francis Lahys around in the late 1700s

Date	Names	Location	Reference
1739	Francis	Upper Moydristan [Registry of Deeds (Property Registration Authority) retains the copyright]	Ref 23
1775	Francis	Ballina	Ref 82
1779	Francis & Rebecca	Lavagh	Ref 20
1779	Francis	Ballina	Ref 34
1784	Francis	Nutfield	Ref 106
1785	Francis & James Lahy of Lavagh	Nutfield	Ref 107
1785	Francis	Ballina	Ref 108
1786	Francis & James of Lavagh	Killconnell	Ref 109
1790	Francis & Burrows		Ref 110
1799	Francis	Lavagh	Ref 87
1809	Francis & Rebecca	Formerly of Lavagh	Ref 63
1814	Francis & Hannagh (Daughter)	Lavagh	Ref 111
1815-1819	Francis Lahy–&	Lavagh	Ref 62

	Wife (Rebecca Burrows) Rebecca Spinster?		

The Marriage articles of 1779 [20] is the first mention of Francis. They don't however specify exactly where he's from however as his father James is from Upper Aghakilmore we can assume Francis also hailed from there.

Notes from the Francis Lahy / Rebecca Burrows Marriage Articles:

Francis Lahy, eldest son and heir at law of James Lahy of Upper Aghakilmore, and Rebecca Burrows, daughter of Robert Burrows of Killiconan and Alexander Burrows and John Lahy of Williamstown.
James Lahy *is now seized and possessed of the several lands herin after mentioned by deed bearing date **2/7/1667** and made by Thomas Coote of Cootehill in the county of Cavan Esq deceased **to Patrick Lahy**, deceased at the yearly rent of one xxxx £60.*
60 Acreas of Upper Aghakilmore, now possessed by the said James Lahy or his under tenants.
James also owns lands in Lavagh
£500 and 5 shillings paid to James Lahy
Grant unto Alexander Burrows and John Lahy
James lives in dwelling in lands of Upper Aghakilmore. £10 pension per annum to Hannah wife of said James if she survives him and pension of £8 per annum for Margaret Groves, widow of Thomas Lahy deceased and £400 for the younger children of James Lahy.
If Francis and Rebecca produce no children then the lands go to the next lawful heir of the Lahy family.
Witnessed by James Sheridan.

The land deeds mention Francis Lahy a few more times - from different locations. Obviously, these could be different Francis; however, I find no other evidence of Francis Lahys in the area owning substantial amounts of land in the area at that time. Why then would Francis give different location for his home address? It's a mystery - maybe he was trying to avoid tax etc., but I'm convinced that it is the same Francis Lahy.

According to Francis Sheridan, Francis Lahy once owned the Mill at Ballyheelan and sold it in 1802.

Conversion Controversy

In the late 1820s Francis became embroiled in a religious conversion controversy which became known to the public via letters to various newspapers at the time. The quotes below are taken from *The Stamford Mercury - Stamford, Lincolnshire, England 4/4/1828.*

Philip O'Reilly Parish Priest of Ballymachugh wrote a letter, to the very Rev Patrick O'Reilly, of Cavan, and the latter then inserted it in the *Morning Register.*

> *Six persons of great responsibility in this parish have within these few days become Catholics....Say also that one of these converts to the Catholic faith (Francis Lahy) is an estated gentleman worth 300/. a year"*

A refutation was then sent to the editor of the Dublin Evening Mail by Nicholas Gosselin, Curate of Ballymachugh:

> *"No Protestants, either of respectability or otherwise have become members of the Roman Catholic church in the parish of Ballymachugh within the last few days or even within the last few years....It is certainly true that a person named Francis Lahy forsook the parish church many years since, in consequence of his daughters having been married to Roman Catholics. The following statement from the mouth of Lahy himself will determine how far the account given of the occurrence by Mr Reilly accords with the truth. Francis Lahy declared to a gentleman of respectability on the 7th inst. that he "goes sometimes to the chapel, to satisfy and keep peace with his children - that he knows the Protestants have the word of God and truth on their side - that were he out of the country, and had the means of living elsewhere he never would go inside a chapel door until he went to the clay....He never authorised the Priest to bring his name before the public."*

However, Francis was not happy with neither the first accusation nor the refutation, and objected to being used as religious propaganda from both sides. Francis wrote an eloquent and lengthy reply which stated [in part]:

> *I find my character unblushingly assailed. It is painful to me, in the vale of years, and after the enjoyment of a long and happy life, to be obliged to step forward in defence of my character, and that parental duty I owe to my children - the endearments of my life - to repel the envenomed and foul ascertains so malevolently couched up in a communication from a minister of the gospel. When I see such execrable attempts resorted to, to repair a falling church I am not sorry not to be one of her members! Any honest Protestant whose mind is not seared against, but open to conviction, must nauseate the conduct of the Cavan gospellers........ It is also stated, that "I go to the chapel sometimes, to satisfy and keep peace with my children" - false; - "that the Protestants have the word of God and truth on their side" - quite false; as my conduct shows by observing the Catholic tenants; - "that were I out of this country and had the means of living elsewhere , I would never go into a chapel door until I went to the clay" - (Chester-School language) - utterly false.....From this tirade and tissue of jumbled and quilted nonsense, and wilful representation, the public can conclude to what extremes the Biblemen must go, to oppose the substantial facts set forth by the Rev Mr O'Reilly. - FRANCIS LAHY.*

A further refutation is published by Orange Wood and John Hanna who swore an oath that:

> *"on Thursday 22nd [March] they called on Francis Lahy of Lowagh [Lavagh] and asked him if he had written a letter which appeared in the Weekly Register of the 7th of March, signed Francis Lahy: the said Lahy positively denied any knowledge of it and that he knew nothing whatever of the letter, that he neither signed it nor authorised any person to sign it for him, nor had he ever heard of it before [Signed Orange Wood & John Hanna.Sworn on 24th March, 1827".*

I'm sure that Francis probably did set foot inside a chapel - given that 3 of his daughters were married in one. However, what we can learn from this is that Francis was quite well educated and eloquent and that he objected to his name being used for religious propaganda by either side and that he didn't have much of an opinion for either the Catholic or Protestant church!

Francis is mentioned along with his wife Rebecca in land deeds in 1809, 1814 and 1819, but not after that. In the 1809 deed [63] it states Francis Lahy *formerly* of Lavagh which implies that he had moved on somewhere else.

It is not known exactly when Francis died [although he lived until at least March 1827 according to newspaper conversion controversy mentioned above] however they are buried in Ballymachugh Church of Ireland in a flat stone grave. My cousin and I attempted to decipher the gravestone using shaving foam and sponge to read the text (see Figure 118) unfortunately no dates are decipherable for Francis. The only text I can decipher is:

> *"SACRED To the memory of Rebecca LAHY alias Burrowes who departed this life 1st March 1818 in the 51st year of her age this monument of respect was erected by her husband Francis Lahy Esq of Lavagh".*

The Church of Ireland burial Record shows no record of either of their burials [Francis was still alive in 1827 (Conversion Controversy)] and the Church of Ireland Records at Ballymachugh begin in 1818. Perhaps they were buried by the Roman Catholic Church? And their bodies interred in Ballymachugh's CoI graveyard? (Both Protestants and Roman Catholics are buried in Ballymachugh).

David Leahy M.Sc.

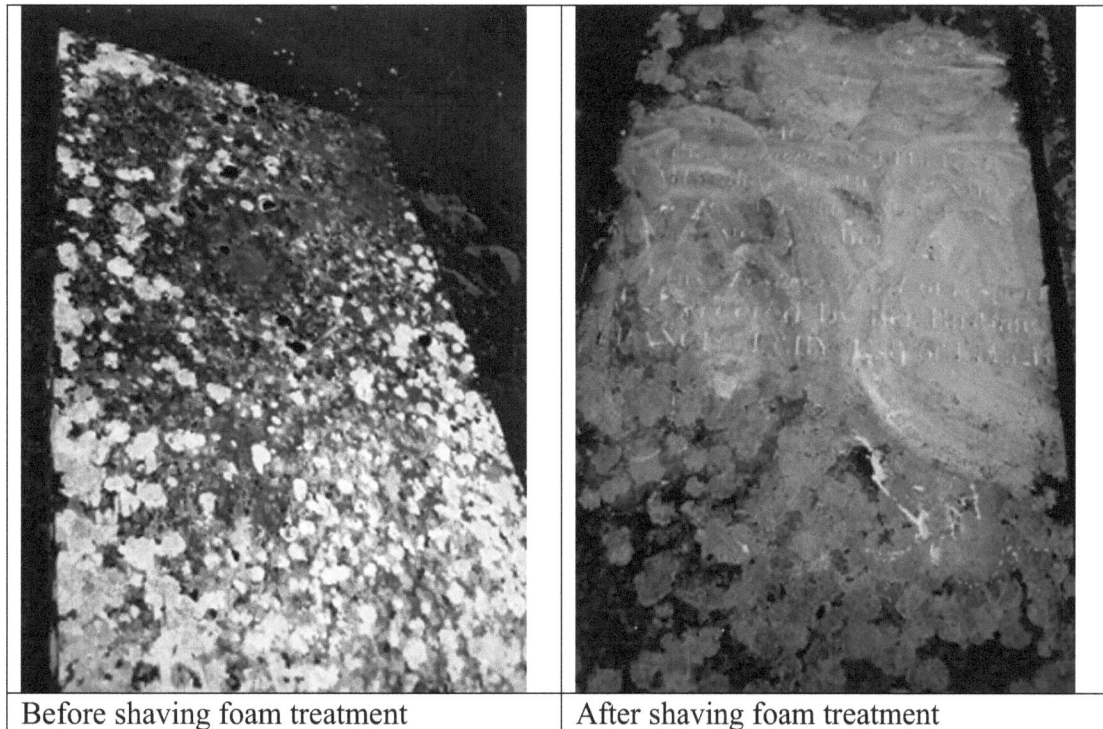

| Before shaving foam treatment | After shaving foam treatment |

Figure 118 Francis Lahy and Rebecca Burrowes Grave

If Rebecca was (as states on the tombstone) 51 when she died in 1818, then that would have made her 12 when she married Francis in 1779! However, there is a birth record of a Rebecca Burrowes on 30/1/1755 (to Robert and Mary Burrowes at Drung, Cavan) which would have made her 24 on her wedding day. Perhaps the text on the gravestone has eroded to such an extent that the dates are indecipherable.

13.3 William of Lavagh

William of Lavagh features in quite a few land transactions dated (1762, 1764, 1766, 1767 1769, 1772, 1773 and 1775) notes on these transactions are shown in Table 18.

Table 18 William of Lavagh's Land Transactions in the mid 1700s [Notes taken from The Registry of Deeds]

From	To	Book No	Page No	Memorial No	Notes	Date
William Lahy	Cheevers	217	280	143827	William Lahy of Lavagh to Thomas Cheevers and Thomas Heaney both of Aghakilmore half of all his lands in Lavagh being the one forth part of the said premesis	1762

From	To	Book No	Page No	Memorial No	Notes	Date
					to hold during the term of 21 years from 1s May next – yearly rent 15 s per acre. Witnessed by Richard Cheevers of Lis Nugent & Oliver Cheevers his son & Hugh Reilly of Finea (Yeoman) and Robert Acheson of Dublin	
William Lahy	Acheson / Cheevers	229	87	149470	William Lahy of Lavagh sell onto Thomas Cheevers of Aughakilmore all that half of the said William Lahys undivided moiety or half part of the lands of Lavagh and Aghacreevy now in the possession of the said William, Lahy, Thomas Lahy and James Lahy as the same is now held by the said Thomas Cheevers the said part undivided thereby demised to the said Thomas Cheevers containing 16 acres to hold for 30 years. Witnessed Robert Cordner, Robert Acheson	1764
William Lahy	Lahy	248	513	160734	16/4/1766. William Lahy of Lavagh £240 paid by James Lahy of Aughakilmore upper lands of Lavagh and Aghacreevy. Witnessed by Thomas Lahy of Aughakilmore Lower..	1766
John Lahy & Wife	Brady & Wife	260	479	174157	William Lahy of Lavagh and Pat Brady of Dublin and John Lahy of Lower Aghakilmore and his mother Susanne Lahy. 35 Acres in Lower Aghakilmore witnessed by Francis David and William McGrath	1767-1769
William Lahy	Lahy	273	349	177801	1769. William Lahy of Lavagh. £240 paid by James	1769

David Leahy M.Sc.

From	To	Book No	Page No	Memorial No	Notes	Date
					Lahy of Aughakilmore Upper lands of Lavagh and Aghacreevy. Witnessed by Thomas Lahy of Aughakilmore Lower	
William Lahy & Wife	Lahy	288	315	190877	1772. William Lahy and Wife Elizabeth of Lavagh. And James Lahy of Mullaghboy	1772
William Lahy	Lahy	290	451	193166	1772. William and Elizabeth and James Lahy of Aughakilmore Upper	1772
William Lahy		297	708	196816	William Lahy of Lavagh and Elizabeth Lahy his wife and James Lahy of Mullaghboy and James Lahy of Ballina. Voluntary settlement, unfair purposes. Witnesses William Cother of Dublin and John Faith of Cortal.	1773
William Lahy		301	652	203250	William Lahy and Elizabeth Lahy his wife of Aughakilmore Upper. James Lahy of Aghakilmore. £148 for land in Lavagh and Achacreevy, now held by Bayan Brady – 8 Acres and 24 Acres purchased by James Lahy from William Lahy. Witnessed by Thomas McManus of Ballyheelin, Henry Lahy of Aghakilmore Lower. Thomas Fitzpatrick of Curivoy, and Francis Lahy of Ballina	1775

William's wife Elizabeth is mentioned in at least half of the deeds. I have a number of theories / Options as to where William is descended from.

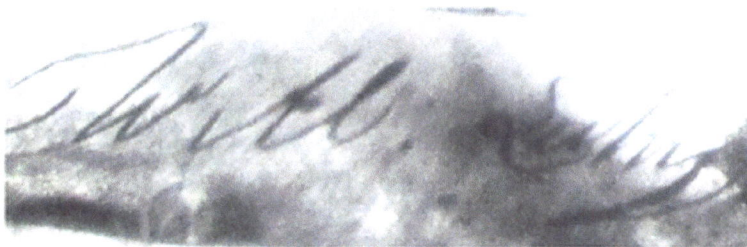

Figure 119 William of Lavagh Signature from 1767 Deed with Brady (and John and Mother Susanna) [52]

[Registry of Deeds (Property Registration Authority) retains the copyright]

Option 1 - William of Lavagh is the son of William of Lower Aghakilmore

This is already mentioned in section 9.2.7 - Option B, but repeated here for clarity:
In the deed dated 1767 [52] John Lahy and his mother Susanne are mentioned alongside William of Lavagh. William of Lavagh seems to be involved in quite a few land transactions (1762, 1764, 1766, 1767, 1769, 1772, 1773 and 1775). Thus, he must have inherited quite a bit of land - mostly in Lavagh and Aghacreevy [where his grandfather had land]. It is a possibility that he was the eldest son (hence being named William) of William (son of John of Lower Aghakilmore). As such he would have inherited the most land. It is a tenuous link, but families back then tended to have many children so I think it is a credible link (see Figure 121).

We know from earlier deeds that Richard had left 70 Acres in Aghakilmore to his son John and 38 Acres in Lavagh. This presumably would have been inherited by his son William - and thence John through to Patrick (land in Aghakilmore) and William (land in Lavagh). William's signature from the 1767 deed is shown in Figure 119.

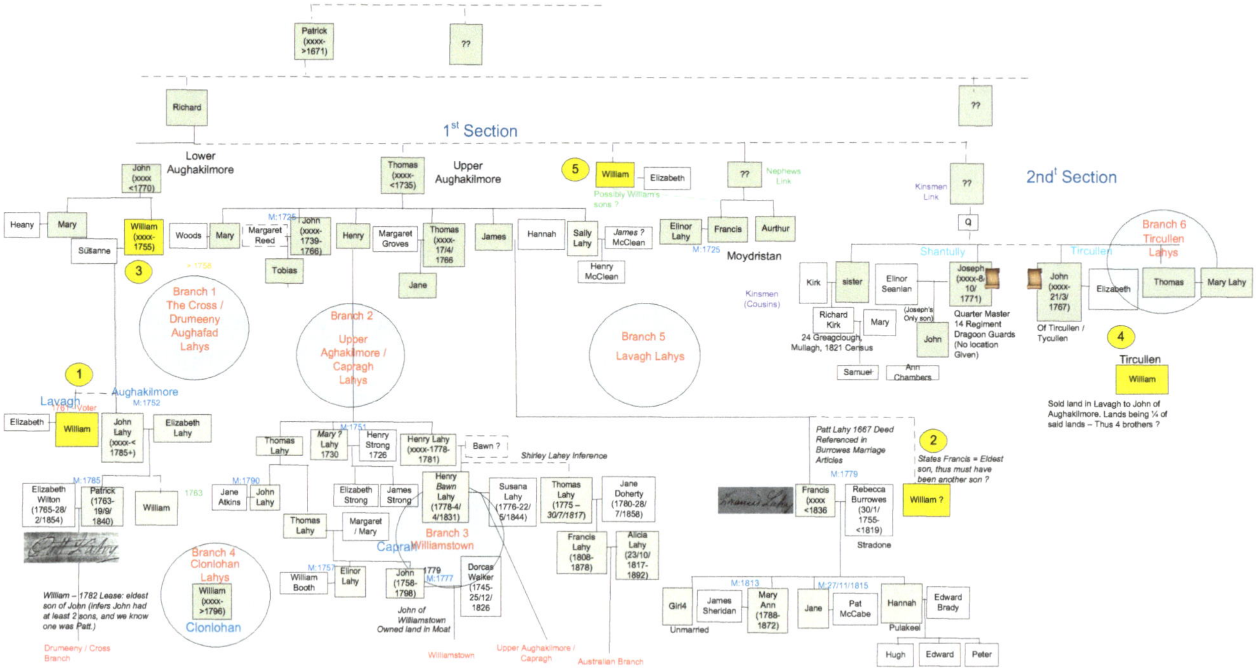

Figure 120 Possible ancestry of William of Lavagh [Options shown in yellow]

Option 2 - William of Lavagh is the son of James of Upper Aghakilmore

William is mentioned in land deeds in conjunction with James Lahy of Upper Aghakilmore in three separate deeds (1769, 1772, and 1775) which could well be a father handing off land to his son. Also, the Francis Lahy / Rebecca Burrowes marriage articles list Francis as the 'eldest son, which implies that James had another son and given that most of his land seemed to be in Lavagh, it would make sense that William was the second son (see Figure 120).

Option 3 - William of Lavagh is the son of John of Lower Aghakilmore

This would explain why William had so much land to sell. However, this William of Lavagh (and his wife Elizabeth) were selling land right up until 1775. John of Lower Aghakilmore's son is mentioned in his daughter's wedding articles in 1719, however his age is not known. Often people mentioned their children in deeds, so it is possible that William was still alive and transacting land in 1773.

Option 4 - William of Lavagh is William of Tycullen

The evidence for this theory consists of the following:
1. William of Tycullen was involved with land transactions involving land in Lavagh.
2. William of Tycullen mysteriously 'disappears' from land transaction records around the same time that William of Lavagh first appears in land transaction deeds records. There is a 1 year overlap (where William of Tycullen is listed as being 'of' Tycullen in 1763 whilst William of Lavagh is first listed in 1762. However, this overlap could be a consequence of how long it took for some land deeds to be processed (some earlier deeds took 15 years to be processed).

Option 5 - William of Lavagh is William of Upper Aghakilmore

There is a possibility that William of Lavagh is the original William of Upper Aughakilmore – mention in section 9.2.4 on page 120 who was transacting land in Lavagh the late 1730s. It is possible he was still alive and transacting land in the mid-1770s.

William Conclusion

I am undecided as to which family 'William' of Lavagh belonged to, he could also be related to other Lahys not mentioned here. However, his last land transaction in 1775 [82] he sold up his land in Lavagh and Aghacreevy and is recorded (with his wife Elizabeth) as now living in Upper Aghakilmore – perhaps he retired back to his roots or where his children were now living. He completed several land transactions with James Lahy of Upper Aghakilmore which suggests a close relative tie. Thomas of Lower Aghakilmore also seemed to be a close friend / relation to William of Lavagh [section 1.1.4 – page 139] as he was a signatory on several of his land deeds.

Hopefully in time further evidence will come to light to enable his direct connection to one of the branches. He did possess and exchange quite a bit of land and was married to a woman called Elizabeth. It is not known if they had any offspring.

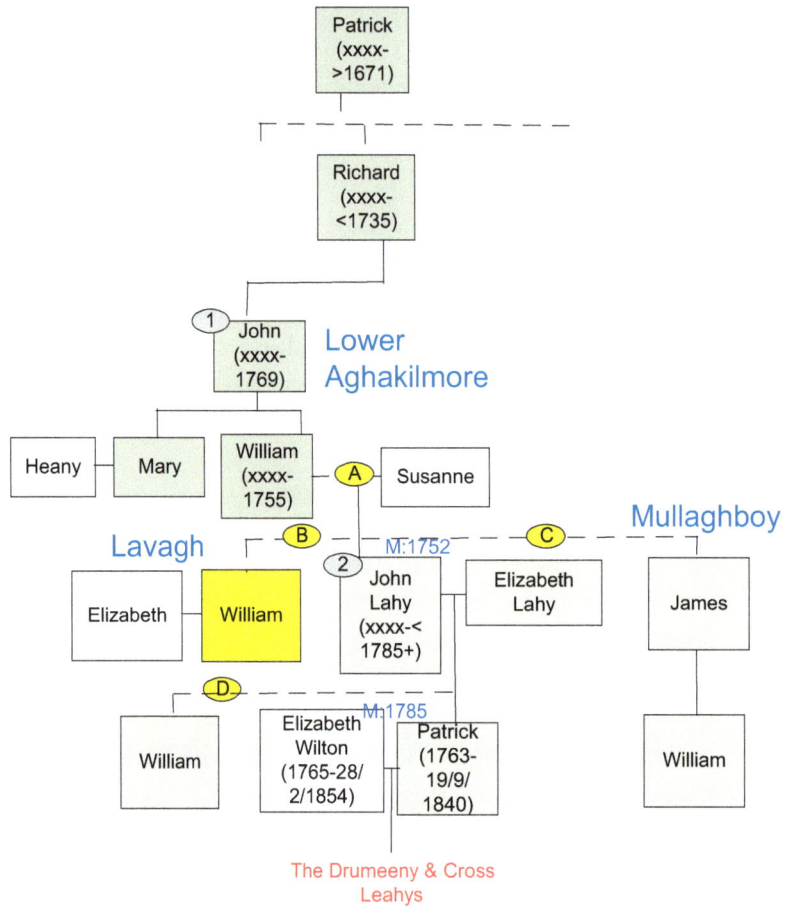

Figure 121 Possible ancestry of William of Lavagh - Option 1

Other Lahys in Lavagh

The land deeds evidence shows the following land transactions involving persons living in Lavagh in the 1700s - Table 19. One could conclude that this indicates William and Elizabeth had a son [James] who then had a son [Francis]. However, it is also possible that these are separate families - who are probably related, but until more evidence comes to light we will not know their exact relationship.

Table 19 Land Deeds evidence of other Lahys in Lavagh in the 1700s

Year	Person(s)	Deed	Reference
1762	William	143827 Ref 90	Ref 90
1764	William	149470 Ref 91	Ref 91
1766	William	160734 Ref 40	Ref 40
1767-69	William	174157 Ref 52	Ref 52
1769	William	177801 Ref 41	Ref 41
1772	William & Elizabeth (Wife)	190877 Ref 21	Ref 21
1773	William & Elizabeth (Wife)	196816 Ref 81	Ref 81
1775	William & Elizabeth (Wife)	203250 Ref 82	Ref 82
1780	James	231422 Ref 89	Ref 89
1786	James	250839 Ref 83	Ref 83
1786	James	250839 Ref 84	Ref 84
1799	Francis	443664 Ref 87	Ref 87

14 Branch 6 - Tircullen

The second section of the tree top is shown in Figure 122 Tree Top - 2nd Section] and the rationale explained below. The dashed lines and question marks at the top are indicators that it is not known exactly how it is connected to the 1st section. Bear in mind that Shantully and Tircullen are very close - within a mile or two (see Figure 123).

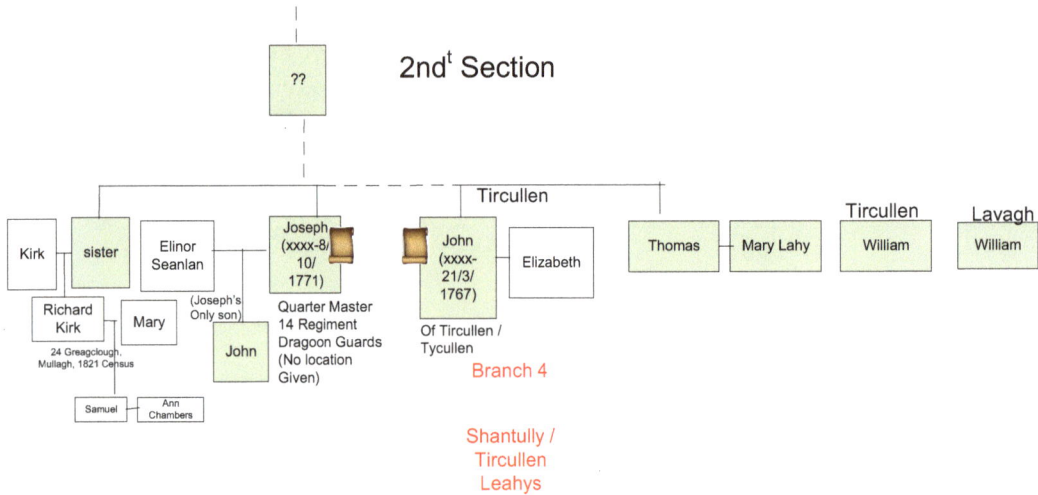

Figure 122 Tree Top - 2nd Section

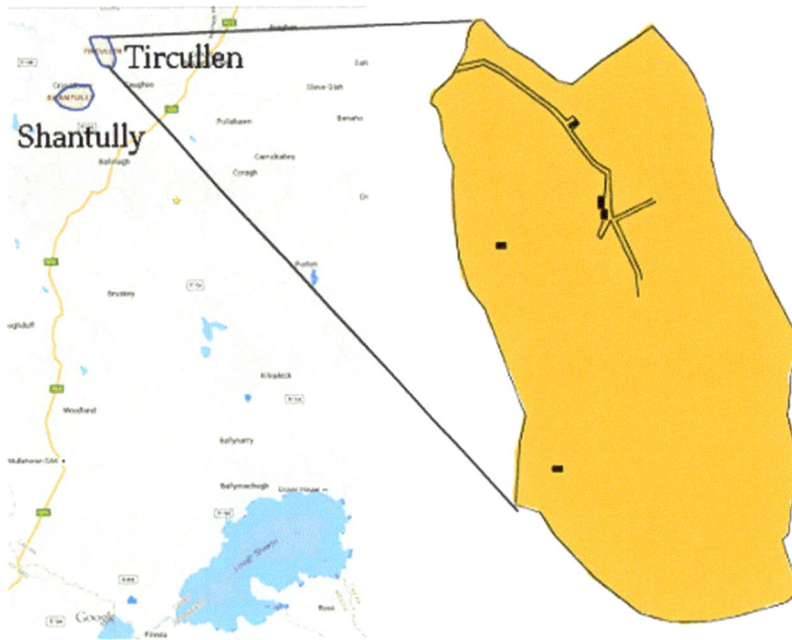

Figure 123 Location of Tircullen and Shantully relative to Lough Sheelin along with dwellings in early 1800s (Courtesy GoogleMaps)

David Leahy M.Sc.

14.1 John of Tircullen

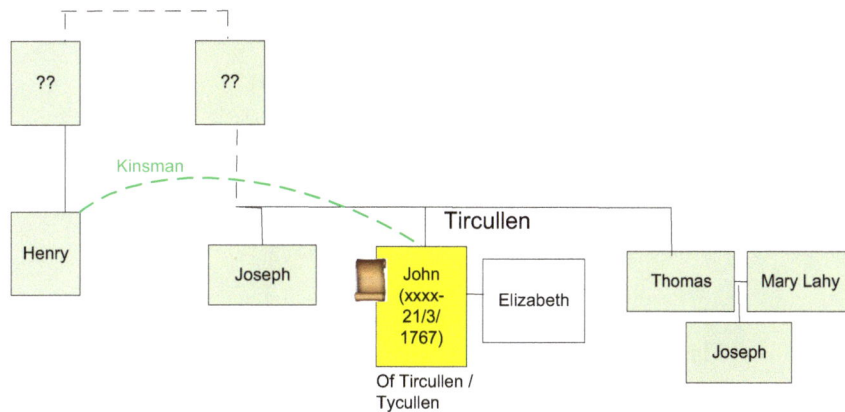

Figure 124 John of Tircullen

The following is a transcription of notes on Irish Wills made by Sir William Betham [Betham Will Abstracts No 153 (Page 60)] [64].

> *Lahy John, Tircullen dated 15/4/1758 - Fri 21 March 1767*
> *Kinsman Henry Lahy*
> *Wife Elizabeth Lahy*
> *Brother Joseph Lahy*
> *Brother Thomas Lacy [Lahy?]*
> *Joseph son of the same*
> *Sister in Law Mary Lahy*

The **'Kinsman'** link could be the Henry of Aghakilmore (who I believe moved from Upper Aghakilmore to Lower Aghakilmore between 1738 -1762). This could be Henry 1 or Henry 2 [see Figure 103]. There is also a land deed in 1758 [30] in which John of Tircullen sold 70 acres to Henry. Also, the brother **Joseph** link is noted and brother Thomas (see Joseph section 15.1.1) There is also a sister-in-law Mary Lahy which suggests that his brother Thomas could have married a Lahy (or it may simply be his brother [Thomas or Joseph]'s wife).

14.2 William of Tircullen

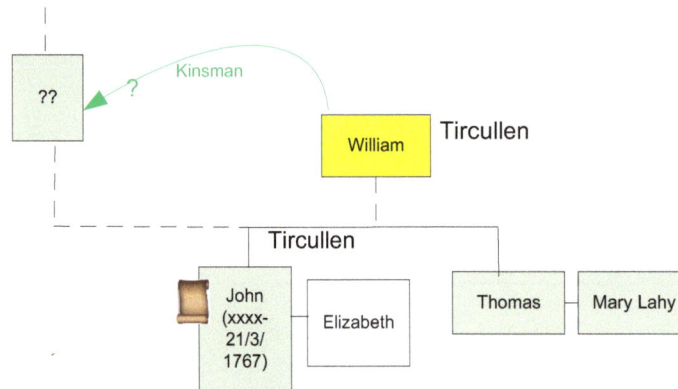

Figure 125 William of Tircullen

There is a land deed dated 1760 [47] in which William Lahy of Tircullen sold John Lahy of Lower Aghakilmore half his right of lands in Lavagh *being one forth part* of the said premises. To me this not only tells us that there was a William in Tircullen, but that he's quite likely the fourth brother at the top level in the 1st Section - who moved to Tircullen (1 of 4 brothers)?

It is very likely that William and John of Tircullen were closely related - as it is a very small townland / homestead - they were likely brothers or more probably father and son. As John didn't mention William in his Will of 1767 as being a son or brother, it is possible that William was the father of John who outlived his son - as depicted in Figure 125.

Another possibility is that William of Tircullen moved to Lavagh – as outlined in the previous section (13.3) where he continued transacting land up until 1775.

In the 1821 census [18] there are no Lahys listed as living at Tircullen thus the Tircullen Lahys may have died out or moved elsewhere / emigrated - perhaps back beside Lake Sheelin were buying and selling land with the other Lahys living these. The 1821 census list residents of '*Turcullen*' and of '*Turcullin*' as separate townlands - no Lahys are mentioned in either.

Figure 126 Tircullen today - the 'Outhouse' was probably an original dwelling

In August 2015, I called at the house and the current residents had no knowledge of previous occupants. However, a neighbour named Sheridan told me that the previous owners (Armstrongs) had spoken about Lahys having once owned the farm. The previous occupants to Armstrongs were Achesons.

15 Branch 7 - Shantully

According to Shirley Lahey, in her book [1] a local historian in the area - Bill Graham, stated that the Lahys moved from Shantully to Aghakilmore in the 1730s.

Shirley has *'William of Shantully'* at the top of her tree - probably born around 1720 - see section 7.6 and Figure 70, however she didn't state the source for this William of Shantully - i.e., where his residence was listed or where she obtained this information.

However as shown before [Patrick Laghy], Lahys were in Aghakilmore in the late 1600s. One branch may have moved to Shantully and then back to Aghakilmore after 1730, however I am unaware of where Bill Graham got this date from for such a move.

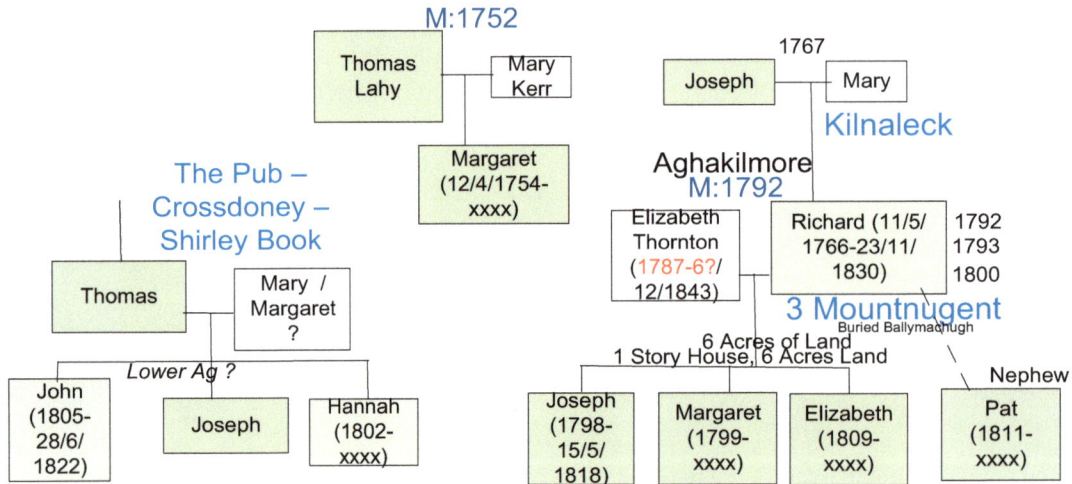

Figure 127 Crossdoney / Shantully Lahys

I am unconvinced that the Lahys in Crossdoney / Shantully owned much land - as they're not included in any land deeds in the 1700s or 1800s, nor were they witnesses to any of the other Lahy deeds except the following:

1. **Joseph** and **Mary** are recorded in a deed dated 1767 [78] selling 76 Acres in Lower Aughakilmore to Andrew Bell of Bellsgrove.

2. **Joesph** sold 70 Acres in Lower Aghakilmore to Henry Lahy in 1770 [25]

Joseph must be directly connected to either the Lower or Upper Aghakilmore Lahys (probably the Lower Aghakilmore as that's where the land was that he sold). However, neither available Will nor deeds currently shed any light on exactly how he was connected.

15.1.1   Joseph (Quarter Master)

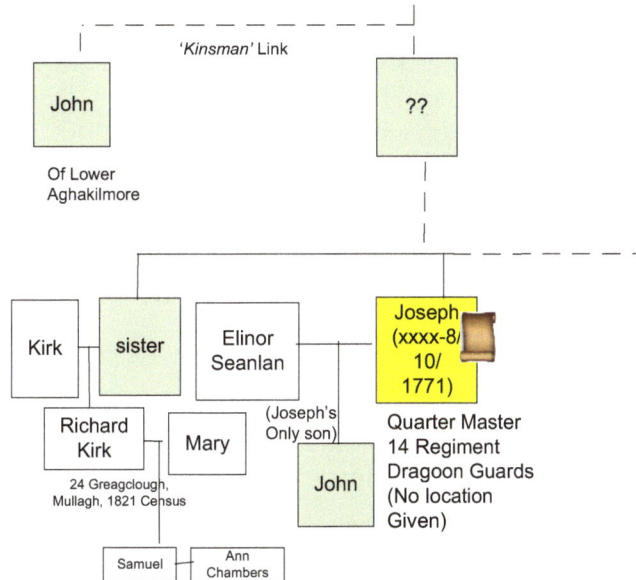

Figure 128 Joseph of Shantully

Joseph (Quarter Master) is recorded as being from Aghakilmore in the 1761 Election Poll [17].

The following is a transcription of notes on Irish Wills made by Sir William Betham [Betham Will Abstracts No 222 (Page 94)] dated 1771 [65].

> *Lahy, Joseph, Quarter Master 14th Regiment of Dragoon Guards.*
> *Only son John*
> *Nephew Joseph*
> *Brother John Lahy*
> *Wife Elinor Lahy (else Seanlan)*
> *Kinsman John Lahy*
> *Nephew Richard Kirk*

He notes a brother John but doesn't say from where which makes it difficult to pin point the correct John however, I have a suspicion it is John of Tircullen (previous section) who also specified a brother Joseph in his Will!

The '*Kinsman*' link is interesting - it is usually taken to be a relative by blood e.g. cousin or uncle. In this case, I think it must mean one of the Johns from Upper or Lower Aghakilmore - thus Joseph's father may have been a brother of either John of Lower Aghakilmore, or John of Upper Aghakilmore. I suspect it is John of *Lower* Aghakilmore as John of Upper Aghakilmore was dead by 1766 [see section 010.1.1] (see Figure 128).

A 'Quarter Master' is a relatively senior soldier who supervises stores and distributes supplies and provisions.

The 14th Regiment of Dragoons regiment was raised in 1715 as a dragoon regiment, named for its first colonel as James Dormer's Regiment of Dragoons, and ranked as the 14th Dragoons. In 1751, it was formally renamed as the 14th Regiment of Dragoons. It later became the 14th King's Hussars. This unit was raised in southern England in 1715 and immediately sent to Preston to face the First Jacobite Rebellion. From 1717 to 1742 it was in Ireland and in 1745 it faced the Jacobites again, this time in Scotland. It then immediately returned to Ireland in 1746 for nearly 50 more years of peacekeeping. [National Arms Museum - http://www.nam.ac.uk/].

Richard Lahy

Richard (son of Joseph and Mary of Kilnaleck) is recorded in three land deeds in the late 1700s which seem to reflect some major financial trouble:

In 1792 [66] Richard is recorded as marrying Elizabeth Thornton (daughter of Francis Thornton) and receiving £113 15s as part of her dowry. There's also mention of £12 a year rent of land in Aghakilmore from her father Francis to Elizabeth.

A year later - 1793 a deed [67] details judgements against Richard by Henry Maxwell of Crover and Richard having to surrender lands known as 'The Cross' until the amount of £479 was paid off at the rate of £28 per year. References are also made to earlier deeds.

Seven years later in 1800 Richard (now moved to Mount Nugent) is selling 72 Acres (arable land) and 5 acres (of bog) to Henry Maxwell of Crover for £1465 15s 9d - a very large amount of money at the time! [68].

We may never know what happened between Richard and Henry Maxwell - but it clearly left Richard so broke that he had to sell up all his land in Aghakilmore.

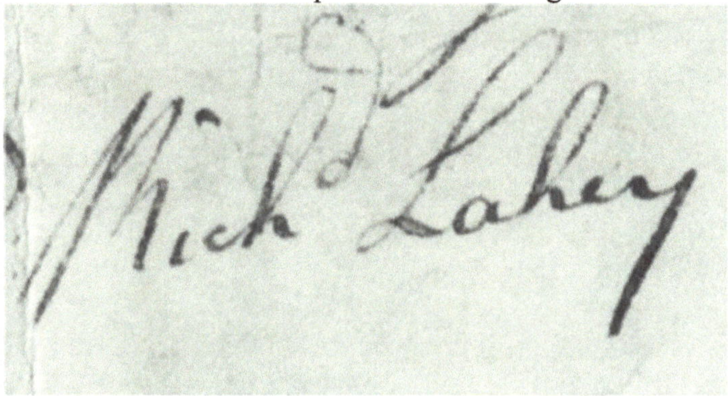

Figure 129 Richard Lahey's Signature from 1800 Deed [68]

David Leahy M.Sc.

Thomas and Mary / Margaret lived in or owned a pub in Crossdoney in 1802 (at the birth of their daughter). There is currently a pub there called the Shantully Arms, however locals told me that this is a relatively new pub and the original pub stood on the other side of the main street.

According to a local historian - Wendy Swan, previous owners were 'Lang' and before that 'Lord' - perhaps the Lord family bought it from the Lahys (who according to Bill Graham then moved to Drumeeny).

One can see from Figure 131 the current building and Figure 130 the building as it was in the 1930s (their appears to be someone looking out of an upstairs window, which looks a bit spooky), In Figure 131 one can see a very old building - probably from the 1700/1800s, this may well have been the Lahy pub at the time.

Figure 130 Crossdoney Spirit Grocer in the 1930s [Courtesy Wendy Swan]

| Crossdoney House in 2015 | Old 'Dwelling' [Original Pub?] behind main house |

Figure 131 Crossdoney Buildings in 2015

16 Branch 8 - Mullagh

Figure 132 Relative positions of the Mullagh Lahys [Greaglough] to Lough Sheelin (courtesy Google Maps)

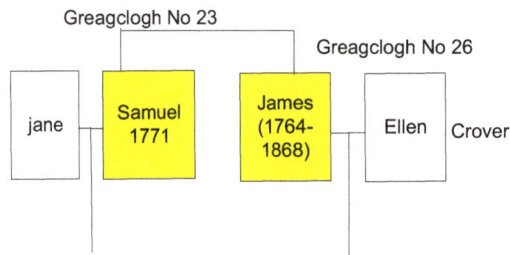

Figure 133 Top of the Mullagh Lahys Tree (from 1821 Census [18])

The origin of the Mullagh Lahys is unclear. They were Protestant and attended the nearby Bailieborough Church of Ireland Church. They were quite a way from the other Lahys around Lough Sheelin (Figure 132) but still close enough to be related. They were not mentioned in the early land deeds as buyers, vendors or witnesses. However, this could just mean that they rented and were less well off than the Lough Sheelin Lahys. They may not be related, but I'm convinced that they are principally because they were Church of Ireland Protestants - whereas the other Lahys in Ireland at the time e.g. in Kilkenny and Tipperary were almost exclusively Roman Catholic. I have two theories as to how they are connected to the Sheelin Lahys:

1. Connected through the Shantully / Tircullen Lahys - Joseph & Richard Kirk
2. Connected through the Crover Lahys

David Leahy M.Sc.

Tircullen Lahys - Joseph & Richard Kirk

In Joseph (of 14th Regiment Dragoon guards) [probably of Tircullen]'s Will [65] he mentioned a nephew Richard Kirk. From the 1821 census [18] we can find a Richard Kirk married to a Mary and who lived at 24 Greaglough. This is literally the house next door to Samuel and Jane Lahy from Mullagh (Figure 133). It would be a very unlikely coincidence if this was just chance. From this one could speculate that the Mullagh Lahys are connected to Joseph Lahy of Shantully.

Ellen - Crover

Another possibility is a connection through the Crover Lahys. James (in Figure 133) married Ellen from Crover. It is possible that James may have lived in Crover as a child and married a local girl. Richard Lahy (son of Joseph of Shantully) owned land in Crover.

Figure 134 Samuel Lahy's House at Greagclough (circled in Figure 135)

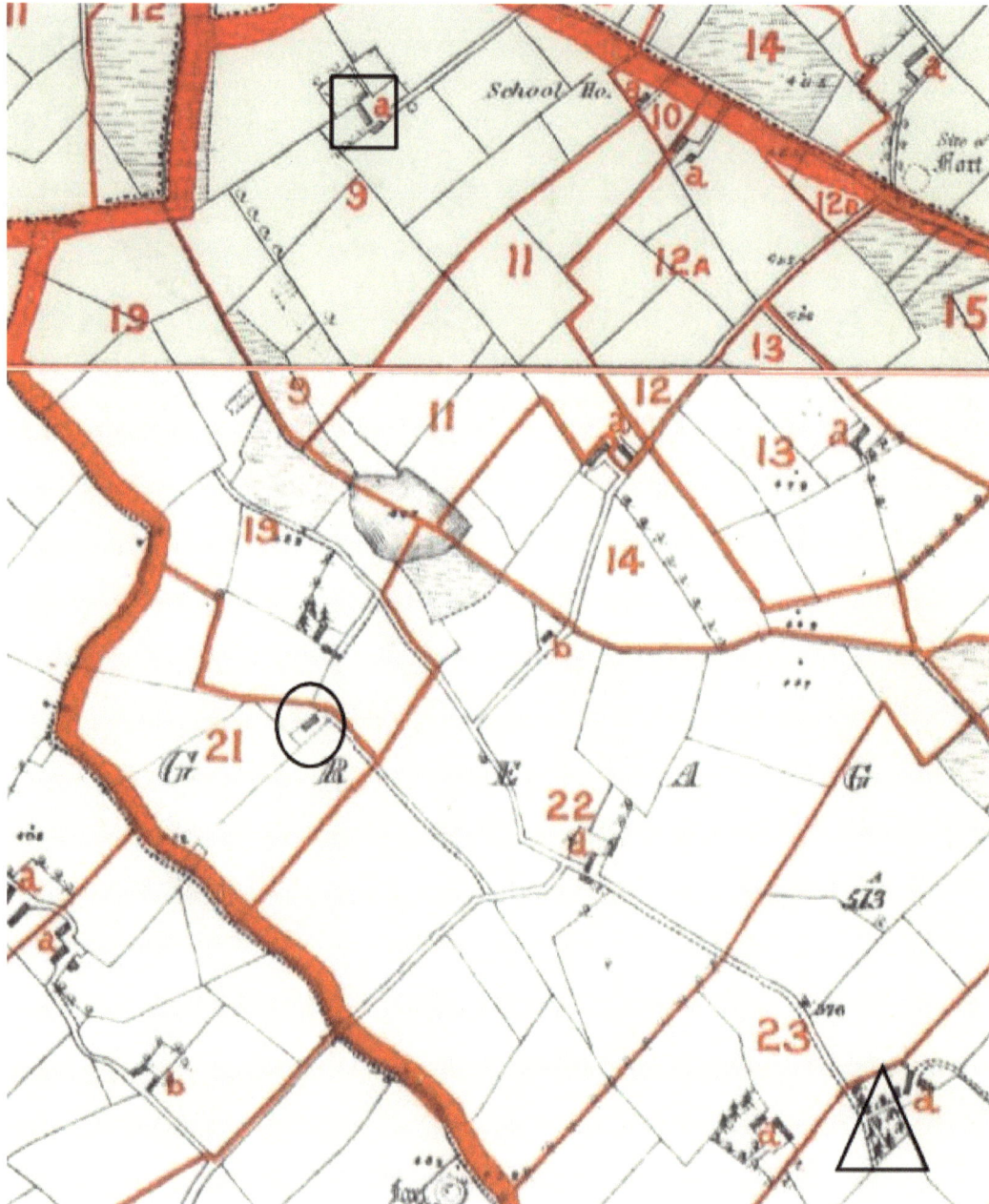

Figure 135 Location of Robert Lahy [Square]. Samuel Lahy [Circle] and Kirke Family [Triangle] (Courtesy AskaboutIreland)

David Leahy M.Sc.

Figure 136 Kirke family dwelling house in Greaglough (Triangle in Figure 135)

Figure 137 The 'Hearth' of the dwelling [inhabited until 1950s]

Robert and Samuel's houses / land rented in the mid 1800s is shown in the Griffiths Valuation [57] (Figure 135). Samuel's house is still standing (Figure 134). Their neighbours the Kirk family's dwelling is also shown – it was occupied until the 1950s according to the present owner.

David Leahy M.Sc.

17 Others

17.1 Thomas and Jane of Kilnahard

There is a record of a **Thomas Lahy** of Kilnahard (see Figure 138) who died owing money to Mr Maxwell in 1818. His wife **Jane** seems to have to take on the debt. I'm not sure how this Thomas links in with the other branches; however, it may be the Thomas Lahy and Jane Doherty at the top of Shirley Lahy's Australian tree (see section 10.1.2 and Figure 99.

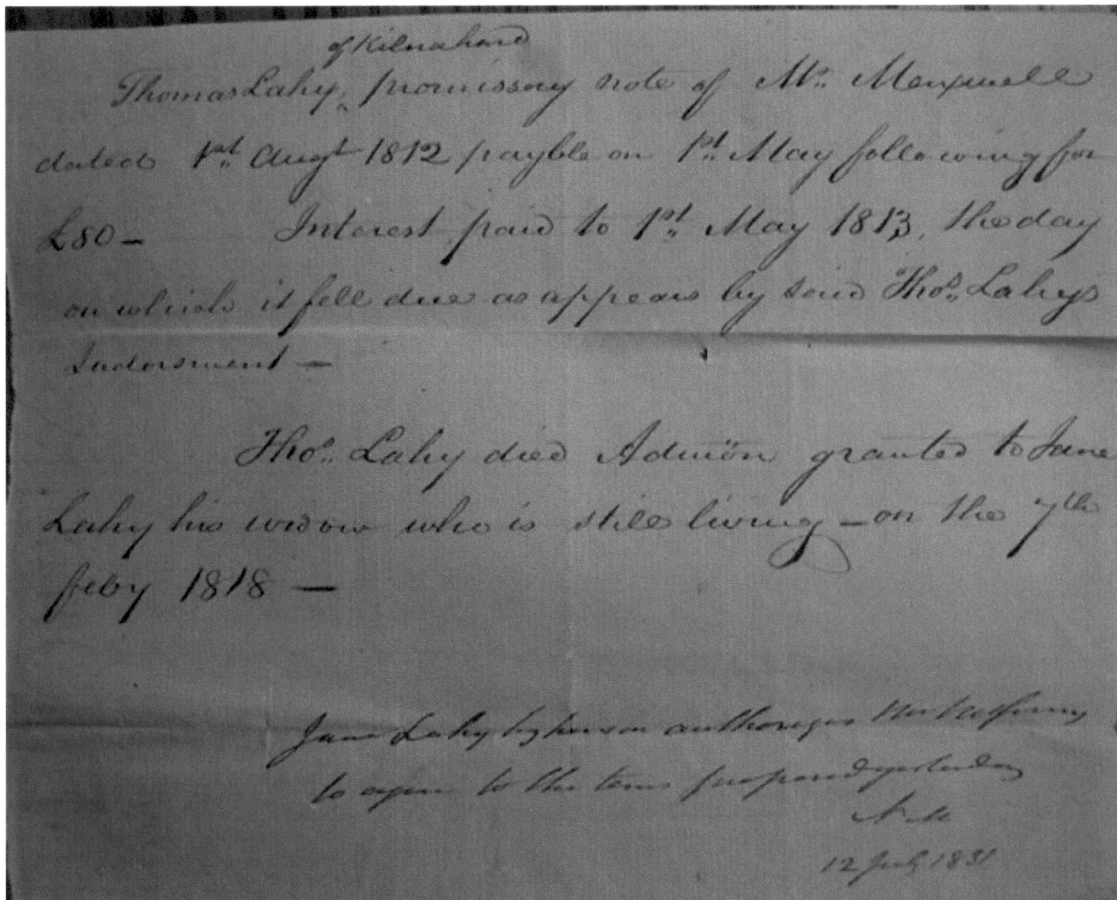

Figure 138 Thomas and Jane Lahy of Kilnahard [69 - NLI]

Transcription:

> *Thomas Lahy of Kilnahard promissory note of Mr Maxwell dated 1st August 1812 payable on 1st May following for £80. Interest paid to 1st May 1813 the day on which it fell due as appears by said Thomas Lahys Indorsement.*

Thomas Lahy died Admin granted to Jane Lahy his widow who is still living on the 7th February 1818.

Jane Lahy by person authorises xxxxx to agree to the terms proposed xxxxx

12 July 1831

One candidate for this Thomas and Jane could be the mother and father of Francis Lahy who emigrated to Australia with his wife Alicia (see Figure 139) – the dates match up – of Thomas's death. Although Janes moved to Kilican (Westmeath) after her husband's death – it is possible that they lived in Kilnahard prior to this.

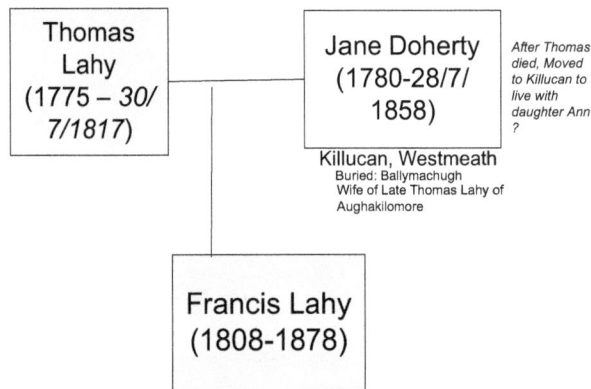

Figure 139 Possible Thomas & Jane from Promissory Note?

17.2 Dragoon Guards

17.2.1   Thomas Lahy - 5th Dragoon Guards

In the National archives [70], there is a record of a Thomas Lahy being discharged in 19/6/1795 (aged 26) from Ballymachugh. Thomas served two years with the regiment in Lt. Col. Taylor's troop whose Colonel was Major General Thomas Bland. Thomas fell of a horse and 'broke his back and spent time in Chelsea Hospital. He was by trade a 'labourer' although I'm sure he wouldn't have returned to labouring with a broken back. It is not known what family he was from.

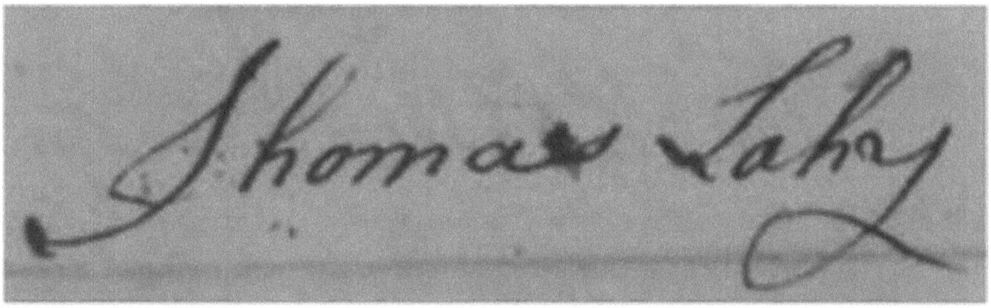

Figure 140 Thomas's Signature in Discharge Paper 1795 [70]

[National Archives retains the copyright]

Napoleonic War Regimental indexes 1806 [71] record Thomas as having enlisted 15/4/1793 as a private.

17.2.2   Francis Lahey - 5th Dragoon Guards

Francis Lahy is recorded in the Chelsea Pensioners discharge documents [99] as being from the parish of 'Wherean' and town of Castle Pollard in County Westmeath, born in 1755 and discharged from the 5th Dragoon Guards (Col being Maj Gen Thomas Bland) in 1795 having served with the regiment for two years. He had received a wound in his leg on the 26th April last at ' Coteau ' which rendered him incapable of further service. I'm sure that Francis probably knew Thomas - there were both from the same area, same surname and joined up and left the same year as each other.

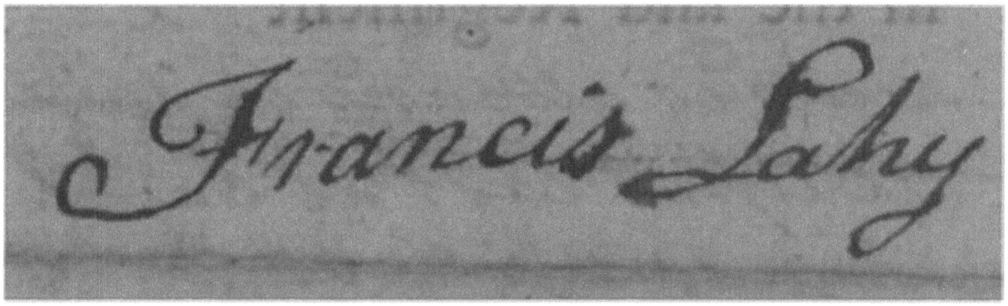

Figure 141 Francis Lahy's signature in 1795

[National Archives retains the copyright]

Battle of Beaumont (1794)

The Battle of Beaumont-en-Cambresis 26 April 1794 (sometimes referred to as the Battle of Coteau, or in France the Battle of Troisvilles) was an action forming part of a multipronged attempt to relieve the besieged fortress of Landrecies, during the Flanders Campaign of the French Revolutionary War. The British and Austrians under the Duke of York defeated a French advance northwards from Cambrai commanded by René Chapuis. Troops attached to the command of General Chapuis had already clashed with the Duke of York two days earlier, when a column had been repulsed with great loss by just 4 squadrons of light cavalry under Rudolf Ritter von Otto at Villers-en-Cauchies. Otto's flanking cavalry meanwhile were drawn up in three lines, the first consisting of six squadrons of Zeschwitz Cuirasiers (Austrian) under Prince Schwarzenberg, the second line of John Mansel's Dragoon brigade (i.e. 2 squadrons each of the Blues, the Royals and the 3rd Dragoon Guards)(British), and the third line of the 1st and 5th Dragoon Guards plus the 16th Light Dragoons (British). - Wikipedia

We can pick up Francis again in 1806 from the British Arms Service Records Transcription [100]. He's listed as having been in the 5th Dragoon guards and pension year 1795 (when he was discharged with his leg injury). He's listed as being specifically with the 1st troop of Horse Guards to 9th Foot.

There is a death record in Ballymachugh church records of 'Darkey' Lahy from Wheran who died aged 82 in 27/12/1826 [88]. I'm sure this must have been a direct relation of this Francis. Darkey is usually a woman's name.

17.2.3   Patrick Lahey - 5th Dragoon Guards

Patrick Lahey from Ballymachugh (Cavan) [72] joined the Dragoon Guards [Colonel General R R Wilford] - Capt Morrison's Troop 2/5/1796 aged 22 years old thus born about 1774. He had brown hair, grey eyes and was 5 feet 9 inches tall and had been a shoemaker by trade. He was discharged on 31 August 1814 at Dundalk barracks due to a 'Reduction' at a final rank of 'Private'.

Figure 142 Patrick's Signature on Discharge Paper 1814

David Leahy M.Sc.

17.2.4   2nd Patrick Lahey 5th Dragoon Guards

There is also a reference to a Corporal Patrick Lahey from the Chelsea Pensioners' discharge documents [98] from the 5th Dragoon Guards with Thomas Bland as Colonel. He was reportedly from the parish of "*Ballymanagh*" in the county of Cavan and is discharged in 1802 having being "*much affected by Rhumatism and bad eyes*", His age is given as 36 and served 10/2 years in the regiment.

Figure 143 Patrick Lahey from 1802 signature

[National Archives retains the copyright]

Obviously, the dates - of service length and age don't match up with the 1st Patrick, however the signatures in Figure 142 and Figure 143 look remarkably similar.

17.2.5   Joseph Lahey - 5th Dragoon Guards

Joseph Lahey from Ballymachugh (Cavan) [73] joined the Dragoon Guards [Colonel General R. R. Wilford] - Capt Morrison's Troop 2/5/1796 aged 18 years old thus born about 1778. He had brown hair, grey eyes and was 5 feet 11 inches tall and had been a Yeoman by trade. He was discharged on 29 September1814 at Dundalk barracks due to a 'Reduction' at a final rank of 'Sergeant'.

Figure 144 Joseph's Signature on Discharge Paper 1814 [73]

[National Archives retains the copyright]

As both Joseph and Patrick joined up on the same day and left the service within a month of each other after 18 years' service, we can probably assume they knew each other very well and were most likely brothers or cousins. It is possible that Joseph and Pat were direct relatives of Joseph (Quarter Master) 14th Regiment of Dragoons [14th King's Hussars] of Shantully who died in 1768 (section 15.1.1).

During the period 1796 - 1814 the 5th Dragoon Guards seen action in:

1793 - 1802 French Revolutionary Wars
1808 - 1814 Peninsular War

17.2.6   Thomas Lahy - 5th Dragoon Guards

This Thomas [74] (from Ballymachugh) joined the 5th Dragoon Guards on 15/4/1793 at the age of 22 and was discharged 28/1/1817. He was in Capt. Lane's Troop and the Colonel of his regiment was Sax Cobourg stationed in Dublin. He had brown hair and grey eyes and was 5 feet 8 inches tall with a dark complexion. He was a labourer before joining up for 23 years & 289 days' service. His discharge reason was given as "'being worn out" - I'm not surprised after 23 years!

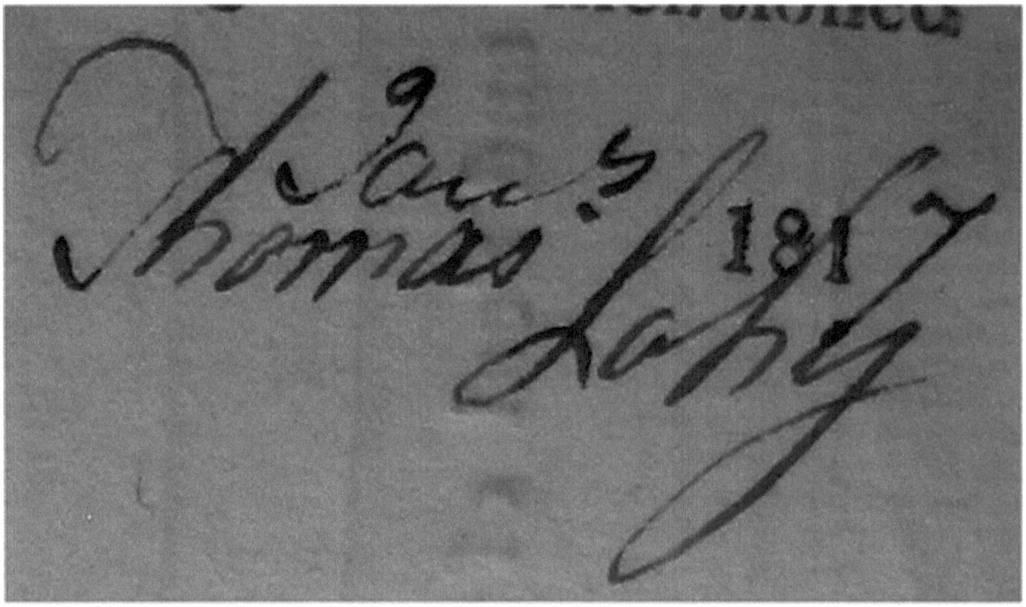

Figure 145 Thomas's signature from his discharge papers

[National Archives retains the copyright]

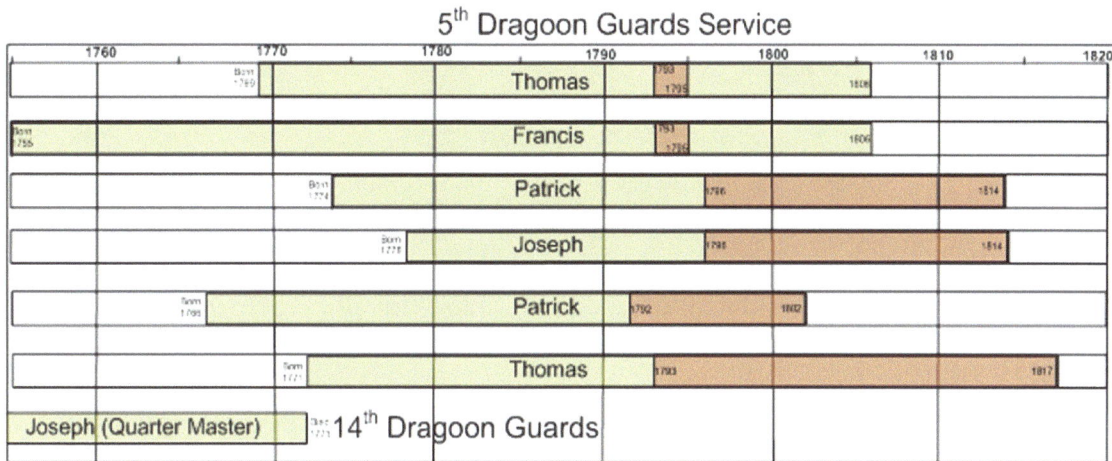

Figure 146 Lahys from Ballymachugh 5th Dragoon Guards Service periods (Orange)

Figure 146 illustrates the above Lahys and their lifespan (yellow) and period of service in the 5th Dragoon Guards (Orange). After they were discharged it is not known what became of them or when they died. One can see that Thomas and Francis may have known each other having joined up for almost exactly the same two-year period. Patrick and Joseph too seemed to join up and leave at the same time (after 18 years of service!). In fact, Ballymachugh is such a small area that it is very likely that they all knew each other and probably influenced each other's military careers. It's just not clear at this time as to exactly which families they hailed from. It is also worth noting that in the 1761 Poll (Section 7.4 & [17]) A Joseph Lahy Quarter Master (of the 14th Dragoon Guards) is listed [see section 15.1.1] – a Quarter Master was usually taken to mean a "relatively senior soldier who supervises stores and distributes supplies and provisions". – Wikipedia. Thus, Joseph is the earliest known Lahy to have been in the Military. Joseph (Quarter Master) is listed in 13.1.1.3 as leaving a Will in 1771.

18 DNA Evidence

18.1 Rationale

DNA tests can be used to 'support' paper trails (of Church and land deeds records and census data etc), or can be used to rule out certain connection lines (perhaps due to an adoption, or an un-marriage related birth).

I took the opportunity to give a DNA sample to **familytreeDNA** to look for matches for the Y-Chromosome - which is the Male Only line. The results can be complicated and difficult to interpret. I had a 67 Marker test performed [the more marker then the more accurate a match can be made]. If a 67 Marker match is found then it means very little if there is no surname match.

To briefly explain what happens in a DNA comparison:

Each male has a Y-Chromosome which he inherits directly from his father who in turn inherited from his father etc. etc. Over time mutations (changes) occur to the Y-Chromosome during its 'copying' in reproduction. Most of these changes are very small and inconsequential; however, they occur at a measured rate which can be predicted. By comparing the Y-Chromosome material from two males one can predict the natural occurring (by chance) changes and those that show for example the same changes as male ancestors. By comparing these mutations one can predict the probability of a common male ancestor at each generation.

The DNA testing enables one to directly compare one individual in the database against another to determine exactly how many generations ago they are linked.

One might ask - why not directly compare the DNA with a male DeLahaye descendant? This is difficult for two reasons:
1. Due to the cost, there are currently not a lot of people on the DNA database.
2. DeLahayes on the database may be from a completely different part of Europe.

As I am a descendant of the *John of Lower Aghakilmore branch* I thought it also worth getting a sample tested from a descendant of the **Thomas (Senior) line [mostly from Upper Aughakilmore and Capragh**]. This would help to provide evidence to substantiate the 'assumed' link at the top of the tree (i.e. that John of Lower Aughakilmore and Thomas Senior were brothers).

The *'paper trail'* would indicate that myself (David) descended from the Lower Aughakilmore line and L. Leahy (from the Upper Aughakilmore line) should be directly connected 8 or 9 generations back.

The result could basically fall into three categories:

1. **The match is 3 to 5 generations back**. This would mean that the connection is more recent than the paper trail suggests and that there are more recent unknown ancestors to be discovered,

2. **The match is e.g. 15-20 generations back.** This would mean that the current top of the tree is wrong and the 'common' link between the two (Upper and Lowe) Aughakilmore Leahys is much further back - perhaps even before Pat Laghy.

3. **The match is as predicted** - about 8 or 9 generations back - which would back up the paper trail data and assumptions represented in this book.

The result of the comparison is shown in Figure 147.

18.2 DNA Results

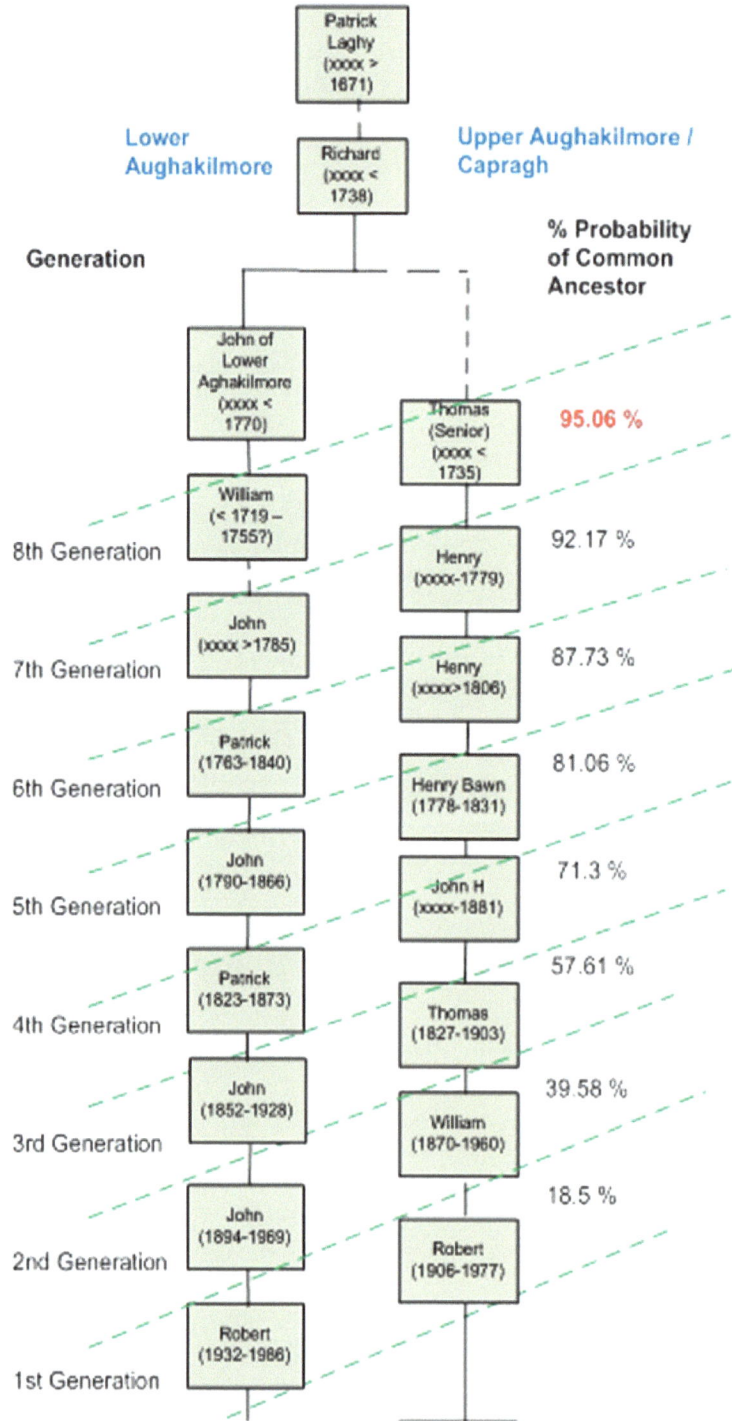

Figure 147 Summary of DNA Comparison between Lower & Upper Aughakilmore Descendants

David Leahy M.Sc.

I checked with the Family Tree DNA site and they stated that:

> *"The DNA cannot confirm which generation the common ancestor is to be found. It is only able to provide a probability as to a range they are likely to be found. The further back in time we go the more likely it is any two men would share a common ancestor. At the 67-marker level, it is saying there is a 95% chance that the common ancestor would be found within 8 generations. If the paper trail is supporting this then you have very likely found the specific common ancestor."*

The two generation lines don't match up exactly as people lived different amounts of time and birth dates obviously varied. Nevertheless, the result I believe confirms the top of the tree link between the *Lower* and *Upper* Aughakilmore Lahys which on the tree diagram is about **8 generations** back. The DNA evidence suggests that there is over a **95 % probability** that this is the case. There is a 5% chance that this is not the case, however given the paper trail of evidence in the form of quoted Wills and Deeds in this book, I believe this to be unlikely.

If the reader has a DNA - Y Chromosome test performed of a male member of their family [e.g. at https://www.familytreedna.com/], they can compare the results with the Lower and Upper Aghakilmore tested here, in Appendix C.

It should be noted that both individuals tested compared quite closely with males with the surname 'Ryan' that exist in the FTDNA database. The 'Ryan' connection (if any) is currently unknown to me. There are currently not a lot of individuals on the DNA database, as it is quite expensive to test and the results can be complex and difficult to interpret (especially if no paper trail exists).

19 Outstanding Questions

The following are outstanding questions relating to the early Lahys which I can't currently answer, but future researchers may be able to cast some light on:

1. How were Patrick and John 'Laughy' [named in 1689 Bill of Attainder] related?
2. Exact relationship between the earliest Patrick and Richard?
3. What was the John [Tircullen] 'Kinsman' link?
4. Tircullen Lahys - How are they linked in to the Agakilmore Lahys?
5. Shantully Lahys - How are they linked in to the Agakilmore Lahys?
6. What was the Joseph [Shantully] 'Kinsman' link?
7. Exactly how the Lower and Upper Lahys connected?
8. What happened to the 'black sheep' 'Richard' Lahy (son of Joseph)?
9. Did Patrick (1667) have any brothers / sisters with him?
10. How does Patrick link to the Huguenot Francois Delahaye ?
11. Did the Lahys spend time in England before moving the Ireland?
12. How are the Mullagh Lahys connected?
13. What was the outcome of the 1767 'Will' dispute?
14. How are the Longford Lahys connected?
15. How were Joseph & Mary of Kilnaleck connected?
16. Was Shirley Leahy's 'Thomas' at the top of her tree connected to the Henrys of Capragh?
17. Who were William and Elizabeth who conducted so many land transactions?
18. Who was the assumed 4th brother at the top of the tree? [nephew link]
19. Lower Aghakilmore - why is there no more evidence of John's son William's land transactions?
20. Exactly how are the Clonloaghan Lahys connected?

David Leahy M.Sc.

20 Tree Top - Next Generations

Some branches 'discontinued' as a 'Lahy' line due to no male children surviving to marriageable age and producing male heirs (e.g. the Francis Lahy & Rebecca Burrows line who produced only girls). Others have 'discontinued' due to no further information being obtainable about their offspring (if any) or perhaps they moved away - for example the Tircullen and Shantully branches. The fate of the 8 main branches mentioned at the start is shown in Table 20.

Table 20 Main Branches Fate

Branch No	Main Abode	Fate
1	Lower Aghakilmore	Remained in Lower Aghakilmore farming land there and eventually purchased the ''Cross' pub. Some moved to USA & Australia and some to N. Ireland and others still live in the area today.
2	Upper Aghakilmore	Remained in Upper Aghakilmore and Capragh some emigrated to Canada and the USA & Australia. Some still live in the area today.
3	Williamstown	Farm put up for sale in 1894 [155 acres], however remained in Williamstown until the early 1900s when the land was seized by the Land Commission following the formation of the Republic of Ireland
4	Clonloaghan	Some [Mary] emigrated to USA (New York). Others fate unknown, however the Lower Aghakilmore Lahys also owned a farm in Clonloaghan
5	Lavagh	Francis & Rebecca branch produced only girls thus 'Lahy' line ended – however other Lahys from the other branches subsequently moved to Lavagh
6	Tircullen	Fate unknown. Land went to Achesons.
7	Shantully	Fate unknown although some may have joined the Military [Dragoon Guards] see section 17
8	Mullagh	Involved in many petty sessions court cases in 1800s. Samuel resident there until his death in 1903. Many of the family emigrated to New York around the time of the famine.

20.1 Lower Aghakilmore Next Generation

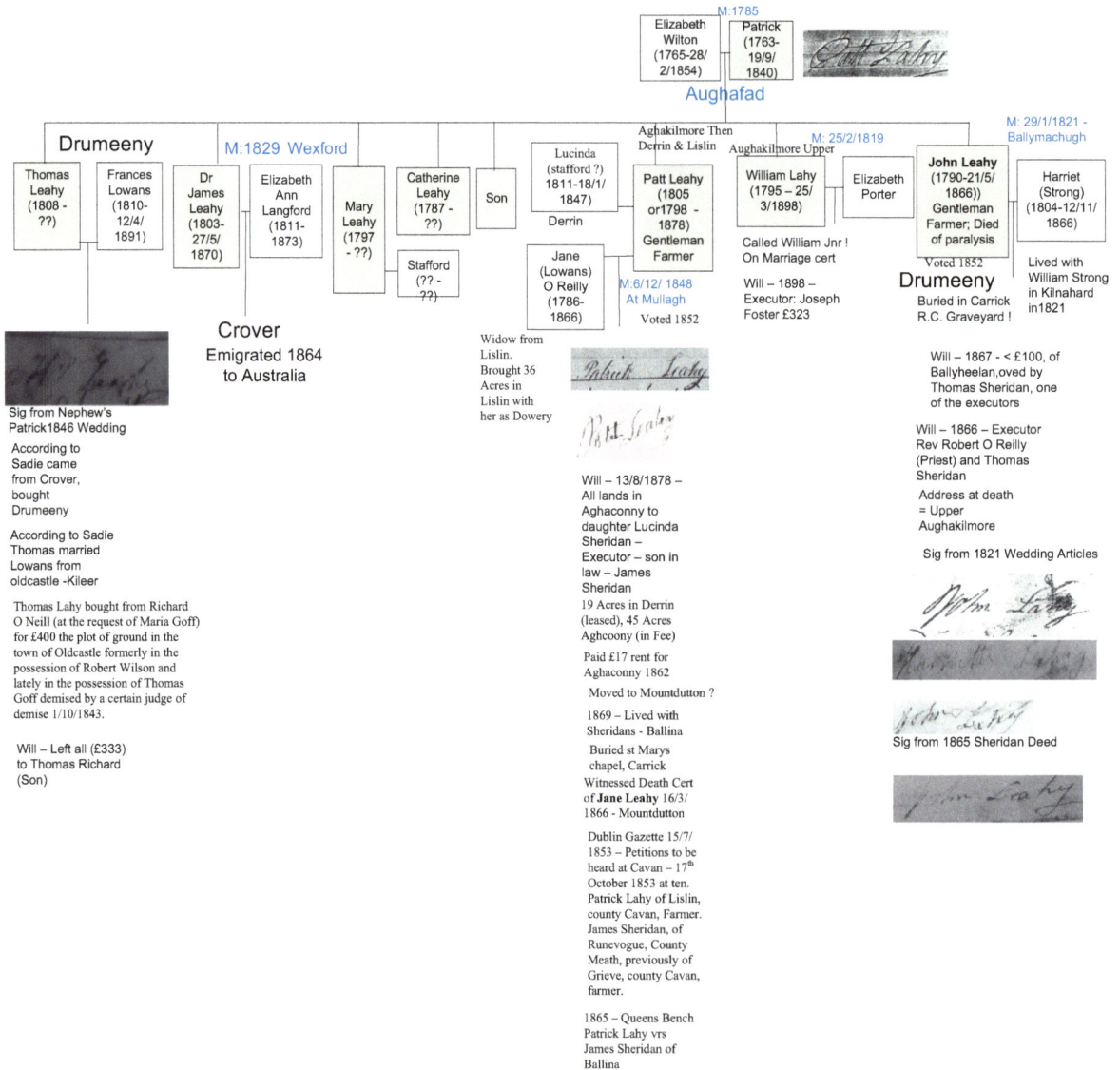

M:1785

Elizabeth Wilton (1765-28/2/1854)

Patrick (1763-19/9/1840)

Patt Leahy [signature]

Aughafad

Drumeeny

M:1829 Wexford

Aghakilmore Then Derrin & Lislin

Aughakilmore Upper

M: 25/2/1819

M: 29/1/1821 - Ballymachugh

Thomas Leahy (1808 - ??)

Frances Lowans (1810-12/4/1891)

Dr James Leahy (1803-27/5/1870)

Elizabeth Ann Langford (1811-1873)

Mary Leahy (1797 - ??)

Catherine Leahy (1787 - ??)

Son

Lucinda (stafford ?) 1811-18/1/1847

Derrin

Patt Leahy (1805 or1798 - 1878) Gentleman Farmer

William Lahy (1795 – 25/3/1898)

Elizabeth Porter

John Leahy (1790-21/5/1866)) Gentleman Farmer; Died of paralysis

Harriet (Strong) (1804-12/11/1866)

Stafford (?? - ??)

Jane (Lowans) O Reilly (1786-1866)

M:6/12/ 1848 At Mullagh

Voted 1852

Called William Jnr ! On Marriage cert

Voted 1852

Drumeeny

Buried in Carrick R.C. Graveyard !

Lived with William Strong in Kilnahard in1821

Crover

Emigrated 1864 to Australia

Widow from Lislin. Brought 36 Acres in Lislin with her as Dowery

Patrick Leahy [signature]

Patt Leahy [signature]

Sig from Nephew's Patrick1846 Wedding

According to Sadie came from Crover, bought Drumeeny

According to Sadie Thomas married Lowans from oldcastle -Kileer

Thomas Lahy bought from Richard O Neill (at the request of Maria Goff) for £400 the plot of ground in the town of Oldcastle formerly in the possession of Robert Wilson and lately in the possession of Thomas Goff demised by a certain judge of demise 1/10/1843.

Will – Left all (£333) to Thomas Richard (Son)

Will – 13/8/1878 – All lands in Aghaconny to daughter Lucinda Sheridan – Executor – son in law – James Sheridan

19 Acres in Derrin (leased), 45 Acres Aghcoony (in Fee)

Paid £17 rent for Aghaconny 1862

Moved to Mountdutton ?

1869 – Lived with Sheridans - Ballina

Buried st Marys chapel, Carrick

Witnessed Death Cert of **Jane Leahy** 16/3/ 1866 - Mountdutton

Dublin Gazette 15/7/ 1853 – Petitions to be heard at Cavan – 17th October 1853 at ten. Patrick Lahy of Lislin, county Cavan, Farmer. James Sheridan, of Runevogue, County Meath, previously of Grieve, county Cavan, farmer.

1865 – Queens Bench Patrick Lahy vrs James Sheridan of Ballina

Will – 1898 – Executor: Joseph Foster £323

Will – 1867 - < £100, of Ballyheelan,oved by Thomas Sheridan, one of the executors

Will – 1866 – Executor Rev Robert O Reilly (Priest) and Thomas Sheridan

Address at death = Upper Aughakilmore

Sig from 1821 Wedding Articles

John Lahy [signature]

[signature]

John Lahy [signature]

Sig from 1865 Sheridan Deed

[signature]

Surnames include: Langford, Lowans, Stafford, Porter, Wilton

20.2 Upper Aghakilmore – Next Generation

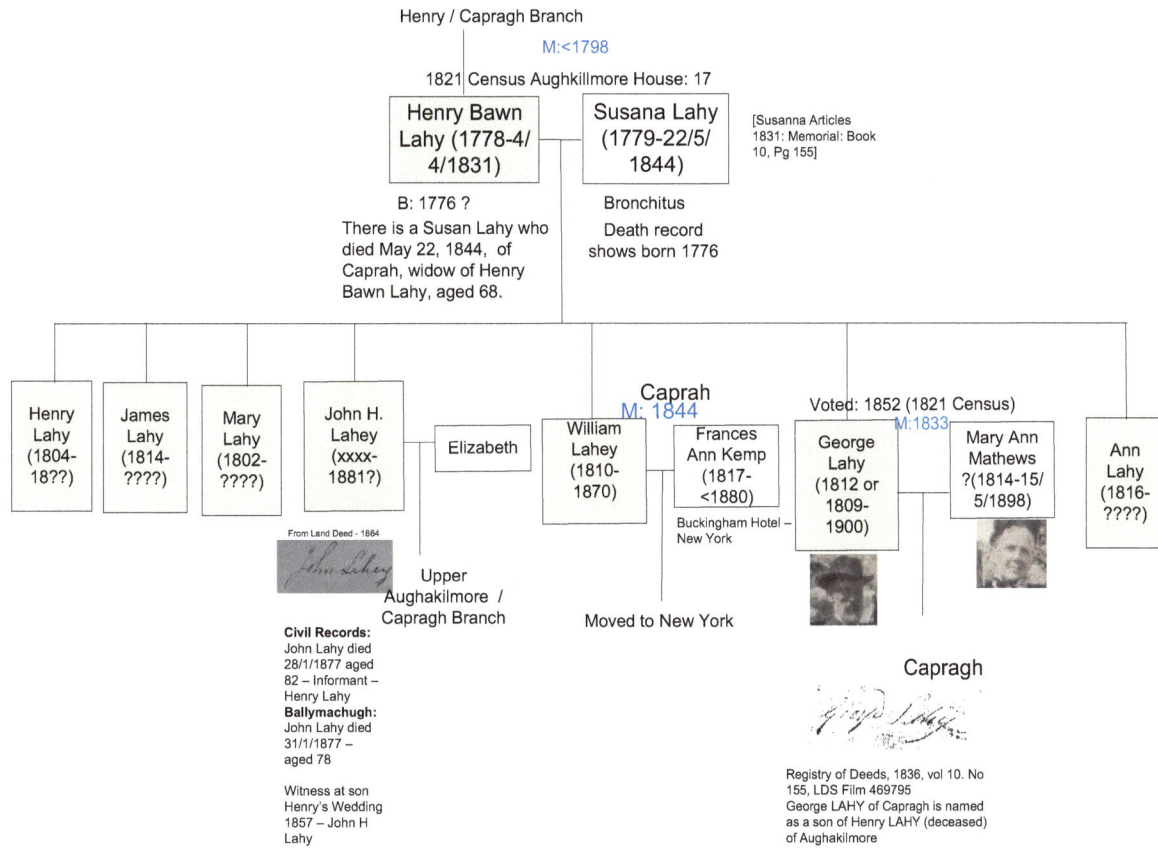

Henry / Capragh Branch

M:<1798

1821 Census Aughkillmore House: 17

Henry Bawn Lahy (1778-4/4/1831)

Susana Lahy (1779-22/5/1844)

[Susanna Articles 1831: Memorial: Book 10, Pg 155]

B: 1776 ?

There is a Susan Lahy who died May 22, 1844, of Caprah, widow of Henry Bawn Lahy, aged 68.

Bronchitus

Death record shows born 1776

Henry Lahy (1804-18??)

James Lahy (1814-????)

Mary Lahy (1802-????)

John H. Lahey (xxxx-1881?)

Elizabeth

Caprah
M: 1844

William Lahey (1810-1870)

Frances Ann Kemp (1817-<1880)

Buckingham Hotel – New York

Voted: 1852 (1821 Census)
M:1833

George Lahy (1812 or 1809-1900)

Mary Ann Mathews ?(1814-15/5/1898)

Ann Lahy (1816-????)

From Land Deed - 1864

Upper Aughakilmore / Capragh Branch

Civil Records:
John Lahy died 28/1/1877 aged 82 – Informant – Henry Lahy
Ballymachugh:
John Lahy died 31/1/1877 – aged 78

Witness at son Henry's Wedding 1857 – John H Lahy

Moved to New York

Capragh

Registry of Deeds, 1836, vol 10. No 155, LDS Film 469795
George LAHY of Capragh is named as a son of Henry LAHY (deceased) of Aughakilmore

Surnames include: Kemp, Mathews

20.3 Williamstown Next Generation

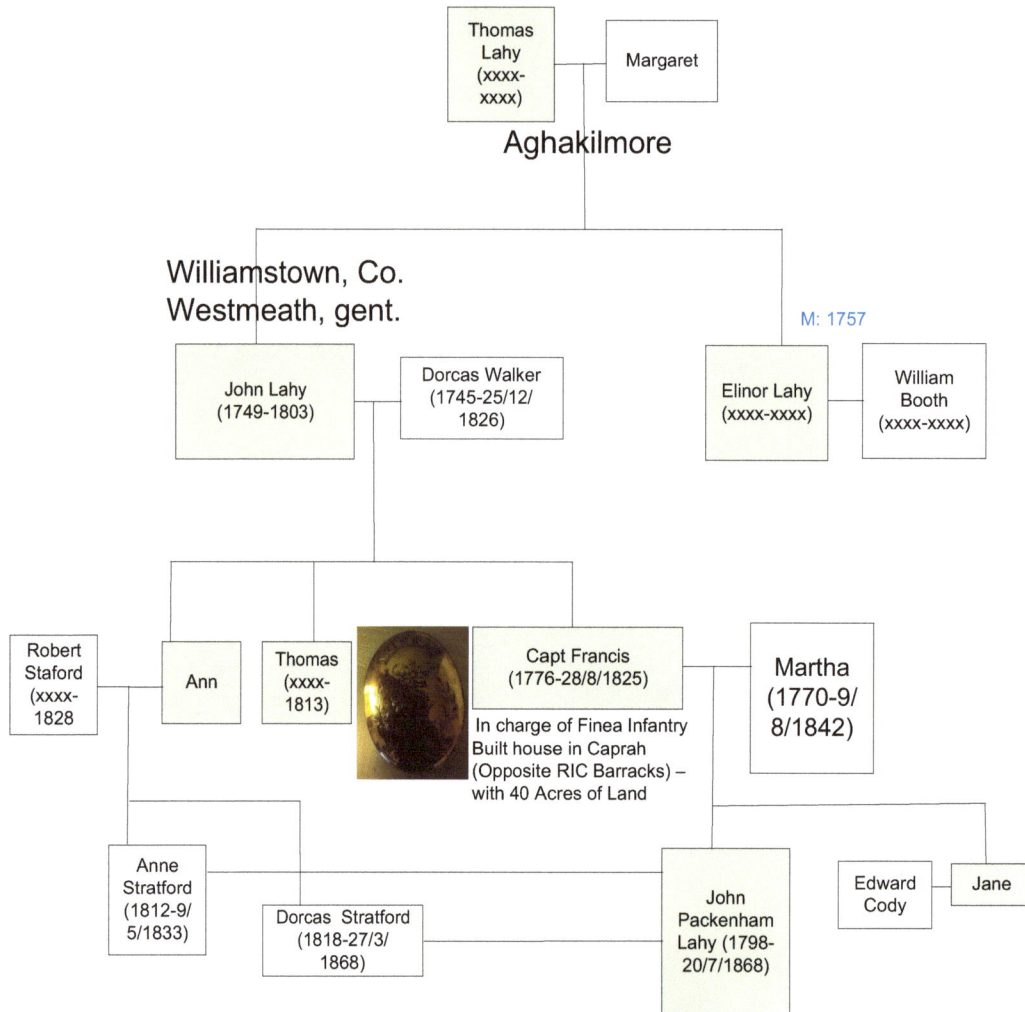

Thomas Lahy (xxxx-xxxx) — Margaret

Aghakilmore

Williamstown, Co. Westmeath, gent.

John Lahy (1749-1803) — Dorcas Walker (1745-25/12/1826)

M: 1757

Elinor Lahy (xxxx-xxxx) — William Booth (xxxx-xxxx)

Robert Staford (xxxx-1828) — Ann

Thomas (xxxx-1813)

Capt Francis (1776-28/8/1825)

In charge of Finea Infantry
Built house in Caprah
(Opposite RIC Barracks) –
with 40 Acres of Land

Martha (1770-9/8/1842)

Anne Stratford (1812-9/5/1833)

Dorcas Stratford (1818-27/3/1868)

John Packenham Lahy (1798-20/7/1868)

Edward Cody — Jane

Surnames include: Booth, Cody, Packenham, Stratford, Walker

David Leahy M.Sc.

20.4 Clonloaghan - Next Generation

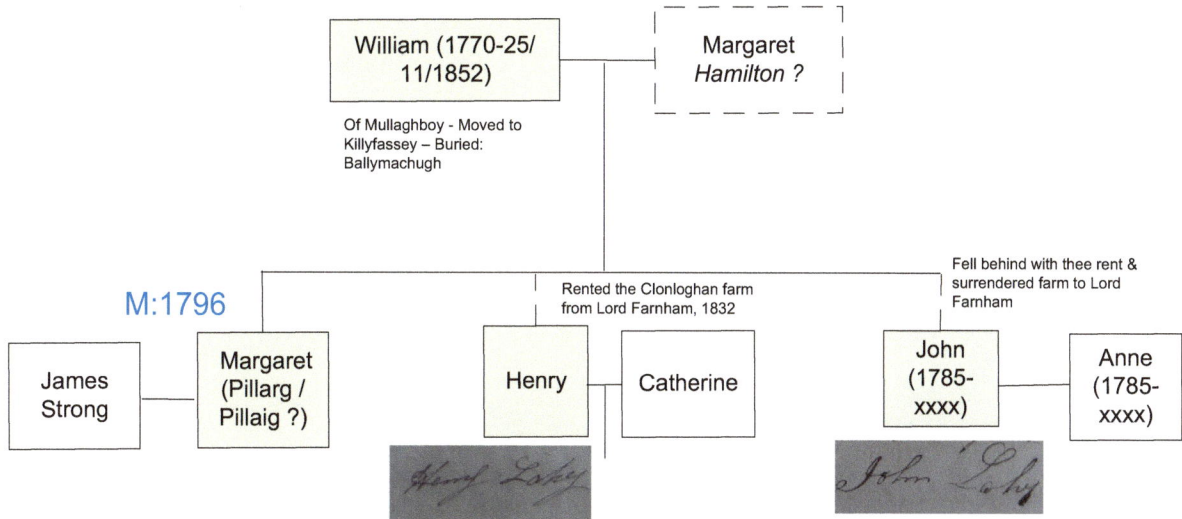

William (1770-25/11/1852)

Of Mullaghboy - Moved to Killyfassey – Buried: Ballymachugh

Margaret Hamilton ?

M:1796

James Strong

Margaret (Pillarg / Pillaig ?)

Rented the Clonloghan farm from Lord Farnham, 1832

Henry

Catherine

Fell behind with thee rent & surrendered farm to Lord Farnham

John (1785-xxxx)

Anne (1785-xxxx)

Surnames include: Hamilton, Strong

20.5 Mullagh - Next Generation

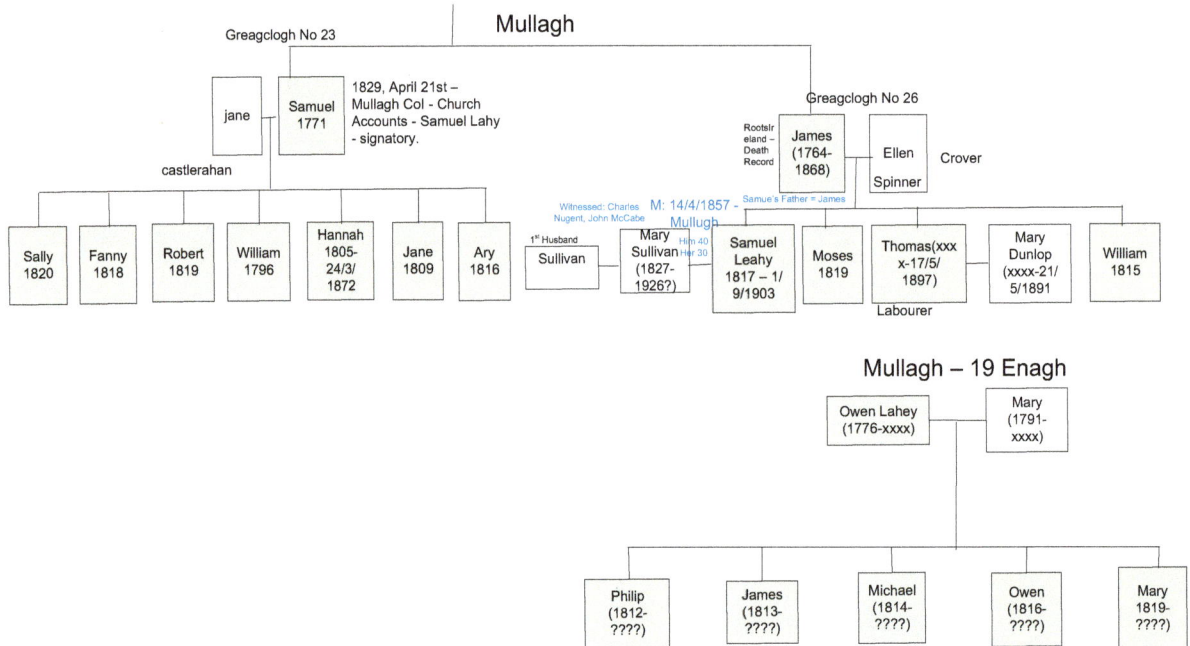

Mullagh

Greagclogh No 23

jane

Samuel 1771

1829, April 21st – Mullagh Col - Church Accounts - Samuel Lahy - signatory.

castlerahan

Greagclogh No 26

RootsIreland – Death Record

James (1764-1868)

Ellen Spinner

Crover

| Sally 1820 | Fanny 1818 | Robert 1819 | William 1796 | Hannah 1805-24/3/1872 | Jane 1809 | Ary 1816 |

Witnessed: Charles Nugent, John McCabe

M: 14/4/1857 - Mullagh

Samue's Father = James

1st Husband Sullivan

Mary Sullivan (1827-1926?)

Him 40 Her 30

Samuel Leahy 1817 – 1/9/1903

Moses 1819

Thomas(xxxx-17/5/1897)

Labourer

Mary Dunlop (xxxx-21/5/1891)

William 1815

Mullagh – 19 Enagh

Owen Lahey (1776-xxxx)

Mary (1791-xxxx)

| Philip (1812-????) | James (1813-????) | Michael (1814-????) | Owen (1816-????) | Mary 1819-???? |

Surnames include: Dunlop, Spinner, Sullivan,

21 Conclusion

In terms of origins, it still remains unclear until more documentary evidence presents itself from the 1600s. My gut feeling is that the Huguenot origin sounds the most plausible, explains why the Cavan Leahys are mostly Protestant and the theory has several different sources. The Mary 'Lahy' Walker Huguenot referenced obituary to the (probable) Clonloaghan originated Mary ties in with the other 'independent' sources (e.g., Michael Leader letter – [116]) citing this theory. Shirley Laheys account [1] of the Huguenot migration is quite detailed and seems unlikely to have been purposefully fabricated however the chapter in her book describing the story is aptly named *'Without Proof'*. However documentary proof one way or the other is difficult to come by for events that long ago.

It is not surprising that the emigrant's descendants have maintained a verbal history of their Huguenot heritage (Australian [Shirley Lahey] & American [Mary 'Lahy' Walker]). There was probably a drive to keep a historical link with the 'home' country and not let their children / grandchildren forget where they came from. That included stories about the old country and what came before. However, the Lahy's that remained in Cavan also passed down the Huguenot origin story to this day, and unless there was a 'mass conversion' to Protestantism by a branch of the Tipperary, Cork or Kilkenny Lahy's then it seems likely that the Huguenot origin story is the only one that can explain the large number of Protestant Leahy's in County Cavan (as opposed to the rest of Ireland where 90% of the Leahy's are Roman Catholic).

Update: Since the first publication of this book a descendant of the Lahaie family who emigrated from Ireland to Canada in the late 1600s (Jean Lahaie 1666 – 1738) has got in touch with me to verify the 'Lahayville' origin of the family, stating that *"What I heard for as long as I can remember is that we came from a place called Lahayville."* She stated that when her father told the children this that they laughed as they thought he had made it up. A descendant of the 'Drumeeny' line also got in touch to state that her father had always told them that they were of Huguenot descent.

Lahys / Laheys / Leahys did live in neighbouring Counties - notably County Longford (Granard), Leitrim, Westmeath (Streete) and Meath - however there is no evidence of them living there before the late 1700s so I believe they are 'overspill' from the County Cavan Leahys who branched out from the original Lough Sheelin Lahys.

Hopefully I have managed to put some structure on what previously seemed to be a haphazard array of disjointed and un-related Lahys at the top of the known tree. The more I researched, the more and more obvious it became that this group of Lahys in County Cavan (and surrounding areas) are in fact all related. There are still many broken links between the main branches and gaps in data. I have pages of Lahys who I can't connect to any of the branches. It has been difficult to determine if one person e.g. 'John' in a named location also owned land in another location or if it was a different person. Many of the Lahys listed in Early Births (see 7.1) Early Marriages (see 7.2) and Early Deaths (see 7.3) are unaccounted for in the tree I have described - as there is currently no evidence to connect them - but I am sure that they ARE connected. We're just awaiting the evidence.

Despite the 8 'branches' that I have described - the evidence tends to suggest that all of these 'branches' emanate from two 'main' branches:

1. *Upper Aghakilmore*
2. *Lower Aghakilmore*.

Even these two branches merge back into one about 8 or 9 generations back - as evidenced by DNA samples.

Certain established customs / practices e.g. naming conventions see (Table 21) and the fact that the eldest boy usually inherited the farm etc. do help to make some assumptions about missing or ambiguous data. Should more data / evidence come to light from the 1700s or even 1600s; the Top of the Tree structure will undoubtedly need to change. I don't pretend that it is 100% accurate, but as more evidence becomes available hopefully we can edge it closer to that goal. It has been a great detective adventure and enjoyable experience uncovering new data and checking where it fits in – usually opening up even more questions. It has also been great to talk to the current Leahy family in the area (as well as their neighbours), they have all been very interested and helpful and it has been a pleasure meeting them and hopefully staying in touch! Sadly, some of those I've talked to have passed on but I'm glad we managed to get a contribution from them. My only regret is that I didn't start the research 20 or 30 years ago when a lot more of them were around to talk to!

Note that if the reader disagrees with my conclusions or has further information to add to the early Lahy story then please get in touch. In addition, if the reader has access to stories or old photographs of Lahy homesteads, correspondence and people then also get in touch and I will endeavour to include them in the next volume.

If a male member of your lahy / lahey / leahy family has done a DNA test with for example www.familytreedna.com then get in touch and we can compare how close a match we are.

Note I have also written notes on all of the Lahy/Lahey/Leahy land Deeds that exist in the Registry of Deeds, Henrietta Street, Dublin [1708-1950] – [120].

My email address is cavanleahys@gmail.com

I have also set up a **FaceBook Group** called **Cavan Leahys** to enable sharing of pictures / stories / queries etc. of the Leahys – and it is also welcome to other Leahys of other Counties and Countries as no doubt there are links!

David Leahy M.Sc.

Table 21 Irish Naming Conventions

Sons	Daughters
First born son named after his father's father	First born daughter named after her mother's mother
Second born son named after his mother's father	Second born daughter named after her father's mother
Third born son named after his father	Third born daughter named after her mother
Fourth born son named after his father's oldest brother	Fourth born daughter named after her mother's oldest sister
Fifth born son named after his father's 2nd oldest brother or his mother's oldest brother	Fifth born daughter named after her mother's 2nd oldest sister or her father's oldest sister

22 Future Work

In the next volume, I shall break out the 8 or so main branches. More detail becomes available in the 1800s of church baptisms, marriages and burials. More details emerge from Newspaper archives and the legal system giving us insight to what battles the various families were fighting and also how they helped their neighbours out and what prizes they won at various local fairs etc. If new information comes to light relating the top of the tree outlined here then I shall update this volume.

From 1800 onwards, the tree grows exponentially and so presents a very real representation / visualisation problem for the printed page – especially with families with 10 or more children! However, on the plus side there is more information about what happened to a lot of individuals, where they lived, where they emigrated to etc. Also, after 1860 there are photographs available, so we get to see what some of the Lahys looked like rather than just their signatures.

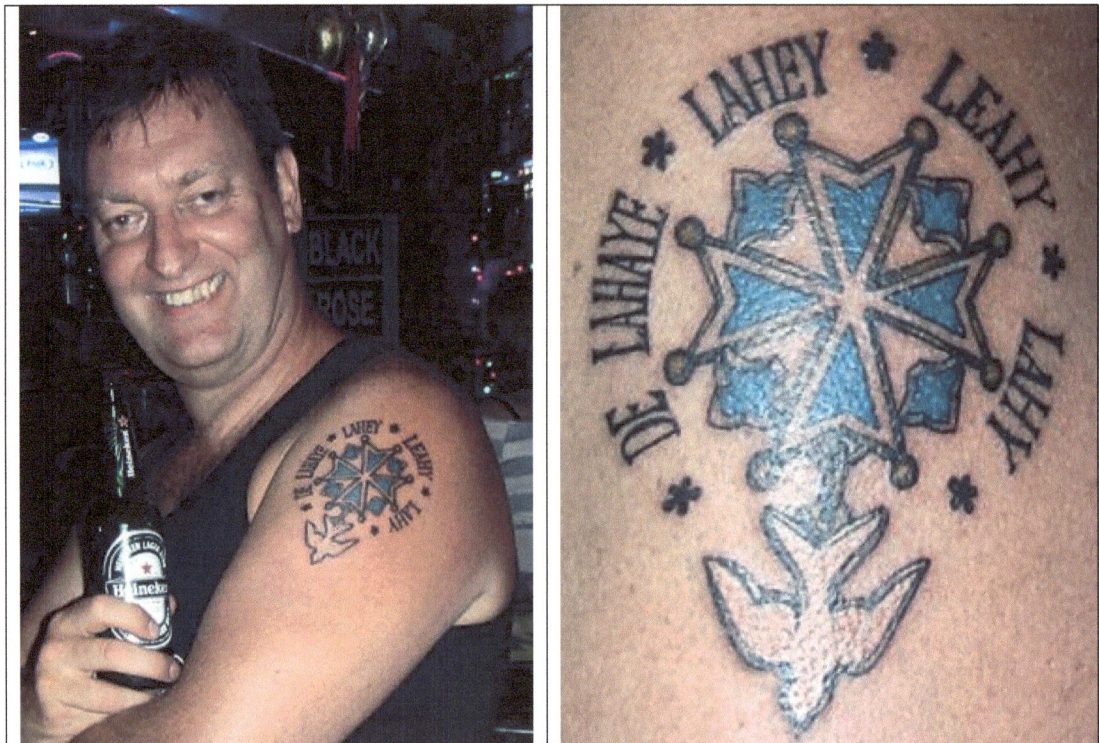

Figure 148 A little piece of Leahy History on me

23 Appendix A - Timeline Data

The following diagrams are data I took from various sources and placed on a timeline organised by townland area in order to identify who was where and when. It doesn't necessarily mean that the individuals lived in that townland at that time, just that there is a record saying that they were there (perhaps as tenants perhaps as landowners). It was a first step to trying to identify what families were possibly connected. I have colour coded the source data according to where it came from (e.g. marriage record, death record, newspaper record, land deed record etc.). There are many dotted lines crossing the townlands - these signify that either:

1. The two individuals listed may in fact be the same person
2. The two individuals are probably directly related
3. The individual has moved (e.g. to start married life in a new townland)

They may appear to be confusing diagrams, but they helped me to initially structure the data from which I could then build the actual family tree. They took a long time to construct, so I thought it worth including them here for reference.

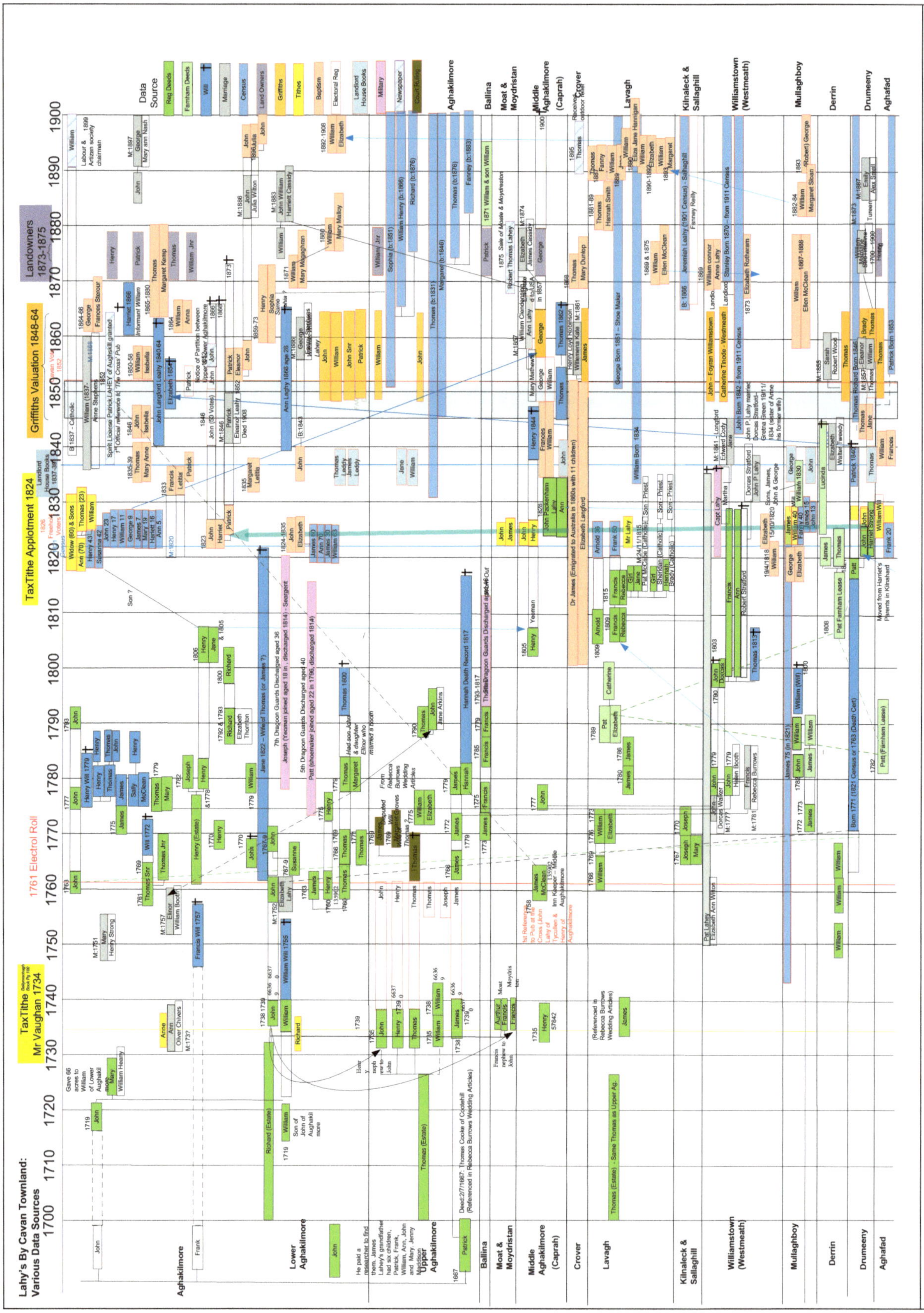

Figure 149 Timeline Data – Part 1

David Leahy M.Sc.

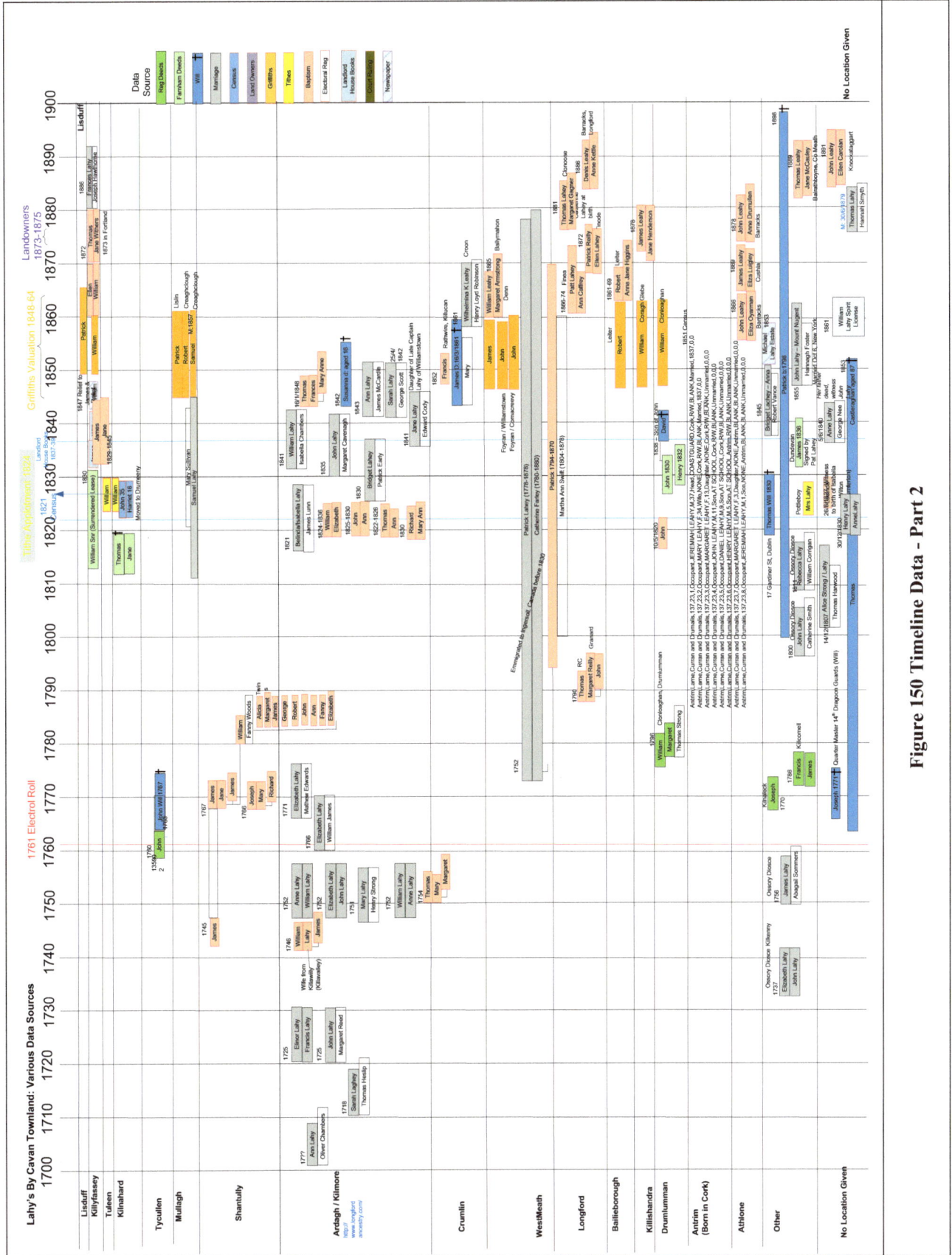

Figure 150 Timeline Data – Part 2

24 Appendix B – References & Notes

Ref No	Date	Reference	Type	Notes
1	2004	ISBN: 0646427644	Book	The Laheys: Pioneer settlers and sawmillers – Shirley Lahey.
2	1247	NLI	Manuscript	Pedigree of Delahay, c 1247 1362, c 1300 c 1420 - Manuscript, National Library of Ireland
3			Web E-Book	The Sacred and the Secular: The Augustinian Priory of Kells in Ossory, 1193-1541 .C. A. Empey .Irish Historical StudiesVol. 24, No. 94 (Nov., 1984), pp. 131-151 (article consists of 21 pages) Published by: Irish Historical Studies Publications Ltd http://archive.org/stream/historyandantiq05carrgoog /historyandantiq05carrgoog_djvu.txt
4	1881		Book	The English in Ireland in the eighteenth century. JAMES ANTHONY FROUDE, M.A. LONDON: LONGMANS, GEEEN, AND CO. 1881.
5			Book	Irish pedigrees; or, The origin and stem of the Irish nation (1892), by John O'Hart, - Volume: 1 & Volume 2. https://archive.org/details/irishpedigreesor_01ohar
6	1911		Book	The French blood in America by Fosdick, Lucian J. (Lucian John), b. 1849. Published 1911. https://archive.org/details/frenchblood00fosdrich
7	1942,		Book	Lahey, Edith Marion.: Laheys of Bellissima Forest : a short history / compiled by Edith M. Lahey.
8	1863		Web Page	The army lists of the Roundheads and Cavaliers, 1642, ed. by E. Peacock https://archive.org/details/armylistsroundh00armygo og
9	1661-1685		Book	Daltons Irish Army Lists, 1661-1685. Ref: IET0060 ISBN: 1-84630-076-2 http://www.eneclann.ie
10	1630		Poll	1630 Muster Rolls for C Cavan (LDS #1279327, Item 6)
11	1692		Manuscript	Deputy Keeper of the Records, Public Record Office of Northern Ireland 15 March 1692- 25 March 1692 La Haye. Arrived there with the King - PRONI (D638/12/70)
12	1667	Private	Deed	1667 Patrick bought land in Aughakilmore from Thomas Coote and in Taulaught from Walter Ward – 2 deeds [1667] – Source = FS
13	1677	Private	Deed	Deed 11/1/1677 - 29th Year of Charles II Reign.

Ref No	Date	Reference	Type	Notes
				Parties: 1. Walter Ward of Drogheda 2. Patrick Laghy of Aughakilmore Patrick gave Walter Ward £50 for 70 Acres in Aughakilmore – Source = FS
14			Book	Ballymachugh & Drumloman South - Ballymachugh History & Heritage Committee, 2008. ISBN 9780955831003. R & S Printers Ltd, Monaghan, Ireland
15	< 1616		Book	O'Donovan, John (ed. and tr.). Annála Rioghachta Éireann. Annals of the Kingdom of Ireland by the Four Masters, from the earliest period to the year 1616. Edited from MSS in the Library of the Royal Irish Academy and of Trinity College Dublin with a translation and copious notes. 7 volumes Royal Irish Academy. Dublin, 1848–51. Second edition, 1856
16		National Archives of Ireland	Wills	Ardagh Wills 1690-1857 - Will Abstracts, Ardagh Diocese
17	1761		Poll	Cavan Poll Book Proni T1522 Cavan Co. Library
18	1821		Census	1821 Census – National Archives of Ireland
19	1600s	Book	The National Archives, Kew, UK	State papers Ireland 1509-1782.
20	1779	NLI	Manuscript	Rebecca Burrows Marriage Articles 1779 - NLI
21	1709	Private	Notes on Deeds	[Rev Peter Brady Notes on Deeds] - FS - William to James – 16 Acres in Lavagh & Aghacreevy - 1709 – Deed Richard Lahy to John Lahy – 70 Acres Aughakilmore & 38 Acres in Lavagh - William Lahy & Elizabeth his wife to James Lahy (Gent) - 8 Acres of Lavagh & Aghacreevy .- 1738 – John to Henry 35 Acres Aughakilmore & 19 Acres in Lavagh - 1739 John Lahy to Thomas Lahy - 38 Acres Lavagh & Aghacreevy & 70 Acres Aughakilmore
22	1738	63321	Deed	Richard the father of John of Lower Aughakilmore. Deed – 63321- 1738
23	1739	66435	Deed	1739 - Arthur and Francis received part of the

Ref No	Date	Reference	Type	Notes
				'estate' of Richard (his grandsons ?) – Deed 66435 – 1739. Witnessed by Thomas – Uncle ?
24	1719	58573	Deed	John lahy of aghakilmore to William (his son) and to Mary his daughter and wife of William Heeny (son in law) – lands of lower aghakilmore. Witnessed by Thomas Heany of upper castletown Westmeath, and John Lahy of Upper Aghakilmore, Hugh Flanagan of Mill Castle Westmeath and Phil Reilly of Dublin
25	1770	183906	Deed	Deed: 183906 – 1770. Joseph of Kilnaleck 70 Acres in Aughakilmore to Henry Lahy. Executed by John Lahy (Late) of Aughakilmore. Witnessed by James Lahy of Upper Aughakilmore.
26	1739	66371	Deed	Henry (of Upper Aghakilmore) is the nephew of John of Lower Aughakilmore [Deed: 66371 – 1739 – Witnessed by James + John of Upper Ag.
27	1739	66370	Deed	John Lahy of Lower Aghakilmore and Francis Lahy (nephew) of Upper Moydristan in county Afones. 66 Acres in Upper Moydristan in Parish of Ballymachugh. Witnessed by William Lahy of Lower Aghakilmore, Thomas Lahy and John Lahy of Upper Aghakilmore
28	1766	Private	Will	1766 – Will Thomas Lahy of Upper Aughakilmore – Source = FS
29	1779	Betham Abstracts	Will	1779 Will Henry of Aughakilmore – Betham Abstracts
30	1758	135902	Deed	John Lahy of Tycullen & Henry Lahy of Aughakilmore Lower (1760). 135902 Henry paid £60 for 70 Acres in Lower Aughakilmore. Witnessed by James McClean Innkeeper of Aughakilmore Middle, Henry Strong farmer and James Killroy, Schoolmaster and Thomas Lahy of Aughakilmore Lower.
31		NAI & Salt Lake City	Court Record	1769 Will Dispute – Margaret (Wife) and James (Brother) challenge Will of Thomas - Morman Records. 276 Prerogative Case Paper 1769, Salt Lake City – Family History Centre Film# 596411, T, Box & Order# 2915 of 2943 Pg 276 of 301
32	1725	National Archives of Ireland	Marriage	Kilmore Marriages – NLI

Ref No	Date	Reference	Type	Notes
33	1777	214253	Deed	Deed: 214253 - 1777 - John Lahy of Caprah. Marriage between John and Dorcas Walker. Lands of Williamstown formerly in the possession of widow duffy and half of lands in Togher in possession of Alex Walker. The said John Lahy in possession of lands of Moat and Middle Aghakilmore.
34	1779	222030	Deed	Deed: 222030 – 1779 - Thomas Lahy of Lower Aughakilmore and Wife Mary / Margaret, and John Lahy of Williamstown & Elinor Booth (otherwise Lahy). 13/12/1779. Henry Lahy. 60 Acres of UPPER Aughakilmore 5 Schillings. Thomas sold land to John for 5 Schillings. Witnessed by William Lahy & Francis Lahy of Ballina.
35	1781	227627	Deed	Deed: 227627 - 1781 – Joseph Lahy of Aughakilmore and Henry Lahy great second son and heir at law of Henry Lahy late of Aughkilmore. 20/7/1764 - £ 120
36	1805	388775	Deed	Henry Lahy of Capragh and Anthony. Gilroy of Granard. Henry in consideration of £220 was lent and advanced a further sum of 5 shillings 14 Acres in Capragh for 500 years witnessed by Pat Brady and xxx Murphy and John O Reilly.
37	1806	390529	Deed	Henry Lahy of Capragh (Yeoman) and Jane Lahy of Aughakilmore in said County, Widow of the other part reciting articles entered into by the said Henry and Jane Lahy bearing date 4th day of June last and consisting of several covenants and agreements....concerning town and lands of Upper Aughakilmore and Lower Aughakilmore....shall be lawful for said Jane and her children to enter into premises and use half part of the lands of Upper and Lower Aughakilmore and the rent and profits etc.. to which said Henry Lahy is entitled, should be subject to the payment of half such debts.... Contracted or created by the different persons of the name of Lahy (and Jane's children which when reach age of 21 will also be subject to this agreement).Witnessed by Andrew Bell Esq and Owen Keogh.
38	1762	143828	Deed	Deed 143828 – 1762 - Thomas Lahy of Lower Aghakilmore sold to Thomas Cheevers of Upper Aghakilmore half of Upper Aghakilmore for the term of 21 years. Lease commencing 1st May 1763

Ref No	Date	Reference	Type	Notes
				at yearly rent of £14 5s 6d. Witnessed by Richard Cheevers of Lis Nugent & Oliver Cheevers his son & William Lahy and Henry Lahy of Lower Aghakilmore.
39	1763	146370	Deed	Deed: 146370 – 1763. William Lahy of Tycullen and John Lahy of Aughakilmore – William released and granted onto said John all part of the town and lands of Aughakilmore wheron the John then Lived & agreed for fee £5 Sterling. Witnessed by Thomas, Henry & James of Lower Aghakilmore
40	1766	160734	Deed	Deed: 160734 – 1766. William of Lavagh sold land to James of Aghakilmore Upper. Witnessed by Thomas of Ag Lower.
41	1769	177801	Deed	Deed: 177801 – 1769. William Lahy of Lavagh. £240 paid by James Lahy of Aughakilmore Upper lands of Lavagh and Aghacreevy. Witnessed by Thomas Lahy of Aughakilmore Lower
42	1790	296468	Deed	Deed: 296468 – 1790. Thomas and John Lahy of Lower Aghakilmore and Thomas Atkins of Killgolough, Cavan and Jane Atkins (daughter).£150 dowry and lands in upper and lower Aughakilmore. Witnessed by John Lahy of Williamstown, John Married Jane Arkins
43	1761	143581	Deed	Deed: 143581 – 1761. Mentions Thomas the Elder and Thomas the Junior of Aughakilmore
44	1793	319919	Deed	Deed:319919 – 1793 - Thomas Lahy and John Lahy of Aughakilmore – fell behind in rent to Pat Kilroy of Killeadrean
45	1831		Deed	Henry Lahy (Sen) of Capragh and William and George (a minor) his brother (sons). Henry owns 27 acres in Capragh. £240 to be paid to the sons. Witnessed by: Thomas Lahy of Aughakilmore, James Lahy of Tawlaught, Henry Lahy of Clonloaghan George Carmichael, Dublin Charles McCreedy of Dublin
46	1803	391569	Deed	1803 – Deed 391569 – Ann Married to Robert Stratford. Father = John of Williamstown (deceased). She has £250 Dowry and £30 / year from Father's Will. Witnessed by Patt Lahy
47	1760	135904	Deed	William in Tycullen Deed 135904 – 1760 – Transferred to John of Lower Ag – half his lands in

Ref No	Date	Reference	Type	Notes
				Lavagh. Being ¼ of said premises (land divided between 4 brothers ?) Witness: Thomas of Aughakilmore
48	1734	55583	Deed	John, Henry and Thomas (of Upper Aughakilmore) sold 3/4 of the estate of Thomas Also owned land Lavagh (dec'd). Deed 55583 - 1734
49	1735	57842	Deed	Thomas William & John all witnessed Deed 57842 – 1735 of Henry of Upper Aughakilmore – supports them being brothers
50	1738	66369	Deed	1738 – deed 66369: John Lahy of Lower Aghakilmore and William Lahy of Up Aghakilmore. 35 Acres in lower aghakilmore. Witnessed by William Blakely of Aughafad, Jam(es) Lahy and John Lahy of Upper Aghakilmore & Bxxx Delaney (Dublin Gent). 19 Acres in Lavagh and Aughacreevy.
51	1758		Will	Testamentary - Ardagh Admin Bonds - National Archives of Ireland
52	1767	174157	Deed	Deed 174157 - 1767-1769 William of Lavagh to John of Aughakilmore & his mother Susanna.
53	1785	202256	Deed	Deed:202256: - 1785 John Lahy & Elizabeth father & Mother of Patrick – marriage settlement 1785 – To Elizabeth Wilton from Derrin
54	1785	Private Source	Deed	Francis Lahy of Ballynidrumma - County Meath - witnessed by Pat Lahy
55	1782	NLI	Deed	1782 Aughafad Deed [Farnham Papers] - Royalties Turf Bogs reserved lives of Patt Lahy Lessee, William Lahy eldest son of John Lahy Lessee and William Lahy eldest son of James Lahy of Mullaghboy
56	1796	345139	Deed	Deed:345139 – 1796. William Lahy of Clonlohan, parish of Drumluman on behalf of his daughter Margaret Lahy. James strong took his wife Pillarg Lahy
57	1848-1864	NAI	Land Census	Individuals who occupied property in Ireland between 1848 and 1864. National Archives, Dublin. http://www.askaboutireland.ie/griffith-valuation/
58	1832	NLI MS 41,137 /3	Manuscript	Farnham Papers. MS 41,137 /3. Clonloaghan: to John Lahey. 3 lives. 1830 Aug. 21. Also, related deed of surrender, 1832 May 21; with draft of same. 1 membrane with map & 2 sheets. Clonloaghan: to Henry Lahy. 3 lives. 1832 Jan. 3. 1 membrane with map.

Ref No	Date	Reference	Type	Notes
59		NLI Mss. 3117-3118	Manuscript	Two volumes giving summaries of applications and representations made by tenants and other persons to the Lords Farnham and decisions made in respect of these, 1832 - 1860. Mss. 3117-3118
60	1886	15	Deed	6/4/1886. William Lahy of Mullaghboy (farmer) and Margaret Lahy his wife and Henry Lahy of Clonloaghan (farmer). Reciting Mortgage dated 6/8/1857 between William Lahy since deceased of the one part and John Hamilton since deceased of the second part to secure the payment of £127 10s as therin charged on the premises and that the estate of the said William Lahy deceased is now vested in the said Henry Lahy and all the estate of said John Hamilton deceased is now vested in said William Lahy and Margaret Lahy said indenture of which this is a memorial witnessed for the considerations therein the said William and Margaret Lahy his wife as Mortgagees did grant and convey onto the said Henry Lahy his heirs and assigns all that and premises at present occupied as a police barracks situate in the lands of Capragh together with a yearly rent of £15. Witnessed Richard Allen, Solicitor and William Henry Clarke (clerk).
61	1814	698	Deed	Marriage Articles (Peter Brady & Hannagh Lahy) Peter Brady of Pullakell and John Brady of Pullakell Francis Lahy of Lavagh, Hannagh Lahy daughter of said Francis and Rebecca and Steward Mulligan of Corsmullo and Hugh Brady of Oldcastle Peter Brady gave land to Steward and Hugh, lands of Garnasallagh and Pullakeel. Francis and Rebecca together with their said daughter lands to Steward and Hugh Brady – lands of Lavagh (70 Acres) and lands leased by Col John Brady – 200 acres and lands of Killymullen and Corsumalla - £20 yearly paid to Hannagh for Life. Witnessed by Patrick McCabe of Lavagh
62	1815	501666	Deed	Pat Mc Cabe and Francis Lahy of Lavagh –& Wife (Rebecca Burrows) and Jane Lahy **4th daughter** of Francis and Rebecca, spinster of the 70 Acres £370. Jane Lahy mentioned (daughter ?).Witnessed by Arnold Lahy of Knocknaheen Co Cavan
63	1809	456417	Deed	Francis Lahy formerly of Lavagh and Rebecca Lahy his wife and Jogn Galligan and Henry Burrows

Ref No	Date	Reference	Type	Notes
				(Rebecca's brother ?). Witnessed by Henry McCabe, Arnold Lahy of Lavagh and Pat Brady.
64	1767	National Archives of Ireland	Will	Betham Will Abstracts. 1767 – John of Tircullen Will – Wife Elizabeth, brothers Joseph & Thomas – son of Thomas = Joseph. Sister in Law Mary, Kinsman Henry
65	1771	National Archives of Ireland	Will	Betham Will Abstracts. 1771 - Joseph Quarter Master 14th Dragoon Guards 27/8/1768 - 8/10/1771.Only son John, nephew Joseph, Brother John Lahy,Wife Elinor Lahy (Else Seanlan), Kinsman John Lahy,Nephew Richard Kirk Betham Will Abstracts No 222 (Page 94)
66	1792	294154	Deed	Deed: 294154 – 1792. Richard Lahy of Aughakilmore and Francis Thornton of Larkhill to Marry
67	1793	300648	Deed	Deed 300648 – 1793 - Richard Lahy of Aughakilmore and Henry Maxwell of Crover, cavan £479 for Lands in Aughakilmore known as the 'Cross'.
68	1800	348967	Deed	Deed:348967 -1800. Rick (Richard) Lahy of Aughakilmore and the late Henry Maxwell. £1465 lands in Aughakilmore
69	1812	National Archives of Ireland	Manuscript	Farnham papers, ca. 1600-ca. 1950.
70		WO 121/22/93	The National Archives, Kew, UK	Chelsea Pensioners' discharge documents 1760-1887
71	1795	WO25 reference 881	The National Archives, Kew, UK	Napoleonic War Regimental indexes 1806. National Archives.
72	1814	WO 119/24/341	The National Archives, Kew, UK	Kilmainham Pensioners British Army Service Records 1771-1821.Kilmainham Reference: A6895.
73	1814	WO 119	The National Archives, Kew, UK	Kilmainham Pensioners British Army Service Records 1771-1821
74		WO 119/39/146	The National Archives,	Kilmainham Pensioners British Army Service Records 1771-1821 Kilmainham Reference: A11665.

Ref No	Date	Reference	Type	Notes
			Kew, UK	
75	1570	D.2753	NLI	Grant by Sir Thomas Lahie, vicar of Kells, to James Archdeacon of the whole vicarage of Kells (in Ossory), Feb. 13, 1570.
76	1572	D. 2837	NLI	Grant by the Earl of Ormonde to Sir Thomas Lahy of the town of the Grange of Kenlis, Co. Kilkenny, for 21 years, July 20, 1572.
77	1578	D.2980	NLI	Grant by Richard Shee, as attorney of the Earl of Ormonde, to Peter Shee and Sir Thomas Lahie, of the altarage of Kilrye and Donnamogane, Co. Kilkenny with all tithes, lands, etc. belonging thereto, for 21 years, Feb. 2, 1578.
78	1767	166410	Deed	Deed 166410 – 1767 Joseph & Wife Mary of Kilnaleck sold 76 Acres in Lower Ag to Andrew Bell of Bellsgrove
79	1772	190877	Deed	Deed: 190877 – 1772 - William Lahy and Wife Elizabeth of Lavagh. And James Lahy of Mullaghboy
80	1772	193166	Deed	Deed: 193166 – 1772. William and Elizabeth and James Lahy of Aughakilmore Upper
81	1773	196816	Deed	Deed: 196816 – 1773. William Lahy of Lavagh and Elizabeth Lahy his wife and James Lahy of Mullaghboy and James Lahy of Ballina. Voluntary settlement
82	1775	203250	Deed	Deed: 203250 – 1775. William Lahy and Elizabeth Lahy his wife of Aughakilmore Upper. James Lahy of Aghakilmore. £148 for land in Lavagh. Witnessed by Henry Lahy of Aghakilmore Lower, Francis Lahy of Ballina
83	1786	250840	Deed	Deed: 250840 – 1786 James Lahy of Lavagh and Francis Lahy of Killcomell, Cavan and John Bell of Creevy, Longford. £567 2s, 8d Debt. Land in Lavagh
84	1786	250839	Deed	Deed: 250839 – 1786. James Lahy of Lavagh and Francis Lahy of Killcomell. 16 Acres and Lavagh lands in the possession of James Lahy
85	1778	216909	Deed	Deed: 216909 – 1778. Henry Lahy of Aghakilmore and Henry Lahy his son. One half of the lands of Aghakilmore.
86	1797	332001	Deed	Deed: 332001 – 1797:Thomas Lahy of Aughakilmore and Terence Joey of Aughakilmore (Publican). 10 Acres in Aughakilmore for 41 years yearly rent of £1 8s 31/2 d
87	1799	443664	Deed	Deed:443664 – 1799 - Francis Lahy of Lavagh to

Ref No	Date	Reference	Type	Notes
				James Strong of Taulaght
88	1800s		Church Record	Ballymachugh Church of Ireland Vestry Records
89	1780	231422	Deed	Deed: - 1780- 231422 -James Lahy of Lavagh and Joseph Lahy of Aghakilmore (Brothers ?) and John Bell from Creevy, Longford. Sold lands in Lavagh (in possession of tenants James Smyth and Henry Gallaghan) and lands in Aghakilmore in possession of Patrick and Lawrence Reilly
90	1762	143827	Deed	Deed 143827 1762 - William Lahy of Lavagh to Thomas Cheevers and Thomas Heaney both of Aghakilmore half of all his lands in Lavagh being the one forth part of the said premises to hold during the term of 21 years from 1s May next – yearly rent 15 s per acre.
91	1764	149470	Deed	Deed 149470 – 1764 - William Lahy of Lavagh sell onto Thomas Cheevers of Aughakilmore all that half of the said William Lahys undivided moiety or half part of the lands of Lavagh and Aghacreevy now in the possession of the said William, Lahy, Thomas Lahy and James Lahy as the same is now held by the said Thomas Cheevers the said part undivided thereby demised to the said Thomas Cheevers containing 16 acres to hold for 30 years. Witnessed Robert Cordner, Robert Acheson
92	1779	222029		Thomas Lahy of Lower Aughkilmore & wife Margaret and John Lahy of Williamstown in the county of Westmeath Seized and possessed of an estate of inheritance in the town and lands of Aghakilmore Upper now in the tenure of Thomas Heany and Lower Aghakilmore in the Possession of John Masterson, Henry Lahy and the said Thomas Lahy containing 60 Acres.Thomas Lahy received 5 shillings from John Lahy.Witnessed by William Lahy of Aughakilmore and George M Farran and Bryan Carry of the city of Dublin.
93	1771	187079		Thomas Lahy of Lower Aghakilmore to Thomas Cheevers of Upper Aghakilmore Lands for 31 years at yearly rent of $14 7s 6d. witnessed by Richard Cheevers, Samuel Cheevers, Thomas McManus & James Sheridan
94	1687			Church of the Latter Day Saints - LDS film no.0845002
95	1660	MS. Carte	The	[MS. Carte 158, p(p). 15. William De Lahaye Back

Ref No	Date	Reference	Type	Notes
		158	National Archives, Kew, UK	Paye claim 1660.
96	1983		Journal Article	Gwynn, Robin. The number of Huguenot immigrants in England in the late seventeenth century. Journal of Historical Geography 9(4):384-395 · October 1983
97	1684-1929		The National Archives, Kew, UK	Royal Kilmainham Hospital, 1684-1929
98	1760-1887	WO 121/0059	The National Archives, Kew, UK	Chelsea Pensioners' discharge documents 1760-1887
99	1760-1887	WO 121/0021	The National Archives, Kew, UK	Chelsea Pensioners' discharge documents 1760-1887
100	1806	WO23/ Piece 136	The National Archives, Kew, UK	British Army Service Records Transcription
101	1738-1804		Notes on Wills	NAI - Thrift Will Abstracts - Diocese of Ossary 1738-1804
102	1755		NLI	Newspaper Archives - Dublin Gazette 1755
103	1708-1950s			The Registry of Deeds, Henrietta Street, Dublin
104	1536-1810		Book	Index to Prerogative Wills of Ireland 1536-1810. Sir Arthur Edward Vicars. Genealogical Pub. Co.
105	1831	155	Deed	Susanna Articles. Book 10 Page 155. Registry of Deeds
106	1784	241032	Deed	Francis Lahy of Nutfield Co Cavan and Mathew Read of Drumhose, Co Cavan. 29 Acres in Nutfield for 31 years rent at £1 per acre. Witnessed by John Reid and Thomas Reilly of Tullygain and Robert Woods. Signed in Clones, Co Monaghan.
107	1785	243816	Deed	James Lahy of Lavagh, Francis Lahy of Nutfield and George Kierr of Finea (Westmeath). Lands in Lavagh (now in the possession of Thomas Cheevers) or their under tenants. 16 Acres in possession of Mc Farnan or his under tenants. *

David Leahy M.Sc.

Ref No	Date	Reference	Type	Notes
				Acres in possession of James Lahy, 42 Acres for 31 years. Rent 13 Shillings 3d per acre for 16 Acres
108	1785	249281	Deed	Francis Lahy of Ballina and Henry Maxwell. Witnessed by xxx Strong of Tawlaught and James Lord of Ballynahxxxx
109	1786	250840	Deed	James Lahy and Francis Lahy of Killconnell, Cavan and John Bell of Creevy, Longford. Said Jo Lahy in debited to John Bell by his bond 24/5/1779 for. £567 2s, 8d Debt. And also by his the said James Lahy and Francis Lahy joint bond for £1000.
110	1790	299871	Deed	Book No 461 Page 514. Registry of Deeds
111	1814	478911	Deed	Francis Lahy of Lavagh, Hannagh Lahy daughter of said Francis and Rebecca and Steward Mulligan of Corsmullo and Hugh Brady of Oldcastle
112	1835			New York passenger lists 1820-1891. https://familysearch.org
113			Newspaper	New York Times Archives
114			Journal	The Churchman - Volume 72 - Page 15.
115			Book	The History and Antiquities of the Diocese of Ossory, Volume 4. William Carrigan Roberts Brooks, 1981 - Ireland. ISBN 0907561004, 9780907561002
116		Irish Genealogical Research Society - London	Members Notes	Notes from Michael Leader File - 1990 - Letter to Registrar, Trinity College Dublin.
117		Web Page		Wexford Martyrs https://en.wikipedia.org/wiki/Wexford_Martyrs
118		Web Page		French Huguenot Officer - William of Orange http://huguenots-france.org/france/refuge/Veterans1.htm
119		Wills	Preogative Court	Ireland Diocesan and Prerogative Wills & Administrations indexes 1595-1858 Transcription
120	1708-1950	Deeds Notes	Book	Leahy Land Deed Notes 1708-1950,. David Leahy 2016. ISBN-13: 978-0995663015 ISBN-10: 0995663017
121	1652		Web Site	Commonwealth Survey Records of 1652 https://cavantownlands.com/
122	1713			W. King, 'The State of the Protestants of Ireland under the late King James's Government', Dublin, 1713.
123				U. H. Foundation, "Ulster Historical Foundation," [Online]. Available:

Ref No	Date	Reference	Type	Notes
				https://www.ancestryireland.com/.
124	2018		Book	W. C. Trimble, The History of Enniskillen, Forgotten Books (21 April 2018), 2018.
125	2016		Book	W. R. Young, Fighters of Derry: Their Deeds and Descendants, Being a Chronicle of Events in Ireland during the Revolutionary Period, 1688–91, Ulster Books, 2016.
126				N. A. of. Ireland, "Ireland Diocesan and Prerogative Will & Administration 1595-1858," NAI, Dublin, 1595-1858.
127				N. A. of. Ireland, Church of Ireland Marriage Licence Bonds Diocese of Kilmore & Ardagh, Dublin: NAI.
128				C. Marriages, "Irish Marriage Records - Co Antrim & Co Down c. 1600-1930," 1690. [Online]. Available: www.ancestryIreland.com.
129				S. W. Betham, "Betham abstracts from Prerogative Wills, to c.1800," National Archives of Ireland & PRONI, Dublin. Belfast.
130				I. Quit Rent Office, Book of Survey and Distribution, https://repository.dri.ie/catalog/5999n680d: National Archives of Ireland, 1641/1703.
131				D. F. C. a. P. Crossle, "Crossle Genealogocal Abstracts," National Archives of Ireland and PRONI, Dublin / Belfast, 1620 to 1804.
132				G. Thrift, "Thrift Genealogocal Abstracts," National Archives of Ireland and PRONI, Dublin / Belfast, 1500s - 1900s.
133				Ireland, Court of Chancery Records, 1633-1851 Chancery: 56th Deputy Keeper's Report, p203: roll of Justiciary Pleadings, 6 & 7 EII, and statue roll, 28 H VIII. Also, a considerable collection of Chancery Bills.. Dublin, Ireland: Microfilm of original records held at the National Archives of Ireland.
134				Ireland, Exchequer Court of Equity Bill Books, 1674-1850.Equity Exchequer Bill Books. Dublin, Ireland: Microfilm of original records held at the National Archives of Ireland.

25 Appendix C - DNA Data

Lower Aughakilmore DNA -Y Chromosome [Male] - 67 Marker

DYS393	DYS390	DYS19	DYS391	DYS385	DYS426	DYS388	DYS439	DYS389-1	DYS392	DYS389-II	
13	25	14	11	11-14	12	12	12	13	13	29	
DYS458	DYS459	DYS455	DYS454	DYS447	DYS437	DYS448	DYS449	DYS		DYS464	
17	9-10	11	11	25	15	19	29			15-15-17-18	
DYS460	GATA-H4	YCAII	DYS456	DYS607	DYS576	DYS570	CDY	DYS442	DYS438		
11	11	19-23	15	15	19	17	33-36	13	12		
DYS531	DYS578	DYF395S1	DYS590	DYS537	DYS641	DYS472	DYF406S1	DYS511			
11	9	15-16	8	10	10	8	10	10			
DYS425	DYS413	DYS557	DYS594	DYS436	DYS490	DYS534	DYS450	DYS444	DYS481	DYS520	DYS446
12	23-23	16	10	12	12	15	8	13	24	21	13
DYS617	DYS568	DYS487	DYS572	DYS640	DYS492	DYS565					
12	11	13	11	11	12	12					

Upper Aughakilmore DNA -Y Chromosome [Male] - 67 Marker

DYS393	DYS390	DYS19	DYS391	DYS385	DYS426	DYS388	DYS439	DYS389-1	DYS392	DYS389-II	
13	25	14	11	11-14	12	12	11	13	13	29	
DYS458	DYS459	DYS455	DYS454	DYS447	DYS437	DYS448	DYS449	DYS		DYS464	
17	9-10	11	11	25	15	19	29			15-15-16-17	
DYS460	GATA-H4	YCAII	DYS456	DYS607	DYS576	DYS570	CDY	DYS442	DYS438		
11	11	19-23	15	15	19	17	32-36	13	12		
DYS531	DYS578	DYF395S1	DYS590	DYS537	DYS641	DYS472	DYF406S1	DYS511			
11	9	15-16	8	10	10	8	10	10			
DYS425	DYS413	DYS557	DYS594	DYS436	DYS490	DYS534	DYS450	DYS444	DYS481	DYS520	DYS446
12	23-23	16	10	12	12	15	8	13	24	21	13
DYS617	DYS568	DYS487	DYS572	DYS640	DYS492	DYS565					
12	11	13	11	11	12	12					

26 Appendix D - Name Index

The surnames Lahy / Lahey and Leahy are not included here as they are mentioned on virtually every page!

R

Reed, **97**, **132**
Rorke, **96**

S

Sax Cobourg, **182**
Seanlan, **169**, **209**
Shee, **23**, **210**
Soily, **114**
Spinner, **194**
Stafford, **146**, **190**
Stratford, **97**, **192**, **206**
Strong, **58**, **96**, **97**, **134**, **147**, **193**, **204**, **211**
Sullivan, **194**

T

Taylor, **179**
Thornton, **97**, **128**, **170**, **209**
Tindall, **131**

W

Walker, **18**, **36**, **97**, **140**, **145**, **192**, **205**
Ward, **57**, **58**, **114**, **202**, **203**
Wilford, **180**, **181**
Wilson, **97**
Wilton, **124**, **190**, **207**
Wood, **88**, **156**

www.ingramcontent.com/pod-product-compliance
Lightning Source LLC
Chambersburg PA
CBHW041419290326
41932CB00042B/21